Default Template for a Base Template Class

```
// default template for a base
template class

template <class T>
class className
{
   public:
      className();
      ~className();
      className(className&
      SourceObject);
      className&
      operator=(className&
      SourceObject);
      // declarations of otherÆ
      public members

   protected:
      // declarations of protected
      members

   private:
      // declarations of private
      members
};

template <class T>
className::className()
{
   // statements
}
   // implementation of other
   member functions
```

Default Template for an Abstract Base Class

```
// default template for an
abstract base class

class asbtractClassName
{
   public:
   // declare at least one pure
   virtual member function
      virtual returnType
      memberFunction(parameterList)
      = 0;
   // declarations of other public
   members

   protected:
      // declarations of protected
      members

   private:
      // declarations of private
      members
};
   // implementation of nonpure
   virtual member functions
```

Object-Oriented Programming For Dummies®

COMPUTER
BOOK SERIES
FROM IDG

Cheat
Sheet

Default Template for a Base Class

```
// default template for a base
class

class className

{

  public:

    className();

    ~className();

    className(className&
    SourceObject);

    className&operator=
    (className&SourceObject);

  // declarations of other
  public members

  protected:

  // declarations of protected
  members

  private:

  // declarations of private
  members

};

className::className()

{

  // statements

}

  // implementation of other
  member functions
```

Default Template for a Descendant Class

```
// default template for a
descendant class

class className : public
parentClassName

{

  public:

    className();

    ~className();

    className(className&
    SourceObject);

    className&
      operator=(className&
      SourceObject);

  // declarations of other public
  members

  protected:

   // declarations of protected
   members


   private:

   // declarations of private
   members

};

className::className()

  : parentClassName()

{

  // statements

}

  // implementation of other
  member functions
```

...For Dummies: #1 Computer Book Series for Beginners

OBJECT-ORIENTED PROGRAMMING FOR DUMMIES®

Namir C. Shammas

IDG Books Worldwide, Inc.
An International Data Group Company

Foster City, CA ♦ Chicago, IL ♦ Indianapolis, IN ♦ Braintree, MA ♦ Southlake, TX

Object-Oriented Programming For Dummies®

Published by
IDG Books Worldwide, Inc.
An International Data Group Company
919 E. Hillsdale Blvd.
Suite 400
Foster City, CA 94404

Library of Congress Catalog Card No.: 95-77590

ISBN: 1-56884-332-1

Printed in the United States of America

10 9 8 7 6 5 4 3 2 1

1E/QR/QU/ZW/IN

Distributed in the United States by IDG Books Worldwide, Inc.

Distributed by Macmillan Canada for Canada; by Computer and Technical Books for the Caribbean Basin; by Contemporanea de Ediciones for Venezuela; by Distribuidora Cuspide for Argentina; by CITEC for Brazil; by Ediciones ZETA S.C.R. Ltda. for Peru; by Editorial Limusa SA for Mexico; by Transworld Publishers Limited in the United Kingdom and Europe; by Al-Maiman Publishers & Distributors for Saudi Arabia; by Simron Pty. Ltd. for South Africa; by IDG Communications (HK) Ltd. for Hong Kong; by Toppan Company Ltd. for Japan; by Addison Wesley Publishing Company for Korea; by Longman Singapore Publishers Ltd. for Singapore, Malaysia, Thailand, and Indonesia; by Unalis Corporation for Taiwan; by WS Computer Publishing Company, Inc. for the Philippines; by WoodsLane Pty. Ltd. for Australia; by WoodsLane Enterprises Ltd. for New Zealand.

For general information on IDG Books Worldwide's books in the U.S., please call our Consumer Customer Service department at 800-762-2974. For reseller information, including discounts and premium sales, please call our Reseller Customer Service department at 800-434-3422.

For information on where to purchase IDG Books Worldwide's books outside the U.S., contact IDG Books Worldwide at 415-655-3021 or fax 415-655-3295.

For information on translations, contact Marc Jeffrey Mikulich, Director, Foreign & Subsidiary Rights, at IDG Books Worldwide, 415-655-3018 or fax 415-655-3295.

For sales inquiries and special prices for bulk quantities, write to the address above or call IDG Books Worldwide at 415-655-3200.

For information on using IDG Books Worldwide's books in the classroom, or ordering examination copies, contact the Education Office at 800-434-2086 or fax 817-251-8174.

For authorization to photocopy items for corporate, personal, or educational use, please contact Copyright Clearance Center, 222 Rosewood Drive, Danvers, MA 01923, or fax 508-750-4470.

 is a trademark under exclusive license to IDG Books Worldwide, Inc., from International Data Group, Inc.

About the Author

Namir C. Shammas

Namir C. Shammas is a full-time author who specializes in object-oriented programming and Windows programming books. He has written and coauthored more than 50 programming books, such as *Foundations of C++ Programming* (IDG Books Worldwide, Inc.). Namir holds B.S. and M.S. degrees in chemical engineering.

ABOUT IDG BOOKS WORLDWIDE

WINNER
Eighth Annual
Computer Press
Awards ≥ 1992

WINNER
Ninth Annual
Computer Press
Awards ≥ 1993

IDG
BOOKS
WORLDWIDE

Welcome to the world of IDG Books Worldwide.

IDG Books Worldwide, Inc., is a subsidiary of International Data Group, the world's largest publisher of computer-related information and the leading global provider of information services on information technology. IDG was founded more than 25 years ago and now employs more than 7,700 people worldwide. IDG publishes more than 250 computer publications in 67 countries (see listing below). More than 70 million people read one or more IDG publications each month.

Launched in 1990, IDG Books Worldwide is today the #1 publisher of best-selling computer books in the United States. We are proud to have received 8 awards from the Computer Press Association in recognition of editorial excellence and three from Computer Currents' First Annual Readers' Choice Awards, and our best-selling ...*For Dummies*® series has more than 19 million copies in print with translations in 28 languages. IDG Books Worldwide, through a joint venture with IDG's Hi-Tech Beijing, became the first U.S. publisher to publish a computer book in the People's Republic of China. In record time, IDG Books Worldwide has become the first choice for millions of readers around the world who want to learn how to better manage their businesses.

Our mission is simple: Every one of our books is designed to bring extra value and skill-building instructions to the reader. Our books are written by experts who understand and care about our readers. The knowledge base of our editorial staff comes from years of experience in publishing, education, and journalism — experience which we use to produce books for the '90s. In short, we care about books, so we attract the best people. We devote special attention to details such as audience, interior design, use of icons, and illustrations. And because we use an efficient process of authoring, editing, and desktop publishing our books electronically, we can spend more time ensuring superior content and spend less time on the technicalities of making books.

You can count on our commitment to deliver high-quality books at competitive prices on topics you want to read about. At IDG Books Worldwide, we continue in the IDG tradition of delivering quality for more than 25 years. You'll find no better book on a subject than one from IDG Books Worldwide.

John J. Kilcullen

John Kilcullen
President and CEO
IDG Books Worldwide, Inc.

IDG Books Worldwide, Inc., is a subsidiary of International Data Group, the world's largest publisher of computer-related information and the leading global provider of information services on information technology. International Data Group publishes over 250 computer publications in 67 countries. Seventy million people read one or more International Data Group publications each month. International Data Group's publications include: **ARGENTINA:** Computerworld Argentina, GamePro, Infoworld, PC World Argentina; **AUSTRALIA:** Australian Macworld, Client/Server Journal, Computer Living, Computerworld, Digital News, Network World, PC World, Publishing Essentials, Reseller; **AUSTRIA:** Computerwelt, PC TEST; **BELARUS:** PC World Belarus; **BELGIUM:** Data News; **BRAZIL:** Annuario de Informática, Computerworld Brazil, Connections, Super Game Power, Macworld, PC World Brazil, Publish Brazil, SUPERGAME; **BULGARIA:** Computerworld Bulgaria, Networkworld/Bulgaria, PC & MacWorld Bulgaria; **CANADA:** CIO Canada, ComputerWorld Canada, InfoCanada, Network World Canada, Reseller World; **CHILE:** Computerworld Chile, GamePro, PC World Chile; **COLUMBIA:** Computerworld Colombia, GamePro, PC World Colombia; **COSTA RICA:** PC World Costa Rica/Nicaragua; **THE CZECH AND SLOVAK REPUBLICS:** Computerworld Czechoslovakia, Elektronika Czechoslovakia, PC World Czechoslovakia; **DENMARK:** Communications World, Computerworld Danmark, Macworld Danmark, PC World Danmark, PC World Danmark Supplements, TECH World; **DOMINICAN REPUBLIC:** PC World Republica Dominicana; **ECUADOR:** PC World Ecuador, GamePro; **EGYPT:** Computerworld Middle East, PC World Middle East; **EL SALVADOR:** PC World Centro America; **FINLAND:** MikroPC, Tietoverkko, Tietoviikko; **FRANCE:** Distributique, Golden, Info PC, Le Guide du Monde Informatique, Le Monde Informatique, Reseaux & Telecoms; **GERMANY:** Computer Business, Computerwoche, Computerwoche Extra, Computerwoche Focus, Electronic Entertainment, GamePro, I/M Information Management, Macwelt, PC Welt; **GREECE:** GamePro, Macworld & Publish; **GUATEMALA:** PC World Centro America; **HONDURAS:** PC World Centro America; **HONG KONG:** Computerworld Hong Kong, PCWorld Hong Kong, Publish in Asia; **HUNGARY:** ABCD CD-ROM, Computerworld Szamitastechnika, PC & Mac World Hungary, PC-X Magazine; **INDIA:** Computerworld India, PC World India, Publish in Asia; **INDONESIA:** InfoKomputer PC World, Komputek Computerworld, Publish in Asia; **IRELAND:** ComputerScope, PC Live!; **ISRAEL:** PC World 32 BIT, People & Computers; **ITALY:** Computerworld Italia, Computerworld Italia Special Editions, Lotus Italia, Macworld Italia, Networking Italia, PC Shopping, PC World Italia, PC World/Walt Disney; **JAPAN:** Macworld Japan, Nikkei Personal Computing, SunWorld Japan, Windows World Japan; **KENYA:** East African Computer News; **KOREA:** Hi-Tech Information/Computerworld, Macworld Korea, PC World Korea; **MACEDONIA:** PC World Macedonia; **MALAYSIA:** Computerworld Malaysia, PC World Malaysia, Publish in Asia; **MEXICO:** Computerworld Mexico, GamePro, Macworld, PC World Mexico; **MYANMAR:** PC World Myanmar; **NETHERLANDS:** Computable, Computer! Totaal, LAN Magazine, Macworld, Net Magazine; **NEW ZEALAND:** Computer Buyer, Computerworld New Zealand, MTB, Network World, PC World New Zealand; **NICARAGUA:** PC World Costa Rica/Nicaragua; **NIGERIA:** PC World Africa; **NORWAY:** Computerworld Norge, Computerworld Privat, CW Rapport Klient/Tjener, CW Rapport Nettverk & Telecom, CW Rapport Offentlig Sektor, IDG's KURSGUIDE, Macworld Norge, Multimedia World, PC World Ekspress, PC World Nettverk, PC World Norge, PC World's Produktguide, Windows Spesial; **PAKISTAN:** Computerworld Pakistan, PC World Pakistan; **PANAMA:** GamePro, PC World Panama; **PARAGUAY:** PC World Paraguay; **P. R. OF CHINA:** China Computerworld, China Infoworld, Computer & Communication, Electronic Product World, Electronics Today, Game Camp, PC World China, Popular Computer Week, Software World, Telecom Product World; **PERU:** Computerworld Peru, GamePro, PC World Profesional Peru, PC World Peru; **POLAND:** Computerworld Poland, Computerworld Special Report, Macworld, Networld, PC World Komputer; **PHILIPPINES:** Computerworld Philippines, PC Digest, Publish in Asia; **PORTUGAL:** Cerebro/PC World, Correio Informático/Computerworld, Mac•In/PC•In Portugal; **PUERTO RICO:** PC World Puerto Rico; **ROMANIA:** Computerworld Romania, PC World Romania, Telecom Romania; **RUSSIA:** Computerworld Rossiya, Network World Russia, PC World Russia; **SINGAPORE:** Computerworld Singapore, PC World Singapore, Publish in Asia; **SLOVENIA:** MONITOR; **SOUTH AFRICA:** Computing S.A., Network World S.A., Software World; **SPAIN:** Computerworld España, COMUNICACIONES WORLD, Dealer World, Macworld España, PC World España; **SWEDEN:** CAP&Design, Computer Sweden, Corporate Computing, MacWorld, Maxi Data, MikroDatorn, Nätverk & Kommunikation, PC/Aktiv, PC World, Windows World; **SWITZERLAND:** Computerworld Schweiz, Macworld Schweiz, PCtip; **TAIWAN:** Computerworld Taiwan, Macworld Taiwan, PC World Taiwan, Publish Taiwan, Windows World; **THAILAND:** Thai Computerworld, Publish in Asia; **TURKEY:** Computerworld Monitör, MACWORLD Turkiye, PC WORLD Turkiye; **UKRAINE:** Computerworld Kiev, Computers & Software Magazine, PC World Ukraine; **UNITED KINGDOM:** Acorn User, Amiga Action, Amiga Computing, Amiga, Appletalk, CD Powerplay, CD-ROM Now, Computing, Connexion, GamePro, Lotus Magazine, Macaction, Macworld, Open Computing, Parents and Computers, PC Home, PC Works, The WEB; **UNITED STATES:** Cable in the Classroom, CD Review, CIO Magazine, Computerworld, Computerworld Client/Server Journal, Digital Video Magazine, DOS World, Electronic, InfoWorld, I-Way, Macworld, Maximize, MULTIMEDIA WORLD, Network World, PC World, PUBLISH, SWATPro Magazine, Video Event, WebMaster; **URUGUAY:** PC World Uruguay; **VENEZUELA:** Computerworld Venezuela, GamePro, PC World Venezuela; and **VIETNAM:** PC World Vietnam   10/17/95a

Dedication

To Emily Rennie, who resides in my soul.

Acknowledgments

This book is the fruit of the efforts of many people. I would like to thank the Publisher, Milissa L. Koloski, and the editorial manager, Mary Corder, for sharing my vision in this book. Many thanks to my literary agent, Carol McLyndon of Waterside Productions, for encouraging me and pursuing this project. I would also like to thank the technical editor, Greg Guntle, who has edited my most successful books. Many thanks to the project editor, John Pont, and the editor, Pat Seiler, for their patience in shaping the manuscript. Let's do it again, guys!

(The Publisher would like to give special thanks to Patrick J. McGovern, without whom this book would not have been possible.)

Credits

Senior Vice President and Publisher
Milissa L. Koloski

Associate Publisher
Diane Graves Steele

Brand Manager
Judith A. Taylor

Editorial Managers
Kristin A. Cocks
Mary C. Corder

Product Development Manager
Mary Bednarek

Editorial Executive Assistant
Richard Graves

Editorial Assistants
Constance Carlisle
Chris H. Collins
Jerelind Davis
Kevin Spencer

Marketing Assistant
Holly N. Blake

Acquisitions Assistant
Gareth Hancock

Production Director
Beth Jenkins

Production Assistant
Jacalyn L. Pennywell

Supervisor of Project Coordination
Cindy L. Phipps

Supervisor of Page Layout
Kathie S. Schnorr

Supervisor of Graphics and Design
Shelley Lea

Reprint Coordination
Tony Augsburger
Elizabeth Cárdenas-Nelson
Todd Kleme
Theresa Sánchez-Baker

Blueline Coordinator
Patricia R. Reynolds

Media/Archive Coordination
Leslie Popplewell
Melissa Stauffer
Jason Marcuson

Project Editor
John W. Pont

Editors
Pat Seiler
Suzanne Packer

Technical Reviewer
Greg Guntle

Project Coordination Assistant
Regina Snyder

Graphic Coordination
Gina Scott
Angela F. Hunckler

Production Staff
Cameron Booker
Brett Black
Kate Snell
Ron Riggan
Marti Stegeman

Proofreaders
Arielle Carole Mennelle
Christine Meloy Beck
Gwenette Gaddis
Dwight Ramsey
Carl Saff
Robert Springer

Indexer
Sherry Massey

Cover Design
Kavish + Kavish

Contents at a Glance

Cartoons at a Glance

By Rich Tennant
Fax: 508-546-7747
E-mail: the5wave@tiac.net

Page 7

Page 95

Page 339

Page 261

Table of Contents

Introduction

· ·

*O*bject-oriented programming (OOP) has gained popularity among programmers and end users alike. The past 16 years have seen the advent of OOP languages such as SmallTalk, Eiffel, and C++. Even non-OOP programming languages, such as Ada and COBOL, are getting object-oriented programming features as part of their new American National Standards Institute (ANSI) standards. So it is easy to see that OOP is happening!

About This Book

This book introduces you to the world of object-oriented programming using C++. I assume that you are already familiar with C++. If you are not, I suggest that you get *C++ For Dummies* by Stephen R. Davis (published by IDG Books Worldwide, Inc.). That book does an excellent job of explaining C++, so I don't need to discuss C++. Instead, I focus on the object-oriented aspects of C++. Consequently, I expect that you already have a C++ compiler (it could be running under DOS, Windows, UNIX, or the Macintosh operating system, to name a few) and know how to write *console* applications (generic programs that use the standard input and output streams).

About the Code in This Book

This book contains the general syntax of classes, member functions, and so on. Here is a simple example that shows you the style I use:

```
class className
{
    public:
        // public members
    protected:
        // protected members
};
```

The example shows that nonreserved keywords (in this case, *className*) appear in italic, and reserved words (such as *class, public,* and *protected*) appear as normal text. I also use square brackets to show optional components. When I present the general syntax for a particular C++ feature, I often use comments to describe elements of that syntax in general terms.

The book contains sample sessions with the programs that I present. In these examples, I use boldface to highlight any input that the user provides.

Sometimes, you will see a curved arrow (↵) at the end of some lines of code. This means that the line of code will appear as one line on your screen. We just didn't have the space to fit all the characters on one line.

How This Book Is Organized

The four parts of this book contain 17 chapters and a glossary that guide you on your trek through the world of object-oriented programming. Each chapter contains programming examples that show you the details of various aspects of object-oriented programming. Typically, programmers prefer listings over long-winded text that dances around (and avoids) concrete details. In a sense, a program listing is like a picture — it's worth a thousand words. Moreover, I've been burned many times by inaccurate code snippets, especially in technical manuals. That's why I prefer showing you a complete program listing that works! I sometimes use code snippets, but I keep them to a minimum.

Part I: Basic OOP Concepts

In Part I, which includes Chapters 1 through 3, you read about the basics of object-oriented programming, classes, and objects.

Chapter 1 gives you the big picture by discussing the pillars of object-oriented programming: classes, objects, methods, inheritance, and polymorphism. This chapter introduces you to the fundamental notions (and buzzwords) of object-oriented programming.

Chapter 2 looks at classes and shows you how to declare them. The chapter examines the various components of a class (data members and member functions). The chapter also discusses the various roles played by member functions.

Chapter 3 presents the life cycle of an object and shows you how to declare, initialize, manipulate, and finally destroy an object.

Part II: Cruising at Comfortable Levels

Part II includes Chapters 4 through 10 and presents the meat and potatoes of object-oriented programming.

Chapter 4 focuses on static data members and member functions and shows you how they relate conceptually to the class instead of to the class instances. The chapter provides examples of using static members. These examples illustrate instance counting, common error management, and shared information.

Chapter 5 talks about class design and focuses on cohesion and coupling — two criteria that relate to the design of member functions. The chapter gives you an example of an ill-designed class and then shows you its improved version.

Chapter 6 discusses inheritance in C++ classes. The chapter focuses on single inheritance and shows you how to declare and use descendant classes. The chapter also discusses constructors for child classes and the use of nonpublic descendants.

Chapter 7 looks at *polymorphism*, an OOP feature that provides unified response in the members of a class hierarchy. The chapter discusses how virtual member functions support polymorphism in C++.

Chapter 8 discusses class hierarchy design and offers guidelines for a good design. The chapter shows an example of an inefficient class hierarchy and then compares it with an improved version.

Chapter 9 presents multiple inheritance and shows you how to declare descendant classes that use the multiple inheritance scheme. The chapter shows you an example of a descendant class that comes from distinct parent classes. The chapter also presents an example of a descendant class that comes from parent classes that share a common lineage.

Chapter 10 compares containment with multiple inheritance. The chapter shows you how containment relates different classes without using a multiple inheritance scheme. The chapter includes a programming example that uses containment and compares it with the example of multiple inheritance in Chapter 9.

Part III: Advanced OOP Features

In Part III, which includes Chapters 11 through 14, I present advanced object-oriented programming topics.

Chapter 11 discusses abstract classes and shows you how to declare them. The chapter provides examples of a single abstract class hierarchy and a multiple abstract class hierarchy.

Chapter 12 presents templates, a relatively new C++ feature. The chapter discusses the benefits of templates and shows you how to declare a class template, how to define the member functions of a class template, and how to instantiate a class template. In addition, the chapter shows you how to create a hierarchy of class templates.

Chapter 13 looks at exceptions (run-time errors) and shows you how C++ uses classes and objects to manage exceptions. The chapter discusses the standard exceptions and presents the throw, try, and catch keywords. The chapter also talks about nested try-catch blocks, rethrowing an exception, and associating functions and exceptions.

Chapter 14 describes other ways to relate classes, namely by using friend classes and nested classes. The chapter discusses the benefits of using friend classes and shows you an example of these benefits. The chapter also presents nested classes, discusses their benefits, and presents examples of friend classes and nested classes.

Part IV: The Part of Tens

In keeping with the tradition of other ... *For Dummies* books (or is it David Letterman?), Part IV is the Part of Tens.

Chapter 15 provides a checklist for declaring classes. You can use this handy list to make sure that you don't forget a valuable class component.

Chapter 16 looks at the ten commandments of virtual member functions (featuring Charlton Heston as Moses).

Chapter 17 examines ten common stream I/O objects, member functions, and manipulators. The components are typically involved in C++ console applications, such as the ones I describe in this book.

Last, but not least, the Glossary is the place to look for all those buzzwords and technical terms that stump you.

Icons Used in This Book

Throughout this book, I use the following icons to point out special information:

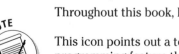

This icon points out a technical note that provides additional comments on a programming feature that I'm presenting.

This icon reminds you of a key programming feature.

This icon highlights a programming tip that can help you enhance your code.

This icon warns you about some bad "mamajama" and saves you from a lot of frustration (and saves me from a lot of hate mail!).

Where Do You Go from Here?

So, here we go! Your trek into the world of object-oriented programming is about to begin. Don't shy away from taking a break if you feel overwhelmed. You may want to have your introductory C++ book (for example, *C++ For Dummies*,) available just in case you want to refamiliarize yourself with some basic C++ terms. Remember that this is your book. So don't hesitate to circle key points, write in the margins, or mark statements in program listings.

And that's all she wrote! I hope this book opens the door for you to enter the world of object-oriented programming.

Happy object-oriented programming!

Part I
Basic OOP Concepts

In this part...

Y ou begin with the basics of object-oriented programming, classes, and objects. The first chapter discusses the pillars of object-oriented programming. The second and third chapters discuss classes and objects as they relate to object-oriented programming.

Chapter 1

Object-Oriented Programming: The Big Picture

. . . .

In This Chapter

▶ Looking at structured programming: the past

▶ Looking at object-oriented programming: the present

▶ Understanding the basic principles of object-oriented programming

. . . .

*T*o get started with object-oriented programming (OOP), you need to understand the big picture. This chapter describes the evolution of programming techniques and the basic pillars of OOP: classes, objects, inheritance, and polymorphism. So sit back and relax. Your OOP journey is just beginning!

Structured Programming: A Walk down Memory Lane

In programming (and many other aspects of life), where you're headed depends on where you've been. Programming technology has evolved, and to understand the importance of OOP, you need to understand what preceded OOP.

Your introduction to object-oriented programming begins with a brisk walk down memory lane (don't worry, you'll be on the fast track). Programming the early computers was a difficult task because it involved working in machine language that used numerically coded instructions. Fortunately, computer scientists quickly recognized the need for programming languages that were more easily understood by humans. These languages replaced numbers with names (that is, *identifiers*) that represent the various parts of the program, such as loops, *if* statements, variables, functions, and procedures.

The popular programming languages during the 1950s and 1960s included BASIC and FORTRAN. The early version of BASIC (which was famous for using line numbers) was a simple programming language with global variables and no separate functions or subroutines. By supporting separate functions and subroutines, FORTRAN was one of the first popular programming languages to foster the reuse of routines and the creation of libraries of routines. These features were lacking in the early BASIC, which supported local GOSUB subroutines (these are subroutines that simply start and end at certain line numbers) that are inferior to FORTRAN's subroutines.

The 1970s witnessed the popularity of Pascal, a programming language that was created by a Swiss professor named Nicklaus Wirth who taught at ETH (the technical university at Zurich). As a structured language, Pascal became popular with university professors who taught sound programming practices. Unlike BASIC (which is rather easygoing, for example, insofar as declaring variables is concerned), Pascal requires that every variable be declared and that a data type be associated with each variable. Pascal also supports formal functions and procedures (which I collectively call *routines*). These routines enjoy a certain level of autonomy in that they can declare their own data types, constants, variables, and nested routines. Thus, Pascal enables you to develop reusable functions and procedures. The evolution of Pascal compilers led to the support of library units that contain reusable data types, constants, variables, functions, and procedures. For a while, programming in Pascal was in style.

The popularity of structured programming also led to the creation of C, the parent language of C++. Initially, C was meant to be a portable high-level assembler to support the UNIX operating system on different machines. However, C also proved to be a useful general-purpose programming language. Historically, C compilers produced tight executable code and programs that run fast. In contrast, Pascal compilers did not have to be efficient because they were mainly used for teaching rather than for flying rockets! For these reasons, C soon surpassed Pascal, becoming the *cool* programming language of the 1980s.

Structured programming focuses primarily on routines and secondarily on data. Even though you start by defining the data structures that represent a piece of information, you quickly shift your focus to writing the routines needed to manipulate that data.

Structured programming techniques support the top-down or the bottom-up approach of creating a tree of callable routines. In the top-down approach, you start by defining the top-level routines and gradually define the lower-level routines that are called by the top-level routines. In contrast, the bottom-up approach starts by defining the low-level routines and works its way up to the top-level routines. Either approach focuses primarily on the routines and how they manipulate the data. Figure 1-1 shows a sample hierarchy of routines that are calling each other and passing data between each other. If you've programmed in C, Pascal, or the newer versions of BASIC, you should be familiar with structured programming techniques.

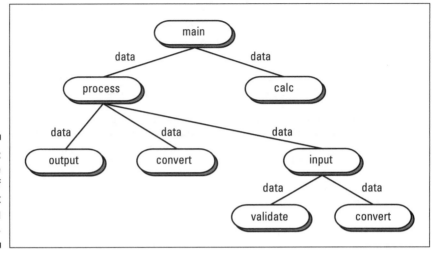

Figure 1-1:
A sample
hierarchy of
routines that
are calling
each other.

Object-Oriented Programming: The Here and Now

We live in a world of objects: the book you are reading, the pen you write with, the computer you use, the car you drive, the TV you watch, and the house in which you live. Some objects are more animated than others. Every object has its own *characteristics* (also called *attributes*), such as color, shape, and weight. The objects that are animated, such as a compact disc player, perform operations like playing music. An object is any *thing*.

Structured programming models real-world objects by defining data types and using them in a hierarchy of loosely related routines that manipulate the information in these data types. This rather loose association between data types and the related routines turned some computer scientists into unhappy campers. These grumpy scientists questioned the efficiency of structured programming techniques, especially for developing large software projects. Among their complaints was the fact that there is no limit to writing routines that manipulate the data types. The object-minded scientists argued for a new way of looking at things. This new way is based on the object that is being modeled rather than on a loose collection of data types and routines.

The Four Pillars of OOP

Object-oriented programming offers a new way of looking at things. The main focus of OOP is the *object,* which is one pillar of OOP. Every object belongs to a category of objects, called a class, which is the second pillar of OOP. In other words, a *class* is a category of very similar objects. The third and fourth pillars of OOP are inheritance and polymorphism. These pillars involve working with families of classes. I discuss these pillars later in this chapter.

Classes: object family values

Object-oriented programming promotes the categorization of objects into classes. Each class describes the characteristics and the operations of its objects. For example, consider a TV model called TV-01. Figure 1-2 shows a sketch of this television model.

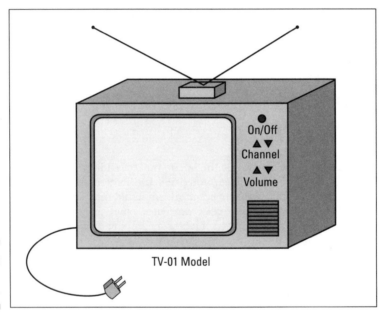

Figure 1-2:
The TV-01
model.

The TV-01 model represents a class of televisions that display images in color and receive UHF and VHF stations. The components of the TV-01 model are:

- Electronic circuits
- A cathode ray tube
- A casing
- A power supply
- An antenna
- Control buttons and knobs

The operations of the TV-01 model include the following:

✔ Turning the TV on or off

✔ Selecting a channel

✔ Changing the volume (preferably, turning it down to keep Mom or Dad happy)

To keep the example simple, I omitted adjusting the screen contrast, brightness, and all that jazz. Thus, the TV-01 model has specific characteristics and operations.

A class is a category of objects that share the same characteristics and operations.

As another example of a class — one that hits closer to home — consider a word processing program that I'll call MyOwnWord Version 1. The program represents a class (or category, if you prefer) of executable files that support a simple word processor. The program has its own attributes that enable it to store and manage text internally and to display text. The word processor performs the following simple tasks:

✔ Creates a new file

✔ Opens a file

✔ Closes a file

✔ Saves a file using the current source filename

✔ Saves a file using a new filename

✔ Edits text

✔ Finds and replaces text

✔ Prints text

✔ Quits

Objects: trains, planes, and . . .

An *object* is an instance of a class. Going back to the TV-01 example, suppose you decide to buy two TV-01 models. You keep one and give the other to your best friend. Each unit you buy represents an object that is an instance of the TV-01 model. In other words, you keep one TV-01 object (or *instance*, if you prefer), and you give your friend the other TV-01 object. Both TV objects share the same capabilities and features. However, you and your friend are not likely to be watching the same program at the same volume level, at the same time.

In OOP terms, the TV program that you are watching and the volume level you choose define the *state* of the TV object. In other words, attributes such as the channel number, the volume level, and the on/off mode define the state of a TV object. Each object has its own state that may or may not match the state of another object. Figure 1-3 depicts the TV-01 class and three of its instances. Each instance has its own state, because each instance is tuned to a different channel.

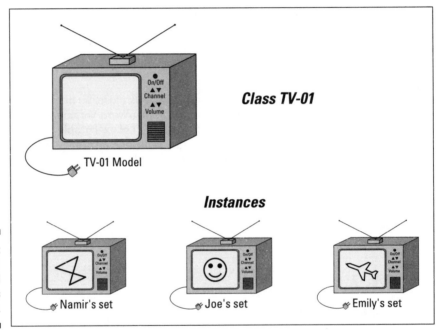

Figure 1-3:
The TV-01 class and three of its instances.

When you turn the TV off or on, change the channel, or alter the volume, you change the state of the TV, because you change the value of one or more of its attributes — the on/off mode, the channel, or the volume.

It is very rare for multiple instances of an object to have the same state. For example, the maker of MyOwnWord sells copies of its executable files to customers directly or through dealers. Each copy of the word processor contains a set of files that represents an instance of the word processor class. The state of each instance depends on the text in the word processor. It is very unlikely that any two computer users who are running copies of MyOwnWord have the exact same text.

An object is a tangible example (or *instance*, if you prefer) of a class.

Methods and messages: can we talk?

In object-oriented programming terms, you interact with an object and manipulate its state by sending it a message. This message tells the object what to do. For example, when you change the channel on the TV set, you use the channel selection knob to send the TV object the message that you want to select a new channel. (I am using the word *message* here in the OOP sense.) Your TV, an object (probably an expensive one at that), responds to the message by selecting and executing a method. (Again, I am using the word *method* here in the OOP sense.) In the case of the TV, changing channels causes its electronics to receive a different signal representing the channel you selected.

In object-oriented programming terms, a *method* tells the object how to respond to a message. Figure 1-4 depicts the message you send to the channel knob and how that knob selects the appropriate method. (Yes, channel knob. TV-01 is an old TV object.) The TV-01 object responds to the following messages:

✔ Turn the television set on and off.

✔ Change the channel.

✔ Change the volume.

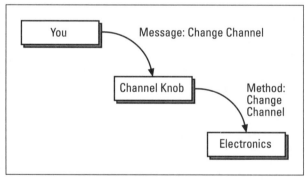

Figure 1-4:
Sending a change channel message to the channel knob.

You can regard a *message* as a relatively abstract command or request. Messages may include *arguments,* which you can view as additional instructions. The object responds to the message by selecting an appropriate method and executing it. The executed method performs all the gory details.

A message tells an object *what* to do. A method tells an object *how* to respond to a message.

Going back to the word processor example, when I use my copy of MyOwnWord, I send the word processor object various kinds of messages. I send some of these messages by invoking menu commands, such as Open, Save, or Find. I generate other messages by pressing the various keys on the keyboard. I can also generate messages by clicking the mouse buttons.

The word processor translates the various messages into methods that respond to menu selection commands, keyboard input, and mouse button clicks. For example, when I issue a Find message by invoking the Find command, the word processor invokes the piece of code that searches for text. The result is that the word processing program displays a Find dialog box that lets me specify the text to search for, whether to look for whole words, and whether to perform a case-sensitive search. The program then searches for the text I specify, in the manner I select.

Inheritance: passing wealth to child classes

Inheritance is a versatile part of object-oriented programming, because it provides for the reuse of classes. Object-oriented programming enables you to declare new classes that are descendants of existing classes (the existing classes are called *parent classes*). A *descendant class* (also called a *subclass* or a *child class*) inherits the attributes and the operations of its parent class. The descendant also defines new attributes and operations and overrides inherited operations that are not suitable for its purposes. Each descendant class represents a refinement of its parent class.

Object-oriented programming enables you to create a hierarchy of classes. The root of a class hierarchy is called the *base class*. The parents of a parent class (or grandparent classes) are called *ancestor classes*.

Figure 1-5 depicts a class hierarchy of color TV sets. The first class is a color TV. Its descendant class has stereo sound. The other descendant class has both stereo sound and a built-in VCR. The plain color TV is the base class for the hierarchy. This model is the parent class to the one with stereo sound and is the ancestor class to the one with both stereo sound and a built-in VCR.

How does inheritance work with the TV and word processor examples? Consider the TV example first.

Suppose that the maker of the TV-01 model decides to create a TV-02 model: a cable-ready TV with the much-cherished remote control. Instead of designing the TV-02 model from scratch, the TV maker uses the design of the TV-01 model but adds circuits and connectors that support cable stations. The TV maker also adds circuits to support the remote control. Thus, the TV-02 model inherits

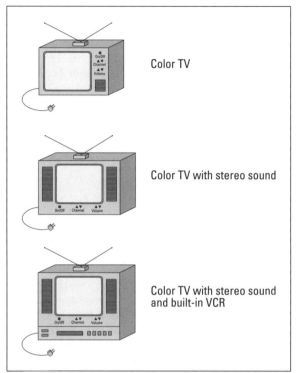

Color TV

Color TV with stereo sound

Color TV with stereo sound
and built-in VCR

Figure 1-5:
An
illustration
of a class
hierarchy.

the color CRT, the on/off knob, and the volume knob. As for the channel selector, the TV maker overrides the inherited channel selector knob with a new digital pad that enables viewers to select TV or cable stations (the inherited channel selector knob is not adequate for the TV-02 model).

In OOP terms, you can say that the TV-02 model is a descendant of the TV-01 model. The descendant model has inherited most of the components of TV-01, added new attributes and operations (to support cable stations and the remote control), and overridden the inherited channel selector.

The TV maker may elect to create yet another model that incorporates a VCR, TV-03. The TV maker builds on TV-02 to create TV-03. The new model uses the same components as TV-02 and supports VCR operations. The TV-03 model has a new casing and uses a new remote control that supports the VCR operations. Thus, TV-03 is a descendant of the TV-02 model. The new descendant class (in *OOPese*) introduces new attributes and operations and overrides some of the inherited ones (such as the casing and the remote control of the TV-02 model). The TV models TV-01, TV-02, and TV-03, form a hierarchy of TV-modeling classes.

To return to the word processor example, perhaps the developer of MyOwnWord creates Version 2 to support text formatting. Rather than recode Version 2 from scratch, the developer adds to the existing code of Version 1. The added code supports text formatting (selecting fonts, character style, paragraph style, and so on). Thus, in OOP terms, Version 2 of MyOwnWord is a descendant of Version 1. The descendant version introduces new attributes and operations to those it inherits from Version 1.

Polymorphism: nifty OOP shapeshifting

Polymorphism is an OOP buzzword that means *different forms*. Polymorphism is a powerful object-oriented programming feature that supports a uniform (or consistent, if you prefer) response among the classes in a class hierarchy. This is not to say that the various classes must behave exactly the same way to offer the uniform response. Quite the contrary, classes in a hierarchy are free to support the uniform response by performing slightly different tasks.

Consider the TV example. The models TV-01, TV-02, and TV-03 each have a volume knob and offer a consistent way to alter the volume. Suppose you are examining and comparing each of these models in a local electronics store. Changing the volume on the TV models should be consistent. Thus, the TV models offer a uniform response regardless of which TV model (which parallels a class) you examine. It may well be that each TV model uses different circuits to control the TV volume. However, turning the volume knob yields the same results in all three TV models. This is polymorphic behavior. Thus, polymorphism ensures that the instances of classes in a class hierarchy offer a uniform response to messages supported throughout the class hierarchy.

Consider the word processor example. The three versions of MyOwnWord support a uniform Find operation. Each version may implement slightly different code for the response to the Find command. However, you issue the Find command the same way in each version. Again, this example shows polymorphic behavior of the three classes of the word processor.

Summary

This chapter presents the basic principles of object-oriented programming. You've learned that classes and objects represent the building blocks of OOP software components. You've also learned about methods and messages and how they affect the state of an object. This chapter also discusses the important role of inheritance in creating new classes from existing ones. Finally, I discuss polymorphism, an OOP feature that supports a uniform response among classes that belong to the same hierarchy.

Chapter 2

Classes: Object Factories

● ●

In This Chapter

▶ Declaring C++ classes

▶ Learning about the sections of a class

▶ Learning about the data members

▶ Learning about the member functions

▶ Understanding the roles of member functions

● ●

*T*his chapter looks at C++ classes and focuses on how they relate to object-oriented programming. I discuss how to build a class to represent an object. This process involves selecting the attributes and the operations for the object that you are modeling.

C++ Classes: OOP Power to the People

C++ enables you to declare classes that represent objects. Classes typically *encapsulate* (that is, bring together) data members and member functions. The *data members* describe the various attributes (or characteristics) of a class of objects. The *member functions* represent the operations that set and query the various attributes of those objects. For example, a class that supports strings (C++ style) has data members that store the characters of the string, the current number of characters, and the maximum number of characters that can be stored. The class would have member functions that set and query the characters, as well as manipulate these characters (for example, make them uppercase, lowercase, and so on).

As you probably remember, you can create a hierarchy of classes, with one or more subclasses derived from a single base class. This chapter looks at base classes (a base class is one that is not derived from any other class). Chapter 6 looks at class hierarchies that declare descendant classes.

You use the following general syntax for declaring a base class:

```
class className
{
  public:
    // declarations of public members

  protected:
    // declarations of protected members

  private:
    // declarations of private members
};
```

The preceding general syntax shows that the declaration of a class consists of the following parts:

- ✔ The keyword `class`, which starts the declaration of the class.

- ✔ The name of the class.

- ✔ The declarations of the class data members and member functions, which are enclosed in a pair of open and close braces. The close brace is followed by a semicolon.

- ✔ The optional public section. This section starts with the keyword `public`, followed by a colon.

- ✔ The optional protected section. This section starts with the keyword `protected`, followed by a colon.

- ✔ The optional private section. This section starts with the keyword `private`, followed by a colon.

I discuss the various sections of a class in more detail in the next section of this chapter. In the meantime, you might ask whether a class must have any section declared. The answer is no. In other words, you can declare an empty class, as in the following example:

```
class myError
{
};
```

Why declare such a class? Well, believe it or not, error handling in C++ uses empty classes in which the name of the class suffices. Chapter 13 describes this weird stuff in more detail.

The Sections of a Class: Controlling Member Access

Through the use of *sections,* C++ provides for three levels of access in a class. This programming feature enables a class to hide some of its details and protects the class from unwarranted access (by class instances and by the member functions and instances of descendant classes) that may corrupt the state of the class instances (that is, objects that belong to the class). The three access levels are provided by the following sections of a class:

- ✓ The public section, which contains members that are accessible to the instances of a class.
- ✓ The protected section, which contains members that are not accessible to the instances of a class.
- ✓ The private section, which contains members that are not accessible to the instances of a class.

For the instances of a base class, the protected and public sections have the same effect. These two sections become more distinct for the descendants of a class.

Keep in mind that all the member functions in a class can access all other members in that class regardless of their access level. By default, the members of a class are private.

For instances of a base class, the protected and private sections have a similar effect. The protected and private sections enforce different access levels with the descendants of the base class. The member functions of the descendant classes can access the protected members of a parent (and ancestor) class, but not the private members.

C++ enables you to declare the public, protected, and private sections in any order you like. Moreover, you can have multiple public, protected, and private sections in the same class, if your heart so desires.

I've seen two general styles for declaring the various sections. The first style uses the sequence of public, protected, and private sections. In other words, the style moves from most accessible to least accessible. The second style arranges the sections in the reverse order. Over the years, I have switched from the second style to the first one. In addition, the style I use lists the data members before the member functions in the protected and private sections and lists the member functions before the data members in the public section.

Using Data Members to Define the State of the Class Instances

The data members in a class describe the various attributes in a class. C++ gurus recommend that you place data members in protected or private sections and avoid placing them in the public section. Why? Placing data members in a public section enables the class instances to access the data members and perhaps corrupt the data in these data members. The gurus recommend that you manage accessing the data members of a class by using access member functions. These member functions return the values of the protected data members.

How do you define the data members in a class? Here are the steps involved:

1. Study the object that you are modeling with the class.

2. Select those attributes that you want to represent in the class and forget about other attributes that are irrelevant to your design.

3. Name the attributes that you selected in Step 2.

4. Associate the appropriate data type with each attribute. Think carefully about which data type is appropriate, and don't rush into picking simple predefined data types such as int or char. For example, using an enumerated type may be more suitable (as in readable) than using an int type. The result of Steps 3 and 4 is a list of data members.

5. Select the access level for each data member. Typically, you place data members in the protected section. As you become a more proficient object-oriented programmer, you will find your own reasons for placing data members in either the private section or (heaven forbid!) the public section.

Figure 2-1 shows the pictorial symbol for a class. The figure shows a round-rectangle shape that contains three parts. The top part defines the name of the class. The middle part lists the attributes of the class. The bottom part lists the methods of the class.

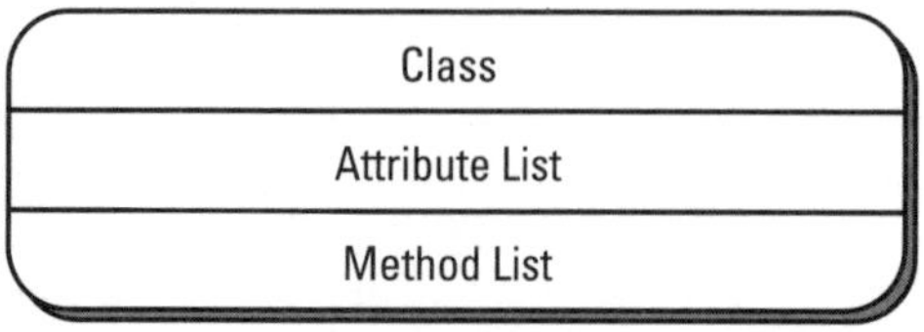

Figure 2-1:
The pictorial representation of a class.

Class
Attribute List
Method List

Who says television has no class?

To understand how you define the data members in a class, you can use the TV-01 example from Chapter 1. The TV-01 model has the following attributes:

- ✔ The On/Off mode
- ✔ The channel number
- ✔ The volume

This list of attributes covers the first two steps (previously mentioned) in defining the data members in a class. To perform Step 3, you give names to the attributes. For example, you can use the following names:

- ✔ IsOn for the On/Off mode.
- ✔ ChannelNumber for the channel number.
- ✔ Volume for the volume.

In Step 4, you associate data types with the names for the attributes. The naming style that I use (which is also recommended by programming gurus) incorporates one or more characters that reflect the data type associated with the data member.

You can represent the On/Off switch with a dual-state value. The candidate types are int (using 0 for off and 1 for on), user-defined logical (true and false), or user-defined enumerated (which specifies on and off values).

Choose the user-defined enumerated type and define the enumerated type OnOffMode with the enumerators tvOff and tvOn. Thus, the name of the data member for the On/Off switch is m_eOnOffSwitch. Notice that this name starts with m_ to specify that you are naming a data member. The letter e following the m_ indicates that the data member is an enumerated type. The string OnOffSwitch completes the name of the data member by appending a descriptive name. Table 2-1 provides a partial list of identifier prefixes.

Table 2-1	A Partial List of Identifier Prefixes	
Data Type	*Prefix Characters*	*Examples*
char	c	cDriveName
int	n	nIndex
long	l	lFileSize
double	f	fVolume

(continued)

Table 2-1 *(continued)*

Data Type	Prefix Characters	Examples
char*	psz	pszMyString
ASCIIZ string	sz	szName
long pointer	lp	lpszDirName
data member	m_	m_nIndex

You can represent the channel number with an integer type. The candidate data types are short, int, unsigned, and byte (which I declare as a typedef of the predefined unsigned char data type). Choose byte because it has a short range of nonnegative values (0 to 255). That way, you don't have to deal with negative channel numbers. Thus, the name of the data member for the channel number is m_uChannelNumber. The characters m_u indicate that the name belongs to a data member that has an unsigned value.

You can represent the volume number similarly to the way you represent the channel number. Thus, the name of the data member for the volume is m_uVolume. The characters m_u indicate that the name belongs to a data member that has an unsigned value.

The last step in defining the data members for the class TV01 is to select the class section in which you declare these data members. Use the default choice: the protected section.

Thus, the partial declaration of class TV01 is:

```
// declare the enumerated type OnOffMode
enum OnOffMode { tvOff, tvOn };

// declare the type byte as an alias to unsigned char
typedef unsigned char byte;

class TV01
{
  public:
    // declarations of public members

  protected:
    OnOffMode m_eOnOffSwitch; // on/off switch
    byte m_uChannelNumber;    // channel number
    byte m_uVolume;           // volume
};
```

This code snippet includes the declarations of the enumerated type `OnOffMode` and the typedefed type `byte`. Figure 2-2 shows the pictorial representation of the class declaration shown in the code (the list of methods is not yet defined).

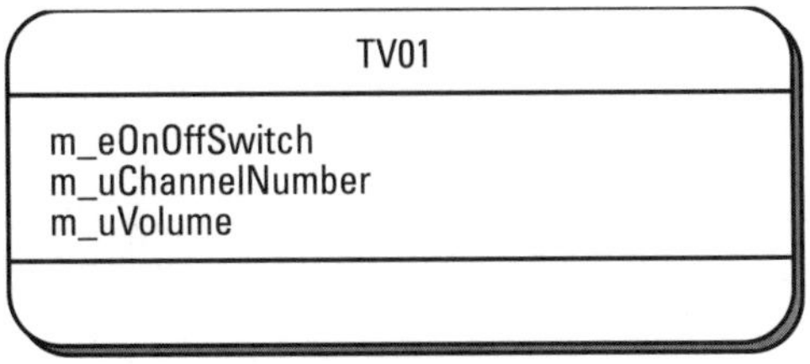

Figure 2-2:
The pictorial representa-
tion of class
TV01.

TV01
m_eOnOffSwitch m_uChannelNumber m_uVolume

A boxing lesson

For another example of defining the data members in a class, consider a cardboard box. The box has dimensions and weight and is made of a certain type of cardboard. This brief study concludes Step 1 (at the beginning of the section "Using Data Members. . ."). Step 2 focuses on the attributes in which you are interested. For this example, you focus on the following attributes:

- ✔ Length
- ✔ Width
- ✔ Height
- ✔ Volume
- ✔ Base area (that is, the area of the bottom surface)

You are not interested in the type of cardboard used to construct the box; nor do you care how much the box weighs when empty.

In Step 3, you name the attributes. Interestingly, you can calculate the base area and the volume of the box by using the first three dimensions. Calculating the base area and the volume is more convenient than storing them in data members and making sure that their values are up-to-date. Thus, the list of attributes you need to name includes only three items:

- ✔ `Length` for the length of the box.
- ✔ `Width` for the width of the box.
- ✔ `Height` for the height of the box.

In Step 4, you associate data types with the list of attributes and you fine-tune the names of these attributes:

- ✔ You can represent the length of the box by using the float or the double data type. For enhanced math precision, select double. Thus, the data member that represents the length of the box is m_fLength. The letters m_f indicate that the name belongs to a data member that has the double type.

- ✔ You can represent the width of the box by using the float or the double data type. Again, I choose the double type, and I end up with the name m_fWidth for the data member.

- ✔ You can represent the height of the box by using the float or the double data type. Once again, I select the double type, and I end up with the name m_fHeight for the data member.

The last step in defining the data members for the class Box is to select the class section in which you declare these data members. Use the default choice: the protected section.

Thus, the partial declaration of class Box (which shows only the data members) is as follows:

```
class Box
{
  public:
  // declarations of public members

  protected:
    double m_fLength; // length of box
    double m_fWidth;  // width of box
    double m_fHeight; // height of box
};
```

Figure 2-3 shows the pictorial representation of the class declaration shown in the code (the list of methods is not yet defined).

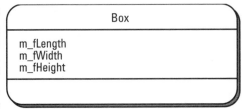

Box

m_fLength
m_fWidth
m_fHeight

Using Member Functions: The Class Enablers

C++ encapsulates data members and member functions in classes. In OOP terms, a member function is also called a *method*. Member functions empower your applications to set and query the state of class instances. Thus, member functions conceptually animate the class instances. Without member functions, you end up with classes that act as mere structures. For example, a class that supports strings needs member functions to assign new characters, obtain the characters, and obtain the number of characters. Without such member functions, the string class is simply a string-storing structure.

The declaration of member functions inside a class resembles the prototyping of nonmember functions. You use the following general syntax for declaring a member function inside a class:

```
returnType functionName(parameterList);
```

The declaration of a member function starts with the return type, followed by the name of the member function, and then the parameter list. The syntax for declaring a member function is similar to declaring function prototypes in C and C++.

C++ enables you to define member functions inside or outside the class declaration. If the definition of a member function includes one or at most two statements, you can include these statements in the class declaration. Otherwise, you need to place the definition of the member function outside the class declaration.

What difference does the placement make? The answer lies in the fact that C++ compilers treat member functions that are defined inside the class declaration as *inline functions*. In other words, when you invoke such member functions, the compiler generates a code that inserts the member function's statements instead of calling that member function. Some compilers count the number of statements inside member functions that are defined within the class and decide whether to expand them as inline functions.

You use the following general syntax for defining a member function outside the class declaration:

```
returnType className::functionName(parameterList)
{
    // statements
}
```

From the syntax, you can see that C++ requires you to qualify the name of a member function by using the name of the *host class* (that is, the class that contains the data members and member functions). The definition separates the names of the class and the member function with two colons.

Here is a simple example of a class declaration followed by the definition of its member functions:

```
class myInt
{
  public:
    void setInt(int nNum);
    int getInt();

  protected:
    int m_nNum;
};

void myInt::setInt(int nNum)
{
  m_nNum = nNum;
}


int myInt::getInt()
{
  return m_nNum;
}
```

The class myInt declares the protected int-type data member m_nNum to store integers. The class declares the member functions setInt() and getInt() to store a new value in the data member and recall the current value in the data member, respectively. The example shows the definition of the member functions outside the class declaration. Because the definition of each member function requires a single statement, I can rewrite the class declaration to incorporate the definitions of the member functions:

```
class myInt
{
  public:
    void setInt(int nNum)
      { m_nNum = nNum; }
    int getInt()
      { return m_nNum; }
```

```
   protected:
      int m_nNum;
};
```

The second version of class my Int is functionally equivalent to the first one.

Selecting Member Functions (Carefully)

Later in this chapter, I provide more details on the various types of member functions in a class. First, however, I present some basic guidelines for selecting the member functions of a class.

As you may know, every class has special member functions called the *constructor* and the *destructor*. When you create a class instance, the run-time system invokes the constructor to initialize that instance. Likewise, when the instance reaches the end of its scope (that is, the range of statements), the run-time system executes the destructor. If you don't declare a constructor or a destructor, the compiler builds one for you. (How nice!) I discuss constructors and destructors in more detail in Chapter 3. For now, keep them in mind as special member functions that initialize and destroy class instances.

Selecting member functions involves the following steps:

1. Determine whether you need to declare a constructor that initializes the attributes of an instance to special values or performs special initialization tasks.

2. Determine whether you need a destructor to clean up after the class instance reaches the end of its scope.

3. Determine which class attributes need to have values assigned to them.

4. Determine which class attributes can be queried by using member functions.

5. Determine what other operations — for example, calculations or other manipulations of attributes — you must implement.

In the following sections, you can see some not too trivial examples of declaring and defining member functions.

Another TV episode

Earlier in the chapter, I defined the data members that represent the TV-01 model. In this section, I focus on the operations of the TV set that I include in the class TV01. Here is a list of operations:

- Turning the TV set on. This task uses the member function turnOn() to set the data member m_eOnOffSwitch to the enumerator tvOn.

- Turning the TV set off. This task uses the member function turnOff() to set the data member m_eOnOffSwitch to the enumerator tvOff.

- Querying the on/off mode of the TV set. This task uses the member function getOnOffMode() to return the enumerator value in the data member m_eOnOffSwitch.

- Selecting a channel. This task uses the member function setChannelNumber(). The function has a parameter that passes the new value for the channel number. The function writes the new channel number to the data member m_uChannelNumber.

- Setting the volume. This task uses the member function setVolume(). The function has a parameter that passes the new value for the volume. The function writes the new volume level to the data member m_uVolume.

- Querying the channel. This task uses the member function getChannelNumber(), which returns the channel number stored in the data member m_uChannelNumber.

- Querying the volume. This task uses the member function getVolume(), which returns the volume level stored in the data member m_uVolume.

Here is the source code for the class TV01:

```
// declare the enumerated type OnOffMode
enum OnOffMode { tvOff, tvOn };

// declare the type byte as an alias to unsigned char
typedef unsigned char byte;

class TV01
{
  public:
   void turnOn()
     { m_eOnOffSwitch = tvOn; }
   void turnOff()
     { m_eOnOffSwitch = tvOff; }
   OnOffMode getOnOffMode()
     { return m_eOnOffSwitch; }
   void setChannelNumber(byte uChannelNumber);
   byte getChannelNumber();
   void setVolume(byte uVolume);
   byte getVolume();
```

```
 protected:
   OnOffMode m_eOnOffSwitch; // on/off switch
   byte m_uChannelNumber;    // channel number
   byte m_uVolume;           // volume
};

void TV01::setChannelNumber(byte uChannelNumber)
{
  m_uChannelNumber = uChannelNumber;
}

byte TV01::getChannelNumber()
{
  return m_uChannelNumber;
}

void TV01::setVolume(byte uVolume)
{
  m_uVolume = uVolume;
}

byte TV01::getVolume()
{
  return m_uVolume;
}
```

Notice that this source code contains definitions of the member functions `turnOn()`, `turnOff()`, and `getOnOffMode()` inside the class declaration. I chose to define the remaining member functions outside the class declaration to remind you of the syntax for defining member functions outside the class declaration. Figure 2-4 shows the pictorial representation of the class `TV01` declaration.

More fun with boxes

Using the box example again, the class `Box` supports the following operations:

✔ Setting the length of the box. This task uses the member function `setLength()`. The function has a parameter that passes the new value for the length. The function writes the new length to the data member `m_fLength`.

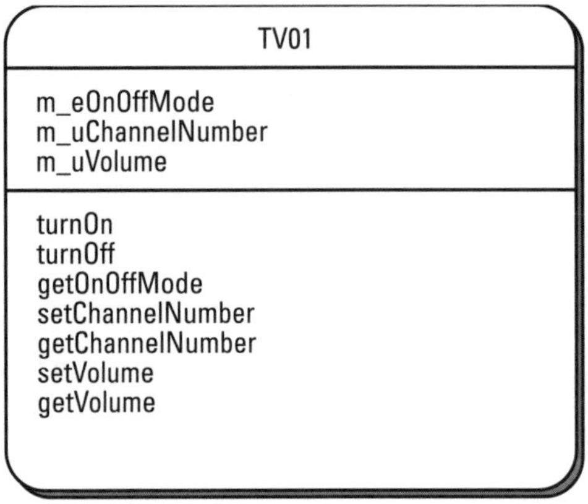

```
                    TV01

    m_eOnOffMode
    m_uChannelNumber
    m_uVolume

    turnOn
    turnOff
    getOnOffMode
    setChannelNumber
    getChannelNumber
    setVolume
    getVolume
```

Figure 2-4:
The pictorial
represen-
tation of the
class TV01.

✔ Setting the width of the box. This task uses the member function
   setWidth(). The function has a parameter that passes the new value for
   the width. The function writes the new width to the data member
   m_fWidth.

✔ Setting the height of the box. This task uses the member function
   setHeight(). The function has a parameter that passes the new value for
   the height. The function writes the new height to the data member
   m_fHeight.

✔ Querying the length of the box. This task uses the member function
   getLength(), which returns the value in the data member m_fLength.

✔ Querying the width of the box. This task uses the member function
   getWidth(), which returns the value in the data member m_fWidth.

✔ Querying the height of the box. This task uses the member function
   getHeight(), which returns the value in the data member m_fHeight.

✔ Returning the calculated value of the base area. This task uses the member
   function getBaseArea(), which calculates the base area using the values
   in the data members m_fLength and m_fWidth.

✔ Returning the calculated value of the volume. This task uses the member
   function getVolume(), which calculates the volume of the box using the
   values in the data members m_fLength, m_fWidth, and m_fHeight.

Here is the declaration of the class Box, including its member functions:

```
class Box
{
  public:
    void setLength(double fLength)
      { m_fLength = fLength; }

    void setWidth(double fWidth)
      { m_fWidth = fWidth; }

    void setHeight(double fHeight)
      { m_fHeight = fHeight; }

    double getLength()
      { return m_fLength; }

    double getWidth()
      { return m_fWidth; }

    double getHeight()
      { return m_fHeight; }

    double getBaseArea()
      { return m_fLength * m_fWidth; }

    double getVolume()
      { return m_fHeight * getBaseArea(); }

  protected:
    double m_fLength; // length of box
    double m_fWidth;  // width of box
    double m_fHeight; // height of box
};
```

This code snippet shows the member functions that I mentioned before the code. Notice that the member function getVolume() calculates the volume of the box by multiplying the height of the box (stored in the data member m_fHeight) by the base area (obtained by calling the member function getBaseArea()). Figure 2-5 shows the pictorial representation of this class declaration.

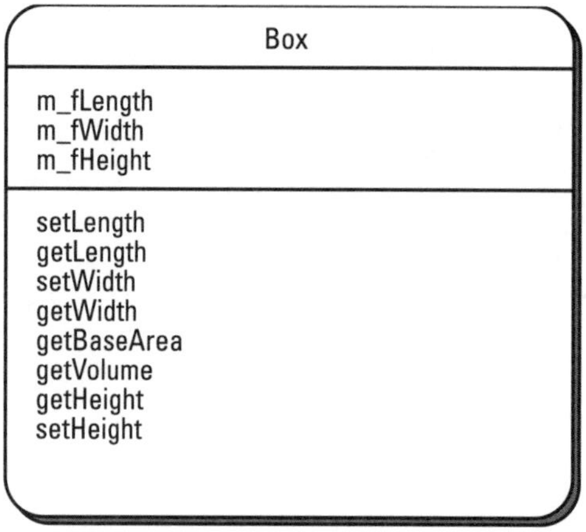

Figure 2-5: The pictorial representation of the class Box.

Storing Class Components

In the preceding examples, the declarations of the classes TV01 and Box are followed by the definitions of their respective member functions. In practice, you place the declaration of a class in a .H (or .HPP) header file and you put the definitions of the member functions in a .CPP file. For example, you would store the declaration for the class TV01 in the file TV01.HPP. The file TV01.HPP contains the following source code:

```
#ifndef _TV01_HPP
#define _TV01_HPP

// declare the enumerated type OnOffMode
enum OnOffMode { tvOff, tvOn };

// declare the type byte as an alias to unsigned char
typedef unsigned char byte;

class TV01
{
  public:
    void turnOn()
      { m_eOnOffSwitch = tvOn; }
    void turnOff()
      { m_eOnOffSwitch = tvOff; }
    OnOffMode getOnOffMode()
      { return m_eOnOffSwitch; }
```

```
    void setChannelNumber(byte uChannelNumber);
    byte getChannelNumber();
    void setVolume(byte uVolume);
    byte getVolume();

  protected:
    OnOffMode m_eOnOffSwitch; // on/off switch
    byte m_uChannelNumber;    // channel number
    byte m_uVolume;           // volume
};

#endif
```

The #ifndef directive ensures that the compiler does not read the declaration more than once, because reading it more than once causes a compile-time error.

I place the definitions of the member functions in the file TV01.CPP, which contains the following code:

```
#include "TV01.HPP"

void TV01::setChannelNumber(byte uChannelNumber)
{
  m_uChannelNumber = uChannelNumber;
}

byte TV01::getChannelNumber()
{
  return m_uChannelNumber;
}

void TV01::setVolume(byte uVolume)
{
  m_uVolume = uVolume;
}

byte TV01::getVolume()
{
  return m_uVolume;
}
```

The file TV01.CPP includes the declaration of the class TV01, the enumerated type OnOffMode, and the type byte by using the #include "TV01.HPP" directive.

Understanding the Roles of Member Functions

Not all member functions are created equal! Each class typically has at least two types of member functions. The class my Int (presented earlier in this chapter) has two types of member functions: the member function setInt() initializes the protected data member m_nNum; the member function getInt() queries the value in that data member. A class might include any of the following types of functions:

- ✔ Initializing functions. These functions set the initial values of some or all data members. These member functions set the stage for a class instance to start out with the proper value.

- ✔ Data broker functions. These functions convert data and perform other data management operations.

- ✔ Implementation functions. These functions perform the main operations of a class. These functions can modify the values of one or more data members and alter the state of a class instance.

- ✔ Access functions. These functions allow a class instance to access some or all of the data members in the class. These member functions ensure that the class instances do not have direct access to critical data members, thereby avoiding possibly corrupting their data.

- ✔ Auxiliary functions. These are helper functions that assist the other kinds of member functions in performing their tasks. The auxiliary member functions usually work behind the scenes, so to speak.

- ✔ const functions. These functions ensure that the code defining them does not alter the value of any data member.

The following sections examine the roles of the preceding member functions.

Initializing functions

Working with uninitialized data items (such as variables, arrays, and pointers) is like traveling with parachute luggage — you're asking (even begging) for trouble! This programming rule also extends to objects. Thus, the first type of member function initializes the instances of a class.

The constructors of a class are special versions of initializing member functions; they are automatically invoked when class instances come into being. In addition to constructors, you can declare initializing member functions that are called by one or more constructors and assist in reinitializing a class instance.

Initialize data members to ensure that they start out with the correct values. Don't rely on arbitrary values that data members initially contain.

In the case of the class TV01, I can add a constructor and the initializing member function `initialize()`. Here is the updated declaration and definition of class TV01:

```cpp
// declare the enumerated type OnOffMode
enum OnOffMode { tvOff, tvOn };

// declare the type byte as an alias to unsigned char
typedef unsigned char byte;

class TV01
{
  public:
    void TV()
      { initialize(); }
    void initialize();
    void turnOn()
      { m_eOnOffSwitch = tvOn; }
    void turnOff()
      { m_eOnOffSwitch = tvOff; }
    OnOffMode getOnOffMode()
      { return m_eOnOffSwitch; }
    void setChannelNumber(byte uChannelNumber);
    byte getChannelNumber();
    void setVolume(byte uVolume);
    byte getVolume();

  protected:
    OnOffMode m_eOnOffSwitch; // on/off switch
    byte m_uChannelNumber;    // channel number
    byte m_uVolume;           // volume
};

void TV01::initialize()
{
  m_eOnOffSwitch = tvOff;
  m_uChannelNumber = 0;
  m_uVolume = 0;
}
```

(continued)

(continued)

```
void TV01::setChannelNumber(byte uChannelNumber)
{
  m_uChannelNumber = uChannelNumber;
}

byte TV01::getChannelNumber()
{
  return m_uChannelNumber;
}

void TV01::setVolume(byte uVolume)
{
  m_uVolume = uVolume;
}

byte TV01::getVolume()
{
  return m_uVolume;
}
```

Note that the constructor merely calls the member function initialize().
The definition of the member function initialize() assigns the values tvOff,
0, and 0 to the data members m_eOnOffSwitch, m_uChannelNumber, and
m_uVolume, respectively. Thus, the constructor initializes the instances of class
TV01 as TV sets that are turned off.

To show how an initializing member function works with class Box, the following declaration of class Box includes a new constructor and the member
function initialize():

```
class Box
{
  public:
  Box(double fLength = 0, double fWidth = 0, double fHeight⤸
  = 0)
    { initialize(fLength, fWidth, fHeight); }

  void initialize(double fLength = 0,
                  double fWidth = 0,
                  double fHeight = 0);
```

```cpp
    void setLength(double fLength)
      { m_fLength = fLength; }

    void setWidth(double fWidth)
      { m_fWidth = fWidth; }

    void setHeight(double fHeight)
      { m_fHeight = fHeight; }

    double getLength()
      { return m_fLength; }

    double getWidth()
      { return m_fWidth; }

    double getHeight()
      { return m_fHeight; }

    double getBaseArea()
      { return m_fLength * m_fWidth; }

    double getVolume()
      { return m_fHeight * getBaseArea(); }

  protected:
    double m_fLength; // length of box
    double m_fWidth;  // width of box
    double m_fHeight; // height of box
};

void Box::initialize(double fLength,
                     double fWidth,
                     double fHeight)
{
  m_fLength = fLength;
  m_fWidth = fWidth;
  m_fHeight = fHeight;
}
```

This code shows that the class Box initializes its instances to have dimensions of zero by default. Otherwise, the constructor can assign nonzero values to the dimensions of the box. The parameter list of the constructor matches that of the member function initialize(). In fact, the constructor merely calls the member function initialize() and passes the values of its arguments to the member function. The member function initialize() assigns values to the three data members. The default arguments of the member function initialize() assign zeros to the data members. The class Box shows greater flexibility in initializing and reinitializing class instances than does class TV01.

Data broker functions

Data broker functions are member functions that perform assignment, memory management, and data type conversion. For example, a data broker function may allocate dynamic memory needed by a class instance. Another data broker function may convert characters to strings. In other words, data broker functions manage data to support other member functions in the same host class.

The following code shows how an *instance-copying member function* (that is, a member function that copies the values in the data members of one class instance into the data members of another class) works with the class Box. In addition to the default constructor, the new class version has a copy constructor (that is, a constructor that creates a new class instance as a copy of an existing class instance) and the member function copy():

```
class Box
{
  public:
    Box(double fLength = 0, double fWidth = 0, double fHeight⊃
    = 0)
      { initialize(fLength, fWidth, fHeight); }

    Box(Box& aBox)
     { copy(aBox); }

    void initialize(double fLength = 0,
                    double fWidth = 0,
                    double fHeight = 0);

    void copy(Box& aBox);

    void setLength(double fLength)
       { m_fLength = fLength; }
```

```
    void setWidth(double fWidth)
      { m_fWidth = fWidth; }

    void setHeight(double fHeight)
      { m_fHeight = fHeight; }

    double getLength()
      { return m_fLength; }

    double getWidth()
      { return m_fWidth; }

    double getHeight()
      { return m_fHeight; }

    double getBaseArea()
      { return m_fLength * m_fWidth; }

    double getVolume()
      { return m_fHeight * getBaseArea(); }

  protected:
    double m_fLength; // length of box
    double m_fWidth;  // width of box
    double m_fHeight; // height of box
};

void Box::initialize(double fLength,
                     double fWidth,
                     double fHeight)
{
  m_fLength = fLength;
  m_fWidth = fWidth;
  m_fHeight = fHeight;
}
void Box::copy(Box& aBox)
{
  m_fLength = aBox.m_fLength;
  m_fWidth = aBox.m_fWidth;
  m_fHeight = aBox.m_fHeight;
}
```

This code snippet shows that the copy constructor invokes the member function copy() to initialize a class instance by using the state of an existing class instance. The member function copy(), as the name suggests, copies the values of the data members of object aBox to those of the targeted instance.

Conceptually, you copy the state of an existing object to the state of another object. In some applications, this copying makes a great deal of sense. For example, copying makes sense in a box factory where you can create new boxes by using the dimensions of existing boxes. Using a copy constructor also makes sense in a string class in which you create a new class instance (that is, a new string object) as a copy of an already existing string object. The two string objects store the same characters.

Implementation functions

Implementation functions perform the main operations of a class. Often, such functions alter the state of a class instance by modifying the values of one or more data members.

The following example shows a class that has implementation functions. The example lists the source code for the class myArray, which models arrays of integers. The class supports the following operations:

- ✔ Creating an internal dynamic array of integers whose size is determined at run time.
- ✔ Deallocating the dynamic space for the internal array of integers.
- ✔ Supporting access of the elements of the internal array.
- ✔ Displaying the elements of the internal array.
- ✔ Sorting the elements of the internal array.

The class has the following two attributes:

- ✔ The pointer to the dynamic array of integers.
- ✔ The number of array elements.

I select the names Array and MaxElems, respectively, for the two attributes. As for associating data types with these names (and updating the names), I select the int* and int types for the names Array and MaxElems. The resulting data member names are m_pnArray and m_nMaxArray. The prefix m_pn indicates that the data member is a pointer to integers. The use of m_n indicates that the name belongs to a data member that is an integer.

Here is a list of the member functions for the operations this class supports:

- ✔ The constructor myArray() creates the dynamic array accessed by data member m_pnArray. The constructor also enables the class instances to initialize the elements of the dynamic array with the value of parameter nInitVal.

- ✔ The destructor deallocates the memory of the dynamic array accessed by data member m_pnArray.

- ✔ The operator [] supports storing and recalling integers in the dynamic array. This operator uses the parameter nIndex as the index of the accessed element.

- ✔ The member function show() displays the elements of the array (accessed by data member m_pnArray). The parameters of this function enable it to display a leading text message, specify the number of array elements to display, and specify whether to display the array in one row or in a single column. Thus, the member function show() enables you to display some of the array elements.

- ✔ The member function ShellSort() sorts the elements of the dynamic array in ascending order.

The member functions show() and ShellSort() are implementation functions; they process the data stored in the class instances. The member function ShellSort() changes the state of the class instances; it reorders the sequence of the array elements. In contrast, the member function show() does not alter the state of the class instance; it merely displays the values in the dynamic array.

Here is the source code for the class myArray:

```cpp
#include <iostream.h>

const int DEFAULT_ELEMS = 10;
enum Logical { FALSE, TRUE };

class myArray
{
  public:
    myArray(int nMaxElems = DEFAULT_ELEMS, int nInitVal = 0);
    ~myArray()
      { delete [] m_pnArray; }
    int& operator[](int nIndex)
      { return m_pnArray[nIndex]; }
```

(continued)

(continued)

```cpp
    void show(const char* pszMsg = "",
              const int nNumElems = DEFAULT_ELEMS,
              const Logical bOneLine = TRUE);
    void ShellSort(int nNumElems = DEFAULT_ELEMS);

  protected:
    int* m_pnArray;
    int m_nMaxElems;
};

myArray::myArray(int nMaxElems, int nInitVal)
{
  m_nMaxElems = (nMaxElems > 1) ? nMaxElems : 1;
  m_pnArray = new int[m_nMaxElems];
  for (int i = 0; i < m_nMaxElems; i++)
    m_pnArray[i] = nInitVal;
}

void myArray::show(const char* pszMsg,
                   const int nNumElems,
                   const Logical bOneLine)
{
  cout << pszMsg << endl;
  if (bOneLine) {
    for (int i = 0; i < nNumElems; i++)
      cout << m_pnArray[i] << ' ';
    cout << endl;
  }
  else {
    for (int i = 0; i < nNumElems; i++)
      cout << m_pnArray[i] << endl;
    cout << endl;
  }
}

void myArray::ShellSort(int nNumElems)
{
  int nOffset = nNumElems;
  Logical bSorted;
```

```
  if (nNumElems < 2 ||
      nNumElems > m_nMaxElems)
    return;

while (nOffset > 1) {
  nOffset = (nOffset - 1) / 3;
  nOffset = (nOffset < 1) ? 1 : nOffset;
  // arrange elements that are nOffset apart
  do {
    bSorted = TRUE; // set sorted flag
    // compare elements
    for (int i = 0, j = nOffset;
         i < (nNumElems - nOffset);
         i++, j++) {
      if (m_pnArray[i] > m_pnArray[j]) {
        // swap elements
        int nSwap = m_pnArray[i];
        m_pnArray[i] = m_pnArray[j];
        m_pnArray[j] = nSwap;
        bSorted = FALSE; // clear sorted flag
      }
    }
  } while (!bSorted);
  }
}
```

This listing declares the global constant DEFAULT_ELEMS to specify the default array size. The source code also declares the enumerated type Logical with its enumerators FALSE and TRUE. The constructor and most of the member functions use default arguments with their parameters.

Access functions

Access functions, as the name suggests, enable you to access one or more data members. Access functions perform three types of operations:

- Returning the values of one or more data members.
- Writing new values to one or more data members.
- Writing new values to one or more data members and returning the old values of these data members.

Typically, an access function accesses a single data member.

Use access member functions to manage the values in data members (which should be placed in the protected and private sections of the class) and prevent direct access to these members by class instances.

The code for the class TV01 contains several access functions. The member functions getOnOffMode(), getChannelNumber(), and getVolume() are examples of access functions that return the values of one or more data members. The member functions turnOn(), turnOff(), setChannelNumber(), and setVolume() are examples of access functions that write new values to one or more data members.

The code for the class Box also includes several access functions. The member functions getLength(), getWidth(), and getHeight() are examples of access functions that return the values of one or more data members. The member functions setLength(), setWidth(), and setHeight() are examples of access functions that write new values to one or more data members.

In the class myArray, the operator [] is an example of an access function that returns the values of one or more data members and writes new values to one or more data members.

None of the previous code in this chapter includes an example of an access function that writes new values to one or more data members and returns the old values of these data members. The following new version of class Box contains this type of access function (the updated member functions appear in boldface):

```
class Box
{
  public:
  Box(double fLength = 0, double fWidth = 0, double fHeight⊃
  = 0)
    { initialize(fLength, fWidth, fHeight); }

  void initialize(double fLength = 0,
                  double fWidth = 0,
                  double fHeight = 0);

  double setLength(double fLength);
  double setWidth(double fWidth);
  double setHeight(double fHeight);
```

```
    double getLength()
      { return m_fLength; }

    double getWidth()
      { return m_fWidth; }

    double getHeight()
      { return m_fHeight; }

    double getBaseArea()
      { return m_fLength * m_fWidth; }

    double getVolume()
      { return m_fHeight * getBaseArea(); }

  protected:
    double m_fLength; // length of box
    double m_fWidth;  // width of box
    double m_fHeight; // height of box
};

void Box::initialize(double fLength,
                     double fWidth,
                     double fHeight)
{
  m_fLength = fLength;
  m_fWidth = fWidth;
  m_fHeight = fHeight;
}

double Box::setLength(double fLength)
{
  double fOldLength = m_fLength;
  m_fLength = fLength;
  return fOldLength;
}

double Box::setWidth(double fWidth)
{
  double fOldWidth = m_fWidth;
  m_fWidth = fWidth;
  return fOldWidth;
}
```

(continued)

(continued)

```
double Box::setHeight(double fHeight)
{
  double fOldHeight = m_fHeight;
  m_fHeight = fHeight;
  return fOldHeight;
}
```

Notice that the new versions of the member functions setLength(), setWidth(), and setHeight() all return the double type. In addition, this source code defines these functions outside the class declaration. The definition of each function declares a local double-type variable that stores the old value of a data member (m_fLength, m_fWidth, or m_fHeight). Each access function updates the value of its related data member with the value of the parameter and then returns the old data member value.

Auxiliary functions

Auxiliary functions are the helping hands, so to speak, of the main implementation functions. When you design a class, you first define the main member functions that support the key operations. Often, these operations requires *other* member functions that perform subtasks or special tasks. These other member functions are the auxiliary functions. For example, auxiliary member functions can swap data, sort data, and search for data.

If you want an auxiliary function to strictly respond to an implementation function, you declare the auxiliary function in the protected or the private section of the class. This way, the class instances cannot access the auxiliary member functions. If you want the class instances to invoke the auxiliary function (which in this case makes the function double up as an implementation function), you declare the auxiliary function in the public section.

Again using the example of class myArray, suppose that you want to add a new operation to this class — one that reverses the order of the array elements. This operation swaps array elements from opposite ends of the array. You may have noticed that the member function ShellSort() also swaps array elements during the sorting process. Therefore, two operations would swap individual array elements.

You can consolidate the swapping of individual elements by using an auxiliary member function. The following source code is a new version of class myArray that contains the new member functions reverseOrder() and swapElems(). The first function is public, and the second is protected.

```
#include <iostream.h>

const int DEFAULT_ELEMS = 10;
enum Logical { FALSE, TRUE };

class myArray
{
  public:
    myArray(int nMaxElems = DEFAULT_ELEMS, int nInitVal = 0);
    ~myArray()
      { delete [] m_pnArray; }
    int& operator[](int nIndex)
      { return m_pnArray[nIndex]; }
    void show(const char* pszMsg = "",
              const int nNumElems = DEFAULT_ELEMS,
              const Logical bOneLine = TRUE);
    void ShellSort(int nNumElems = DEFAULT_ELEMS);
    void reverseOrder(int nNumElems = DEFAULT_ELEMS);

  protected:
    int* m_pnArray;
    int m_nMaxElems;

    void swapElems(int nIndex1, int nIndex2);
};

myArray::myArray(int nMaxElems, int nInitVal)
{
  m_nMaxElems = (nMaxElems > 1) ? nMaxElems : 1;
  m_pnArray = new int[m_nMaxElems];
  for (int i = 0; i < m_nMaxElems; i++)
    m_pnArray[i] = nInitVal;
}

void myArray::show(const char* pszMsg,
                   const int nNumElems,
                   const Logical bOneLine)
{
  cout << pszMsg << endl;
  if (bOneLine) {
    for (int i = 0; i < nNumElems; i++)
      cout << m_pnArray[i] << ' ';
    cout << endl;
```

(continued)

(continued)

```
    }

   else {
     for (int i = 0; i < nNumElems; i++)
       cout << m_pnArray[i] << endl;
     cout << endl;
   }
}

void myArray::ShellSort(int nNumElems)
{
  int nOffset = nNumElems;
  Logical bSorted;

  if (nNumElems < 2 ||
      nNumElems > m_nMaxElems)
    return;

  while (nOffset > 1) {
    nOffset = (nOffset - 1) / 3;
    nOffset = (nOffset < 1) ? 1 : nOffset;
    // arrange elements that are nOffset apart
    do {
      bSorted = TRUE; // set sorted flag
      // compare elements
      for (int i = 0, j = nOffset;
           i < (nNumElems - nOffset);
           i++, j++) {
        if (m_pnArray[i] > m_pnArray[j]) {
          // swap elements
          swapElems(i, j);
          bSorted = FALSE; // clear sorted flag
        }
      }
    } while (!bSorted);
  }
}

void myArray::reverseOrder(int nNumElems)
{
  for (int i = 0, j = nNumElems - 1; j > i; i++, j--)
    swapElems(i, j);
```

```
}

void myArray::swapElems(int nIndex1, int nIndex2)
{
  int nSwap = m_pnArray[nIndex1];
  m_pnArray[nIndex1] = m_pnArray[nIndex2];
  m_pnArray[nIndex2] = nSwap;
}
```

This listing declares the protected member function swapElems() and defines it outside the class declaration. The source code also declares the public member function reverseOrder() and defines it outside the class declaration. The member function swapElems() swaps the array elements specified by the parameters nIndex1 and nIndex2.

If you examine the statements in the member function ShellSort(), you find that the second if statement invokes the member function swapElems() to swap the array elements at indices i and j. If you also examine the statements in the member function reverseOrder(), you find that the function's for loop calls the member function swapElems() to swap the array elements at indices i and j. Thus, the member function swapElems() is an auxiliary function whose sole purpose is to respond to calls from the member functions ShellSort() and reverseOrder().

After presenting the new version of class myArray, perhaps I have second thoughts about the status of the member function swapElems(). Maybe making this member function public isn't a bad idea after all. If the function is public, the class instances can swap their array elements. To make this change, I simply move the declaration of the member function swapElems() to the public section of the class myArray. By doing so, I also change the role of the member function swapElems() from strictly auxiliary to a combination of auxiliary and implementation. Although the function still does the same tasks, it is now accessible to the class instances.

const functions: you can't touch that!

Through the use of const functions, C++ enables you to declare a member function in such a way that it cannot alter the value of any data member. In other words, the function can use the data member to calculate and return anything it wants, but it can't modify the value of the data member. What's the purpose of this feature? It enables a programming team leader to specify that a member function cannot alter the value of any data member. Then if a programmer who implements the definition of a member function fiddles around with data member values, the C++ compiler cries foul.

To declare a const function, place the keyword const after the parameter list, as shown in the following general syntax:

```
returnType functionName(parameterList) const;
```

The const function works well with access functions that return the values of one or more data members. Using const functions with the access functions of class TV01 yields the following version of this class:

```
// declare the enumerated type OnOffMode
enum OnOffMode { tvOff, tvOn };

// declare the type byte as an alias to unsigned char
typedef unsigned char byte;

class TV01
{
  public:
  TV01()
    { initialize(); }
  void initialize();
  void turnOn()
    { m_eOnOffSwitch = tvOn; }
  void turnOff()
    { m_eOnOffSwitch = tvOff; }
  OnOffMode getOnOffMode() const
    { return m_eOnOffSwitch; }
  void setChannelNumber(byte uChannelNumber)
    { m_uChannelNumber = uChannelNumber; }
  byte getChannelNumber() const
    { return m_uChannelNumber; }
  void setVolume(byte uVolume)
    { m_uVolume = uVolume; }
  byte getVolume() const
    { return m_uVolume; }

  protected:
    OnOffMode m_eOnOffSwitch; // on/off switch
    byte m_uChannelNumber;    // channel number
    byte m_uVolume;           // volume
};
```

```
void TV01::initialize()
{
  m_eOnOffSwitch = tvOff;
  m_uChannelNumber = 0;
  m_uVolume = 0;
}
```

Notice that this listing declares the member functions `getOnOffMode()`, `getChannelNumber()`, and `getVolume()` as const functions. You find the keyword `const` after the parameter list in each of these member functions. Thus, the statements inside the member functions `getOnOffMode()`, `getChannelNumber()`, and `getVolume()` cannot change the value of any data member.

Creating a Guessing Game

This section presents an example demonstrating the principles that I describe in this chapter. The example is a high-low number guessing game, in which the computer tries to guess a number you choose. (Isn't it nice to make your PC sweat for a change?)

You pick a secret number between 1 and 1,000, and the program tries to zoom in on that number. The program displays a guess for the secret number and asks you to enter a numeric hint code:

- ✔ 1 indicates that the computer's guess is high.

- ✔ -1 means the computer's guess is low.

- ✔ 0 signifies a match.

The program repeats this process until it guesses the secret number you selected. Because the computer is very trusting, you can easily mislead it by typing the wrong number. Don't do that, however, unless you want to make your computer look like a real idiot.

I chose the following attributes for the game:

- ✔ The limits for guessing the secret number.

- ✔ The guess for the secret number.

- ✔ The hint code that you so kindly enter.

Here are the names for the attributes:

✔ Lo for the lower limit.

✔ Hi for the upper limit.

✔ Guess for the guess.

✔ Hint for the hint code.

Next, I assign data types to the names and update the names accordingly. Because the game deals with integers, the range of numbers and the guess have the int type. Because the hint code has values -1, 0, and 1, I can also use the int type for the hint code. The resulting data member names are as follows:

✔ The int-type data member m_nLo stores the lower limit for the secret number.

✔ The int-type data member m_nHi stores the upper limit for the secret number.

✔ The int-type data member m_nGuess stores the guess for the secret number.

✔ The int-type data member m_nHint stores the hint code.

Next, I focus on the operations involved in the number-guessing game:

✔ Initializing the game. This task displays instructions and initializes data members.

✔ Displaying the guess.

✔ Prompting the player for a hint code and acting on that code.

These operations translate into the following member functions:

✔ startGame().

✔ showGuess().

✔ playMore(). This function returns an integer code that tells the computer whether it should stop.

I chose to add the member function play(), which invokes these member functions. The class guessGame declares the member function play() as public and declares the other member functions as protected. Thus, the member function play() is an implementation function. Here is how the other member functions operate:

✔ The member function startGame() combines the roles of an initializing function and an auxiliary function. As an initializing function, startGame() initializes the data members m_nLo, m_nHi, and m_nGuess. As an auxiliary function, startGame() is a protected member function that serves only the member function play().

✔ The member function showGuess() combines the roles of an access function and an auxiliary function. As an access function, showGuess() displays the value in the data member m_nGuess. As an auxiliary function, showGuess() is a protected member function that serves only the member function play().

✔ The member function playMore() combines the roles of an implementation function and an auxiliary function. As an implementation function, playMore() performs the major tasks of prompting you for a guess, examining your input, updating the values of data members m_nLo and m_nHi, and returning a value that determines whether the computer should continue the game. As an auxiliary function, playMore() is a protected member function that serves only the member function play().

Here is a sample session using the number-guessing program for the secret number 777 (the input is in boldface):

```
Guess a number between 1 and 1000
At hint prompt enter one of the following:
 1 when my guess is high
 0 when my guess is correct
-1 when my guess is low

Guess is 500
Enter hint value : -1
Guess is 750
Enter hint value : -1
Guess is 875
Enter hint value : 1
Guess is 812
Enter hint value : 1
Guess is 781
Enter hint value : 1
Guess is 765
Enter hint value : -1
Guess is 773
Enter hint value : -1
Guess is 777
Enter hint value : 0
End of game!
```

Listing 2-1 shows the source code for the CLASS1.CPP program.

Listing 2-1	CLASS1.CPP

```cpp
// A number-guessing game class

#include <iostream.h>

const int MIN_NUM = 1;
const int MAX_NUM = 1000;

class guessGame
{
  public:
    void play();

  protected:
    int m_nHi;
    int m_nLo;
    int m_nGuess;
    int m_nHint;

    void startGame();
    void showGuess();
    int playMore();

};

void guessGame::play()
{
  startGame();
  showGuess();
  while (playMore())
    showGuess();
}

void guessGame::startGame()
{
  cout << "Guess a number between " << MIN_NUM
       << " and " << MAX_NUM << "\n";
  cout << "At hint prompt enter one of the following:\n"
       << " 1 when my guess is high\n"
       << " 0 when my guess is correct\n"
       << "-1 when my guess is low\n\n";
  m_nLo = MIN_NUM;
  m_nHi = MAX_NUM;
  m_nGuess = (m_nLo + m_nHi) / 2;
```

```
}

void guessGame::showGuess()
{
  cout << "Guess is " << m_nGuess << "\n";
}

int guessGame::playMore()
{
  cout << "Enter hint value : ";
  cin >> m_nHint;

  if (m_nHint == 0) {
    cout << "End of game!\n";
    return 0;
  }
  else if (m_nHint > 0)
    // set upper limit to last guess
    m_nHi = m_nGuess;
  else
    // set lower limit to last guess
    m_nLo = m_nGuess;

  // get new guess
  m_nGuess = (m_nLo + m_nHi) / 2;

  // double-check player is not cheating!
  if (m_nGuess == m_nLo || m_nGuess == m_nHi) {
    cout << "Your secret number must be " << m_nGuess <<
    "\n";
    return 0;
  }
  else
    return 1;
}

main()
{
  guessGame game;

  game.play();

  return 0;
}
```

Summary

In this chapter, I've explained C++ classes and their components. You've learned that a C++ class may have public, protected, and private sections. Each section contains data members and member functions. The data members store information that describes the data stored in the class instances. The member functions manipulate the data members and perform other tasks. I've also discussed the various roles of member functions.

The next chapter discusses the life cycle of objects (that is, class instances). You learn how to create, use, and remove class instances.

Chapter 3

Object Life Cycles: scOOPs on the Life-Styles of the ...

● ●

In This Chapter

▶ Sending messages to objects

▶ Initializing objects

▶ Destroying objects

▶ Working with objects

● ●

*T*his chapter looks at an object's life cycle, which ranges from the moment of inception to the time of an object's demise. An object's life cycle encompasses creation, initialization, manipulation (by sending it C++ messages), and finally, destruction.

The process of creating and initializing an object brings it into being and prepares it to interact with other objects and functions. When an object is destroyed, you need to free up any resources used by that object. Typically, an object spends most of its life cycle interacting with other objects and functions by responding to C++ messages. That's why this chapter starts by focusing on sending messages to objects.

Please Take a Message

Chapter 2 focuses on declaring classes. Most of the examples in Chapter 2 present the source code for various class versions but do not show you how to manipulate the instances of these classes. This section explains how to manipulate a class instance (or object, if you prefer). OOP thinking fosters the notion of interacting with a class instance by sending it a message. The object executes that message by invoking the appropriate method (that is, a member function in C++). The names of the message and the method are identical. A message often includes arguments that it submits for use by the corresponding method.

The TV example (one more time)

The class TV01 once again provides a helpful illustration. Listing 3-1 contains the source code for the OBJECT1.CPP program. The listing contains the declaration of class TV01, the definitions of its member functions, and the definition of the function main(). This function declares two instances of the class TV01: myTV and yourTV. To give you an idea of what the OBJECT1.CPP program does, here is the output from this program:

```
Object myTV is on
Selected channel number is 8
Volume is set at level 5

Object yourTV is on
Selected channel number is 9
Volume is set at level 15
Switching yourTV to channel 8
Switching volume level of yourTV to 2
```

Listing 3-1	OBJECT1.CPP

```cpp
// A C++ program that manipulates
// instances of class TV01

#include <iostream.h>
#include <iomanip.h>

// declare the enumerated type OnOffMode
enum OnOffMode { tvOff, tvOn };

// declare the type byte as an alias to unsigned char
typedef unsigned char byte;

class TV01
{
  public:
  TV01()
    { initialize(); }
  void initialize();
  void turnOn()
    { m_eOnOffSwitch = tvOn; }
  void turnOff()
    { m_eOnOffSwitch = tvOff; }
  OnOffMode getOnOffMode() const
    { return m_eOnOffSwitch; }
```

```
  void setChannelNumber(byte uChannelNumber)
    { m_uChannelNumber = uChannelNumber; }
  byte getChannelNumber() const
    { return m_uChannelNumber; }
  void setVolume(byte uVolume)
    { m_uVolume = uVolume; }
  byte getVolume() const
    { return m_uVolume; }

protected:
  OnOffMode m_eOnOffSwitch; // on/off switch
  byte m_uChannelNumber;    // channel number
  byte m_uVolume;           // volume
};
void TV01::initialize()
{
  m_eOnOffSwitch = tvOff;
  m_uChannelNumber = 0;
  m_uVolume = 0;
}
main()
{
  TV01 myTV;
  TV01 yourTV;

  myTV.turnOn();
  myTV.setChannelNumber(8);
  myTV.setVolume(5);

  if (myTV.getOnOffMode() == tvOn) {
    cout << "Object myTV is on\n"
         << "Selected channel number is "
         << int(myTV.getChannelNumber()) << endl
         << "Volume is set at level "
         << int(myTV.getVolume()) << endl;
  }

   else
    cout << "Object myTV is off!\n";

  cout << endl;

  yourTV.turnOn():
```

(continued)

Listing 3-1 (continued)

```
yourTV.setChannelNumber(9);
  yourTV.setVolume(15);
  if (yourTV.getOnOffMode() == tvOn) {
    cout << "Object yourTV is on\n"
         << "Selected channel number is "
         << int(yourTV.getChannelNumber()) << endl
         << "Volume is set at level "
         << int(yourTV.getVolume()) << endl;

      if (yourTV.getChannelNumber() !=
        myTV.getChannelNumber()) {
      yourTV.setChannelNumber(myTV.getChannelNumber());
      cout << "Switching yourTV to channel "
           << int(yourTV.getChannelNumber()) << endl;
    }
    if (yourTV.getVolume() > 10) {
      yourTV.setVolume((yourTV.getVolume() - 10) / 2);
      cout << "Switching volume level of yourTV to "
           << int(yourTV.getVolume()) << endl;
    }
  }
  else
    cout << "Object yourTV is off!\n";

  return 0;
}
```

Turn your attention to the function main(), which creates and manipulates the instances of the class TV01. This function creates the objects myTV and yourTV as instances of the class TV01 and performs the following tasks:

✔ Turns on the object myTV by sending the C++ message turnOn() to that object. The message has no arguments and results in executing the member function TV01::turnOn().

✔ Sets the channel number of the object myTV by sending the C++ message setChannelNumber() to that object. The message has the argument 8 (the number of a TV channel) and results in executing the member function TV01::setChannelNumber().

✔ Sets the volume of the object myTV by sending the C++ message setVolume() to that object. The message has the argument 5 (the volume level) and results in executing the member function TV01::setVolume().

✔ Determines whether the object myTV is on. This task uses an if statement that compares the result of sending the C++ message getOnOffMode() to the object myTV with the enumerator tvOn. If the two values match, the function main() displays text indicating that the object myTV is on and reports the channel number and the volume. The function main() obtains the channel number by sending the C++ message getChannelNumber() to the object myTV. This message results in executing the member function TV01::getChannelNumber(). Likewise, the function obtains the volume number by sending the C++ message getVolume() to object myTV. This message results in executing the member function TV01::getVolume(). Notice that the output statement typecasts the result of each message into the int type to display an integer instead of a character (remember that the type byte is an alias for the unsigned char type).

✔ Turns on the object yourTV by sending the C++ message turnOn() to that object. The message has no arguments and results in executing the member function TV01::turnOn().

✔ Sets the channel number of the object yourTV by sending the C++ message setChannelNumber() to that object. The message has the argument 9 (the number of a TV channel) and results in executing the member function TV01::setChannelNumber().

✔ Sets the volume of the object yourTV by sending the C++ message setVolume() to that object. The message has the argument 15 (the volume level) and results in executing the member function TV01::setVolume().

✔ Determines whether the object yourTV is on. This task uses an if statement that compares the result of sending the C++ message getOnOffMode() to the object yourTV with the enumerator tvOn. If the two values match, the function main() displays text indicating that the object yourTV is on and reports the channel number and the volume. The function main() obtains the channel number by sending the C++ message getChannelNumber() to the object yourTV. This message results in executing the member function TV01::getChannelNumber(). Likewise, the function obtains the volume number by sending the C++ message getVolume() to the object yourTV. This message results in executing the member function TV01::getVolume(). Again, notice that the output statement typecasts the result of each message into the int type to display an integer instead of a character.

✔ Determines whether the channel numbers of the objects yourTV and myTV differ. This task uses an if statement that sends the C++ message getChannelNumber() to each of the two objects. If the results of the messages don't match, the function main() sets the channel number of the object yourTV to that of the object myTV. To perform this task, the function main() sends the C++ message setChannelNumber() to the object yourTV. The argument for this message is the result of sending the

C++ message getChannelNumber() to the object myTV. Thus, this assignment shows that you can use the result of a C++ message as an argument in another C++ message. (How cool!) Finally, the function main() displays a message telling you that it has adjusted the channel number of the object yourTV. The function obtains the new channel number by sending the C++ message getChannelNumber() to the object yourTV.

✔ Determines whether the volume of the object yourTV exceeds 10. This task uses an if statement that compares the integer 10 with the result of sending the C++ message getVolume() to the object yourTV. If the message yields a value greater than 10, the function main() adjusts the volume level of the object yourTV and displays the new volume level. To adjust the volume, the function main() sends the C++ message setVolume() to the object yourTV. The argument for this message is the expression (yourTV.getVolume() - 10) / 2. Notice that this expression includes the result of sending the C++ message getVolume() to the object yourTV. The function main() then displays the new volume level by sending the C++ message getVolume() to the object yourTV.

This example shows how the function main() manipulates the objects myTV and yourTV by sending them C++ messages. Some messages need arguments, and sometimes these arguments are the results of other C++ messages or include the results of such messages.

The box example (again!!!???)

Look at the class Box example again — yes, one more time. The OBJECT2.CPP program contains the declaration of the class Box, the definitions of its member functions, and the definition of the function main(). This function declares two instances of class Box: myBox and yourBox.

Here is the output from a sample session with the OBJECT2.CPP program (the input is in boldface):

```
Enter the length of the box : 11
Enter the width of the box : 15
Enter the height of the box : 18
Your box has the following dimensions:
Length     = 11
Width      = 15
Height     = 18
Base area  = 165
Volume     = 2970

My box has the following dimensions:
Length     = 10
```

```
Width      = 10
Height     = 10
Base area  = 100
Volume     = 1000
My box can fit inside your box
```

Listing 3-2 contains the source code for the OBJECT2.CPP program.

Listing 3-2	**OBJECT2.CPP**

```
// A C++ program that manipulates
// instances of class Box

#include <iostream.h>
#include <iomanip.h>

class Box
{
  public:
  Box(double fLength = 0, double fWidth = 0,doublefHeight⊃
  = 0)
    { initialize(fLength, fWidth, fHeight); }

  void initialize(double fLength = 0,
                  double fWidth = 0,
                  double fHeight = 0);

  double setLength(double fLength);
  double setWidth(double fWidth);
  double setHeight(double fHeight);

  double getLength()
    { return m_fLength; }

  double getWidth()
   { return m_fWidth; }

  double getHeight()
    { return m_fHeight; }

  double getBaseArea()
    { return m_fLength * m_fWidth; }
```

(continued)

Listing 3-2 *(continued)*

```cpp
double getVolume()
    { return m_fHeight * getBaseArea(); }

  protected:
    double m_fLength; // length of box
    double m_fWidth;  // width of box
    double m_fHeight; // height of box
};
void Box::initialize(double fLength,
                     double fWidth,
                     double fHeight)
{
  m_fLength = fLength;
  m_fWidth = fWidth;
  m_fHeight = fHeight;
}
double Box::setLength(double fLength)
{
  double fOldLength = m_fLength;
  m_fLength = fLength;
  return fOldLength;
}
double Box::setWidth(double fWidth)
{
  double fOldWidth = m_fWidth;
  m_fWidth = fWidth;
  return fOldWidth;
}
double Box::setHeight(double fHeight)
{
  double fOldHeight = m_fHeight;
  m_fHeight = fHeight;
  return fOldHeight;
}
main()
{
  Box yourBox;
  Box myBox;
  double fX;

  // prompt the user to input the length
  do {
    cout << "Enter the length of the box : ";
```

```
   cin >> fX;
} while (fX <= 0);
// set the length of the box
yourBox.setLength(fX);

// prompt the user to input the width
do {
  cout << "Enter the width of the box : ";
  cin >> fX;
} while (fX <= 0);
// set the width of the box
yourBox.setWidth(fX);

// prompt the user to input the height
do {
  cout << "Enter the height of the box : ";
  cin >> fX;
} while (fX <= 0);
// set the height of the box
yourBox.setHeight(fX);

myBox.initialize(10, 10, 10);

cout << "Your box has the following dimensions:\n"
     << "Length    = " << yourBox.getLength() << endl
     << "Width     = " << yourBox.getWidth() << endl
     << "Height    = " << yourBox.getHeight() << endl
     << "Base area = " << yourBox.getBaseArea() << endl
     << "Volume    = " << yourBox.getVolume() << endl <<
        endl;
 cout << "My box has the following dimensions:\n"
     << "Length    = " << myBox.getLength() << endl
     << "Width     = " << myBox.getWidth() << endl
     << "Height    = " << myBox.getHeight() << endl
     << "Base area = " << myBox.getBaseArea() << endl
     << "Volume    = " << myBox.getVolume() <<↵
        endl;

if (myBox.getLength() < yourBox.getLength() &&
    myBox.getWidth() < yourBox.getWidth() &&
    myBox.getHeight() < yourBox.getHeight())

    cout << "My box can fit inside your box\n";
```

(continued)

Listing 3-2 *(continued)*

```
else if (myBox.getLength() > yourBox.getLength() &&
        myBox.getWidth() > yourBox.getWidth() &&
        myBox.getHeight() > yourBox.getHeight())
    cout << "Your box can fit inside my box\n";
  else
      cout << "Neither box fits inside the other\n";

  return 0;
}
```

The program performs the following tasks:

✔ Prompts you to enter the dimensions of the object yourBox.

✔ Assigns the dimensions of the object myBox.

✔ Displays the dimensions, the base area, and the volume of the object yourBox.

✔ Displays the dimensions, the base area, and the volume of the object myBox.

✔ Determines whether the object yourBox fits inside the object myBox and displays a message if this is true.

✔ Determines whether the object myBox fits inside the object yourBox and displays a message if this is true.

✔ If neither box fits inside the other one, displays a message to that effect.

Turn your attention to the function main(), which creates and manipulates the instances of the class Box. The function creates the objects yourBox and myBox as instances of class Box. It also declares the double-type variable fX. The function performs the following tasks. (Get your ruler out for this one)

✔ Prompts you to enter the length of the box. This task stores your input in the variable fX and uses a do-while loop to ensure that you enter a positive value.

✔ Assigns the length of the object yourBox by sending that object the C++ message setLength(). The argument for this message is the variable fX.

✔ Prompts you to enter the width of the box. This task stores your input in the variable fX and uses a do-while loop to ensure that you enter a positive value.

✔ Assigns the width of the object yourBox by sending that object the C++ message setWidth(). The argument for this message is the variable fX.

✔ Prompts you to enter the height of the box. This task stores your input in the variable `fX` and uses a `do-while` loop to ensure that you enter a positive value.

✔ Assigns the height of the object `yourBox` by sending that object the C++ message `setHeight()`. The argument for this message is the variable `fX`.

✔ Assigns the length, the width, and the height of the object `myBox` by sending that object the C++ message `initialize()`. The arguments for this message are 10, 10, and 10, which represent the length, the width, and the height, respectively.

✔ Displays the dimensions, the base area, and the volume of the object `yourBox`. This task obtains the length, the width, the height, the base area, and the volume of the object `yourBox` by sending the C++ messages `getLength()`, `getWidth()`, `getHeight()`, `getBaseArea()`, and `getVolume()`. These C++ messages have no arguments.

✔ Displays the dimensions, the base area, and the volume of the object `myBox`. This task obtains the length, the width, the height, the base area, and the volume of the object `myBox` by sending the C++ messages `getLength()`, `getWidth()`, `getHeight()`, `getBaseArea()`, and `getVolume()`. These C++ message have no arguments.

✔ Determines whether the object `myBox` can fit inside the object `yourBox`. This task determines whether the length, the width, and the height of the object `myBox` are each less than the corresponding dimensions of the object `yourBox`. If these conditions are true, the function displays the string "My box can fit inside your box."

✔ If these tested conditions are not true, the function determines whether the object `yourBox` can fit inside the object `myBox`. This task determines whether the length, the width, and the height of the object `yourBox` are each less than the corresponding dimensions of the object `myBox`. If these conditions are true, the function displays the string "Your box can fit inside my box."

✔ If neither set of tested conditions is true, the function `main()` displays the string "Neither box fits inside the other."

Overloading member functions: don't blow a fuse!

The examples in the previous sections of this chapter involve a one-to-one relationship between messages and methods. For example, the message `yourBox.setLength()` tells the program to execute the member function `Box::setLength(double)`. As you may know, C++ supports the overloading of functions and member functions. With overloading, you can have two or more member functions (that is, methods) that share the same name but have different parameter lists. In such cases, the compiler can tell which one you are calling by looking at the data types of the arguments. For example, if I overload the member function Box::setLength() by declaring Box::setLength(int nLength) and send a message yourBox.setLength(3), the compiler invokes the member function Box::setLength(int nLength) because the message has an integer argument.

The following example is based on the class TV01. Suppose I declare the enumerated type VolumeLevel representing distinct volume levels: mute, low, medium, and high. I assign the values 0, 3, 8, and 15 to these levels and use the enumerated type to declare another version of the member function setVolume(). This version has an enumerated type parameter.

In this new sample program, OBJECT3.CPP, I have two versions of the member function setVolume(): one with the parameter type byte and the other with the parameter type VolumeLevel. When I send the C++ message setVolume() to a class instance and include an integer, the compiler resolves that message by invoking the member function TV01::setVolume(byte). However, when I send the C++ message setVolume() to a class instance and include an enumerated type variable or an enumerator, the compiler resolves that message by invoking the member function TV01::setVolume(VolumeLevel).

Here is the output from the OBJECT3.CPP program:

```
Object myTV is on
Selected channel number is 8
Volume is set at level 5

Object yourTV is on
Selected channel number is 9
Volume is set at level 8
Switching yourTV to channel 8
```

Listing 3-3 shows the source code for the OBJECT3.CPP program.

Listing 3-3	OBJECT3.CPP

```
// A C++ program that manipulates
// instances of class TV01

#include <iostream.h>
#include <iomanip.h>

// declare the enumerated type OnOffMode
enum OnOffMode { tvOff, tvOn };
// declare the enumerated type VolumeLevel
```

```
enum VolumeLevel { volMute = 0, volLow = 3,
                   volMedium = 8, volHigh = 15 };

// declare the type byte as an alias to unsigned char
typedef unsigned char byte;

class TV01
{
  public:
    TV01()
      { initialize(); }
    void initialize();
    void turnOn()
      { m_eOnOffSwitch = tvOn; }
    void turnOff()
      { m_eOnOffSwitch = tvOff; }
    OnOffMode getOnOffMode() const
      { return m_eOnOffSwitch; }
    void setChannelNumber(byte uChannelNumber)
      { m_uChannelNumber = uChannelNumber; }
    byte getChannelNumber() const
      { return m_uChannelNumber; }
    void setVolume(byte uVolume)
      { m_uVolume = uVolume; }
    void setVolume(VolumeLevel eVolume)
      { m_uVolume = byte(eVolume); }
    byte getVolume() const
      { return m_uVolume; }

  protected:
    OnOffMode m_eOnOffSwitch; // on/off switch
    byte m_uChannelNumber;    // channel number
    byte m_uVolume;           // volume
};
void TV01::initialize()
{
  m_eOnOffSwitch = tvOff;
  m_uChannelNumber = 0;
  m_uVolume = 0;
}
main()
```

(continued)

Listing 3-3 *(continued)*

```
{
  TV01 myTV;
  TV01 yourTV;
  myTV.turnOn();
  myTV.setChannelNumber(8);
  // execute TV01::setVolume(byte)
  myTV.setVolume(5);

  if (myTV.getOnOffMode() == tvOn) {
    cout << "Object myTV is on\n"
         << "Selected channel number is "
         << int(myTV.getChannelNumber()) << endl
         << "Volume is set at level "
         << int(myTV.getVolume()) << endl;
  }
  else
    cout << "Object myTV is off!\n";

  cout << endl;

  yourTV.turnOn();
  yourTV.setChannelNumber(9);
  // execute TV01::setVolume(VolumeLevel)
  yourTV.setVolume(volMedium);
  if (yourTV.getOnOffMode() == tvOn) {
    cout << "Object yourTV is on\n"
         << "Selected channel number is "
         << int(yourTV.getChannelNumber()) << endl
         << "Volume is set at level "
         << int(yourTV.getVolume()) << endl;

    if (yourTV.getChannelNumber() !=
        myTV.getChannelNumber()) {
      yourTV.setChannelNumber(myTV.getChannelNumber());
      cout << "Switching yourTV to channel "
           << int(yourTV.getChannelNumber()) << endl;
    }
    if (yourTV.getVolume() > volMedium ) {
      // execute TV01::setVolume(VolumeLevel)
      yourTV.setVolume(volLow);
      cout << "Switching volume level of yourTV to "
           << int(yourTV.getVolume()) << endl;
```

```
      }
    }
  else
    cout << "Object yourTV is off!\n";

  return 0;
}
```

The new version of class TV01 declares the following overloaded member functions:

```
  void setVolume(byte uVolume)
    { m_uVolume = uVolume; }
  void setVolume(VolumeLevel eVolume)
    { m_uVolume = byte(eVolume); }
```

As I mentioned before the listing, the first version has a byte-type parameter, whereas the second version has the VolumeLevel-type parameter. The source code for the function main() in Listing 3-3 is very similar to the source code for the function main() in Listing 3-1. The main differences between the two versions of function main() can be found in the following statements:

✔ The statement that sets the volume of the object myTV. In this statement, the function main() sends the C++ message setVolume() to the object myTV. The argument of this message is the integer 5. The compiler resolves this message by invoking the member function TV01::setVolume(byte), because the compiler can readily convert the integer argument into a byte (an alias to unsigned char) value.

✔ The statement that sets the volume of the object yourTV. In this statement, the function main() sends the C++ message setVolume() to the object yourTV. The argument of this message is the enumerator volMedium. The compiler resolves this message by invoking the member function TV01::setVolume(VolumeLevel).

✔ The first statement inside the last if statement, which sets the volume of the object yourTV. In this statement, the function main() sends the C++ message setVolume() to the object yourTV. The argument of this message is the enumerator volLow. The compiler resolves this message by invoking the member function TV01::setVolume(VolumeLevel). What would happen to this message if the argument were byte(volLow)? The compiler would invoke the member function TV01::setVolume(byte). What about an argument of int(volLow)? Same answer.

This example shows how a function can send the same message — in this case, `setVolume()` — and end up invoking one of several methods. The compiler examines the argument for this type of message and determines which method is the most suitable response to the message.

Initializing Objects: Where Do I Begin?

Now that you know how to send messages to simple objects, I need to describe how you go about initializing these objects. C++ enables you to automatically initialize class instances by using constructors. You can also explicitly initialize class instances by using initializing member functions. Often, when a class has one or more initializing member functions, you code the constructor(s) of that class to use these member functions.

The advantage of constructors is that they are invoked automatically. C++ offers the following categories of constructors:

- **Automatic default constructors:** These constructors, which the C++ compiler creates when you don't declare constructors, aren't much help. Besides, in many cases, the compiler expects you to declare a constructor.

- **Default constructors:** These constructors have no parameters or have parameters that use default arguments. When you use the default arguments for all the parameters, you end up with a default constructor. A class can only have one default constructor.

- **Copy constructors:** These constructors create class instances by using the state of existing instances. A class can have only one copy constructor.

- **Custom constructors:** These constructors initialize class instances in ways that you choose. A class can have several custom constructors.

Using default constructors: the only game in town

You can use default constructors to initialize the data members of objects in one of two ways:

- By assigning values that represent a neutral state. In this case, the object is asleep, so to speak. You need to assign other values to its data members to get the object up and running.

- By assigning values that represent a working state. In other words, the object gets a jump start and is ready to do business.

Keep in mind that the run-time system invokes the default constructor when you specify no instantiation parameters in the declaration of a new object. The default constructor creates instances that have the same initial state.

Starting up in neutral

The following example shows a class that uses a default constructor to create objects that have a neutral state. The OBJECT4.CPP program implements an abbreviated version of the class TV01 that has a default constructor and access member functions. I created this program by modifying the source code from Listing 3-1. The OBJECT4.CPP program initializes two instances of class TV01 and displays their initial states. That's all it does.

Here is the output from the OBJECT4.CPP program:

```
Initializing instance of class TV01
Initializing instance of class TV01
The state of object myTV is
Object myTV is off
Selected channel number is 0
Volume is set at level 0

The state of object yourTV is
Object yourTV is off
Selected channel number is 0
Volume is set at level 0
```

Listing 3-4 shows the source code for the OBJECT4.CPP program.

Listing 3-4	OBJECT4.CPP

```cpp
// A C++ program that illustrates
// default constructors

#include <iostream.h>
#include <iomanip.h>

// declare the enumerated type OnOffMode
enum OnOffMode { tvOff, tvOn };

// declare the type byte as an alias to unsigned char
typedef unsigned char byte;

class TV01
```

(continued)

Listing 3-4 (continued)

```
{
  public:
    TV01()
      { initialize(); }
    void initialize();

OnOffMode getOnOffMode() const
    { return m_eOnOffSwitch; }
    byte getChannelNumber() const
      { return m_uChannelNumber; }
    byte getVolume() const
      { return m_uVolume; }

  protected:
    OnOffMode m_eOnOffSwitch; // on/off switch
    byte m_uChannelNumber;    // channel number
    byte m_uVolume;           // volume
};
void TV01::initialize()
{
  m_eOnOffSwitch = tvOff;
  m_uChannelNumber = 0;
  m_uVolume = 0;
  cout << "Initializing instance of class TV01\n";
}
main()
{
  TV01 myTV;
  TV01 yourTV;

  cout << "The state of object myTV is\n";
  if (myTV.getOnOffMode() == tvOn)
    cout << "Object myTV is on\n";
  else
    cout << "Object myTV is off\n";

  cout << "Selected channel number is "
      << int(myTV.getChannelNumber()) << endl
      << "Volume is set at level "
      << int(myTV.getVolume()) << endl;

  cout << endl;
```

```
cout << "The state of object yourTV is\n";
if (yourTV.getOnOffMode() == tvOn)
  cout << "Object yourTV is on\n";
else
  cout << "Object yourTV is off\n";

cout << "Selected channel number is "
     << int(yourTV.getChannelNumber()) << endl
     << "Volume is set at level "
     << int(yourTV.getVolume()) << endl;

return 0;
}
```

In Listing 3-4, the class TV01 has the same data members as in Listing 3-1. However, the class has a default constructor and the member functions initialize(), getOnOffMode(), getChannelNumber(), and getVolume(). The default constructor merely invokes the member function initialize(). This member function assigns the values tvOff, 0, and 0 to the data members m_eOnOffSwitch, m_uChannelNumber, and m_uVolume, respectively. In addition, the member function displays the string "Initializing instance of class TV01."

The function main() creates the objects myTV and yourTV as instances of class TV01. The default constructor initializes these instances and displays the string "Initializing instance of class TV01" twice (once for each object). For each object, the function main() then displays the initial values for the on/off mode, the channel number, and the volume. The function obtains this information by sending the C++ messages getOnOffMode(), getChannelNumber(), and getVolume() to each object.

Initializing with working values

The preceding example shows that the default constructor initializes the data members of an object with rather neutral values (that is, values that have no specific relevance). Here's an example of a class that initializes its instances to have working values (that is, values that have relevance).

The OBJECT5.CPP program declares the class Random, which generates pseudo-random numbers between 0 and 1 (exclusive). The class has the double-type data member m_fSeed, which stores the last random number and is used to generate the next random number. The class has the following member functions:

✔ A default constructor, which initializes the data member m_fSeed with the value of the constant INIT_SEED. Why not just assign 0 to the data member? Because the initial value affects the sequence of the random numbers that are generated. Sooner or later, the function getRandom() will start repeating the same sequence of numbers (that's why such numbers are called *pseudo-random numbers*). The count for distinct numbers per sequence depends on the initial seed value. Some initial values generate shorter sequences than others.

✔ The public member function getRandom(), which returns a random number.

✔ The protected member function cube(), which yields the cube value.

✔ The protected member function fraction(), which returns the fractional part of a floating-point number.

The OBJECT5.CPP program declares the objects RN1 and RN2 as instances of class Random and uses these objects to generate two sequences of five random numbers. Because the constructor initializes each class instance to the same state, the two objects RN1 and RN2 generate the same sequence of random numbers! Kinda spooky isn't it?

Here is the output from the OBJECT5.CPP program:

```
Initializing a class instance
Initializing a class instance
Here is a sequence of random numbers:
0.99373
0.717692
0.480483
0.519579
0.0750033
Here is another sequence of random numbers:
0.99373
0.717692
0.480483
0.519579
0.0750033
```

Listing 3-5 shows the source code for the OBJECT5.CPP program.

Listing 3-5	**OBJECT5.CPP**

```
// A C++ program that illustrates
// default constructors that assign
// nonneutral values to objects
```

```
#include <iostream.h>
#include <iomanip.h>
#include <math.h>
const double INIT_SEED = 13.17;
const double PI = 4 * atan(1);
class Random
{
  public:
   Random()
     {
        m_fSeed = INIT_SEED;
        cout << "Initializing a class instance\n";
     }
   double getRandom();
  protected:
    double m_fSeed;
    double cube(double x)
      { return x * x * x; }
    double fraction(double x)
      { return x - long(x); }
};
  double Random::getRandom()
{
  m_fSeed = fraction(cube(PI + m_fSeed));
  return m_fSeed;
}
main()
{
  const int MAX = 5;
  Random RN1;
  Random RN2;
  cout << "Here is a sequence of random numbers:\n";
  for (int i = 0; i < MAX; i++)
    cout << RN1.getRandom() << endl;
  cout << endl;
  cout << "Here is another sequence of random numbers:\n";
  for (i = 0; i < MAX; i++)
    cout << RN2.getRandom() << endl;
  return 0;
}
```

Listing 3-5 declares two constants, the class `Random`, and the function `main()`. The `double`-type constants `INIT_SEED` and `PI` represent the initial seed for the random numbers and the constant pi, respectively. The class `Random` models a pseudo-random number generator. (I say *pseudo* because you can control the sequence of random numbers by the initial seed value.) The class declares protected and public members. The protected members are as follows:

✔ The `double`-type data member `m_fSeed`, which stores the last random number generated and provides the seed for the next random number.

✔ The member function `cube()`, which yields cube values.

✔ The member function `fraction()`, which returns the fractional part of a floating-point number.

The class `Random` declares the following public members:

✔ The constructor, which assigns the initial value to the data member `m_fSeed` and displays the message "Initializing a class instance."

✔ The member function `getRandom()`, which returns the next random number. The function has a double return type and yields a value between 0 and 1 (exclusive). The definition of this member function uses the protected member functions `cube()` and `fraction()`. The member function `getRandom()` generates the next random number by using the values of the data member `m_fSeed` and the constant `PI`.

The function `main()` declares the local constant `MAX`, which specifies the number of random numbers generated in a sequence. The function also declares the objects `RN1` and `RN2` as instances of the class `Random`. The constructor initializes the data member `m_fSeed` in each object by using the value of the constant `INIT_SEED`. The function `main()` then performs the following tasks:

✔ Generates a sequence of `MAX` random numbers by using a `for` loop. Each loop iteration sends the C++ message `getRandom()` to the object `RN1`. This message generates a random number.

✔ Generates another sequence of `MAX` random numbers by using a `for` loop. Each loop iteration sends the C++ message `getRandom()` to the object `RN2`.

Cloning class instances with copy constructors

Copy constructors create class instances from existing ones. Thus, the new class instance starts out having the same value as the source class instance. When you write the source code for a copy constructor, you basically copy all the data members of the source instance into the new instance. This operation is fairly straightforward unless you have one or more data members that are pointers to dynamic data. In this case, you have two choices:

- ✔ Have the copy constructor perform a *shallow copy*, in which it copies the addresses held by the pointer-type data members. The result is that the new instance has data members that point to the same data accessed by the source instance. Having two pointers (in separate class instances) with the same address can be trouble if you do not update these addresses simultaneously.

- ✔ Have the copy constructor perform a *deep copy*, in which it allocates dynamic data and copies the dynamic data from the source instance to the new instance. This scheme is much safer than the shallow copy scheme because the source instance and the new instances don't access the same data. Consequently, the source instance can alter its dynamic data independently of the new instance (and vice versa) without causing memory or address corruption.

Use a copy constructor to create *twin* objects, so to speak. The copy constructor enables you to create a new class instance whose state copies that of an existing instance. Avoid writing copy constructors that perform shallow copies.

Next, you look at an example of a simple copy constructor. Later in this chapter, in the section that discusses destructors ("Destroying Objects: DOOM OOP style!"), I show you a copy constructor that handles dynamic data. Why postpone this example? Because copy constructors that handle dynamic data need destructors to recover the dynamic memory.

The next programming example presents a version of the class Box (which should be old hat by now) that has a default constructor and a copy constructor.

The OBJECT6.CPP program performs the following tasks:

- ✔ Creates three instances of the class Box. The second instance is a copy of the first one.
- ✔ Displays the dimensions, the base area, and the volume for the three instances.
- ✔ Displays the outcome of comparing the first and second boxes (which have equal dimensions).
- ✔ Displays the outcome of comparing the first and third boxes (which have different dimensions).

Here is the output from the OBJECT6.CPP program:

```
Box 1 has the following dimensions:
Length    = 10
Width     = 10
Height    = 10
Base area = 100
Volume    = 1000
Box 2 has the following dimensions:
Length    = 10
Width     = 10
Height    = 10
Base area = 100
Volume    = 1000
Box 3 has the following dimensions:
Length    = 10
Width     = 11
Height    = 10
Base area = 110
Volume    = 1100

Boxes 1 and 2 are equal
Boxes 1 and 3 are not equal
```

Listing 3-6 shows the source code for the OBJECT6.CPP program.

Listing 3-6	OBJECT6.CPP

```
// A C++ program that illustrates
// copy constructors

#include <iostream.h>
#include <iomanip.h>
class Box
{
  public:
    Box(double fLength = 0, double fWidth = 0, double⤸
    fHeight= 0)
      { initialize(fLength, fWidth, fHeight); }

    Box(Box& aBox)
      { copy(aBox); }
    void initialize(double fLength = 0,
                    double fWidth = 0,
                    double fHeight = 0);
    void copy(Box& aBox);
```

```
      void setLength(double fLength)
        { m_fLength = fLength; }
      void setWidth(double fWidth)
        { m_fWidth = fWidth; }
      void setHeight(double fHeight)
        { m_fHeight = fHeight; }
      double getLength()
        { return m_fLength; }
      double getWidth()
        { return m_fWidth; }
      double getHeight()
        { return m_fHeight; }
      double getBaseArea()
        { return m_fLength * m_fWidth; }
      double getVolume()
        { return m_fHeight * getBaseArea(); }

      int operator==(Box& aBox);
      int operator!=(Box& aBox);

    protected:
      double m_fLength; // length of box
      double m_fWidth;  // width of box
      double m_fHeight; // height of box
};
void Box::initialize(double fLength,
                     double fWidth,
                     double fHeight)
{
  m_fLength = fLength;
  m_fWidth = fWidth;
  m_fHeight = fHeight;
}
void Box::copy(Box& aBox)
{
  m_fLength = aBox.m_fLength;
  m_fWidth = aBox.m_fWidth;
  m_fHeight = aBox.m_fHeight;
}
int Box::operator==(Box& aBox)
{
  return (m_fLength == aBox.m_fLength &&
          m_fWidth == aBox.m_fWidth  &&
          m_fHeight == aBox.m_fHeight) ? 1 : 0;
```

(continued)

Listing 3-6 *(continued)*

```
}

int Box::operator!=(box& aBox)
{
return (m_fLength != aBox.m_fLength ||
        m_fWidth  != aBox.m_fWidth   ||
        m_fHeight != aBox.m_fHeight) ? 1 : 0;
}

main()
{
  Box Box1(10, 10, 10);
  Box Box2(Box1);
  Box Box3(10, 11, 10);

  cout << "Box 1 has the following dimensions:\n"
       << "Length    = " << Box1.getLength() << endl
       << "Width     = " << Box1.getWidth() << endl
       << "Height    = " << Box1.getHeight() << endl
       << "Base area = " << Box1.getBaseArea() << endl
       << "Volume    = " << Box1.getVolume() << endl;

  cout << "Box 2 has the following dimensions:\n"
       << "Length    = " << Box2.getLength() << endl
       << "Width     = " << Box2.getWidth() << endl
       << "Height    = " << Box2.getHeight() << endl
       << "Base area = " << Box2.getBaseArea() << endl
       << "Volume    = " << Box2.getVolume() << endl;

  cout << "Box 3 has the following dimensions:\n"
       << "Length    = " << Box3.getLength() << endl
       << "Width     = " << Box3.getWidth() << endl
       << "Height    = " << Box3.getHeight() << endl
       << "Base area = " << Box3.getBaseArea() << endl
       << "Volume    = " << Box3.getVolume() << endl;

  cout << endl;

  if (Box1 == Box2)
    cout << "Boxes 1 and 2 are equal\n";
  else
    cout << "Boxes 1 and 2 are not equal\n";
```

```
if (Box1 != Box3)
  cout << "Boxes 1 and 3 are not equal\n";
else
  cout << "Boxes 1 and 3 are equal\n";

return 0;
}
```

Listing 3-6 declares a special version of the class Box with the following new and relevant members:

- ✔ The default constructor (using the default argument), which initializes the data members m_fLength, m_fWidth, and m_fHeight using the values of the parameters fLength, fWidth, and fHeight, respectively.

- ✔ The copy constructor, which initializes the data members m_fLength, m_fWidth, and m_fHeight using the corresponding data members of parameter aBox. This parameter represents the source instance. The constructor actually calls the member function copy().

- ✔ The member function copy(), which copies the values of the data members from the source instance aBox to the new instance.

- ✔ The operator ==, which tests whether two class instances have the same state. The member function returns 1 if the data members of the instances have the same values. Otherwise, the member function yields 0.

- ✔ The operator !=, which tests whether two class instances have different states. The member function returns 1 if any data member of the instances has a different value. Otherwise, the member function yields 0.

The function main() declares the objects Box1, Box2, and Box3 as instances of class Box. The function uses the default constructor to initialize the instances Box1 and Box3 with different nondefault arguments. The function creates the object Box2 as a copy of the object Box1 using the copy constructor. The function then performs the following tasks:

- ✔ Displays the dimensions, the base area, and the volume of the object Box1.

- ✔ Displays the dimensions, the base area, and the volume of the object Box2.

- ✔ Displays the dimensions, the base area, and the volume of the object Box3.

- ✔ Displays the outcome of comparing the objects Box1 and Box2, using the operator ==. This task uses an if statement to determine the correct text commenting on how the objects compare.

- ✔ Displays the outcome of comparing the objects Box1 and Box3, using the operator !=. This task uses an if statement to determine the correct text commenting on how the objects compare.

Using custom constructors: the price of being unique

You do not need to use default or copy constructors to create all objects. In many cases, using a custom constructor makes far more sense than using a default constructor or a copy constructor. Remember how class Random creates instances that generate the same sequence of pseudo-random numbers? That class would be better served with a custom constructor that enables you to specify the initial seed, thereby allowing different instances to generate different sequences of pseudo-random numbers.

A custom constructor has one or more parameters (with possible default arguments) that enable you to do fine-tuning when you are creating class instances. You can use default arguments to make a custom constructor double up as a default constructor. However, keep in mind that you can use only one default constructor in a class.

Use a custom constructor to create a new instance of a class that has a nondefault state and is not a copy of an existing sibling object. Use custom constructors to create class instances that have unique states.

Examine the new version of class Random that follows. It includes a custom constructor with a single parameter that provides the initial seed value. The parameter has a default argument that enables the constructor to double up as a default constructor.

The OBJECT7.CPP program creates three class instances; each one is initialized separately and differently. The program then generates three different sequences of random numbers, as shown in the following sample output:

```
Initializing a class instance
Initializing a class instance
Initializing a class instance
Here is a sequence of random numbers:
0.99373
0.717692
0.480483
0.519579
0.0750033

Here is a second sequence of random numbers:
0.955013
0.749943
0.933624
0.678703
0.755906
```

```
Here is a third sequence of random numbers:
0.0168981
0.509307
0.66308
0.0746535
0.26962
```

Listing 3-7 contains the source code for the OBJECT7.CPP program.

Listing 3-7	OBJECT7.CPP

```
// A C++ program that illustrates
// custom constructors

#include <iostream.h>
#include <iomanip.h>
#include <math.h>

const double INIT_SEED = 13.17;
const double PI = 4 * atan(1);

class Random
{
  public:
    Random(double fInitSeed = INIT_SEED)
      {
        m_fSeed = fInitSeed;
        cout << "Initializing a class instance\n";
      }

    double getRandom();

  protected:
    double m_fSeed;

    double cube(double x)
      { return x * x * x; }
    double fraction(double x)
      { return x - long(x); }
};

double Random::getRandom()
```

(continued)

Listing 3-7 (continued)

```
{
  m_fSeed = fraction(cube(PI + m_fSeed));
  return m_fSeed;
}
main()
{
  const int MAX = 5;
  Random RN1;
  Random RN2(47.0);
  Random RN3(0.13);

  cout << "Here is a sequence of random numbers:\n";
  for (int i = 0; i < MAX; i++)
    cout << RN1.getRandom() << endl;
  cout << endl;

  cout << "Here is a second sequence of random numbers:\n";
  for (i = 0; i < MAX; i++)
    cout << RN2.getRandom() << endl;

  cout << endl;

  cout << "Here is a third sequence of random numbers:\n";
  for (i = 0; i < MAX; i++)
    cout << RN3.getRandom() << endl;
  return 0;
}
```

Listing 3-7 shows the new version of the class Random. The constructor has the double-type parameter fInitSeed with the default argument INIT_SEED. The constructor assigns the value of the parameter fInitSeed to the data member m_fSeed and then displays a message. Thus, you can use the constructor as a default constructor by omitting the argument. Or you can include an argument for the parameter fInitSeed to select a custom initial seed value.

The function main() creates the objects RN1, RN2, and RN3 as instances of class Random. The function creates the first instance using the default argument of parameter fInitSeed. In contrast, the function creates the other two instances using the values 47.0 and 0.13, respectively. The function uses three for loops to generate the three different sequences of random numbers using the objects RN1, RN2, and RN3.

Destroying Objects: DOOM, OOP Style!

The run-time system removes an object when it reaches the end of its scope. If the state of an object is entirely defined by its own data members, the run-time system quietly and successfully removes the object. In contrast, if the state of the object also depends on data that is stored outside the object (such as dynamic data or a data file), you need to use a destructor to prepare for the removal of that object.

Before I discuss destructors any further, take a step back and look at the big picture. In terms of initialization and destruction, you need to be concerned with three general types of objects:

- ✔ Objects that require no initialization or deinitialization. This type of object does not require you to declare constructors or a destructor.

- ✔ Objects that require the use of constructors to initialize some or all of their data members. This type of object typically does not have dynamic data, data files, or other resources associated with it. Thus, no cleanup is necessary before the run-time system removes such objects.

- ✔ Objects that require the use of constructors and a destructor for the initialization and destruction of some or all of their data members. This type of object has outside resources associated with it. The task of the constructors also includes initializing the outside resources. Likewise, the destructor must clean up the resources. Thus, whatever resources the constructors create and use must be removed by the destructor. For example, if the constructors create dynamic data, the destructor must remove that data. Or if the constructors open a file for input/output, the destructor must close the file.

For a programming example, look at the OBJECT8.CPP program. This program uses the class `myArray` to manage dynamic arrays of integers. The class enables you to specify the number of array elements when you create the class instances. The class has a default constructor, a copy constructor, and a destructor. The constructors create the dynamic array associated with each instance, and the destructor removes the dynamic array from memory.

The OBJECT8.CPP program creates three class instances and manipulates the arrays. The second instance starts out as a copy of the first one. The program initializes the first two class instances with values of 1. The program then uses a loop to update the values in the second instance and calculates the values in the third instance using the values in the first two instances.

Here is the output from the OBJECT8.CPP program:

```
Creating new class instance
Creating new class instance using copy constructor
Creating new class instance
Array 1 is:
1 1 1 1 1 1 1 1 1 1 1 1 1 1 1

Array 2 is:
2 3 4 5 6 7 8 9 10 11 12 13 14 15 16

Array 3 is:
3 4 5 6 7 8 9 10 11 12 13 14 15 16 17

Deleting a class instance
Deleting a class instance
Deleting a class instance
```

Listing 3-8 shows the source code for the OBJECT8.CPP program.

Listing 3-8	OBJECT8.CPP

```cpp
// A C++ program that illustrates
// destructors

#include <iostream.h>
#include <iomanip.h>

const int MINIMUM_SIZE = 10;

class myArray
{
  public:
   myArray(int nMaxSize = MINIMUM_SIZE, int nInitVal = 0);
   myArray(myArray& anArray);
   ~myArray();

   int& operator[](int nIndex)
     { return m_pnArray[nIndex]; }
   void show(int nNumElems, const char* pszMsg = "");

  protected:
   int* m_pnArray;
   int m_nMaxSize;

};
```

```
myArray::myArray(int nMaxSize, int nInitVal)
{
  m_nMaxSize = (nMaxSize < MINIMUM_SIZE) ?
                          MINIMUM_SIZE : nMaxSize;
  m_pnArray = new int[m_nMaxSize];
  for (int i = 0; i < m_nMaxSize; i++)
    m_pnArray[i] = nInitVal;
  cout << "Creating new class instance\n";
}
myArray::myArray(myArray& anArray)
{
  m_nMaxSize = anArray.m_nMaxSize;
  m_pnArray = new int[m_nMaxSize];
  for (int i = 0; i < m_nMaxSize; i++)
    m_pnArray[i] = anArray.m_pnArray[i];
  cout << "Creating new class instance using copy
          constructor\n";
}
myArray::~myArray()
{
  // delete array
  delete [] m_pnArray;
  cout << "Deleting a class instance\n";
}
void myArray::show(int nNumElems, const char* pszMsg)
{
  cout << pszMsg;
  for (int i = 0; i < nNumElems; i++)
    cout << m_pnArray[i] << ' ';
  cout << endl;
}
main()
{
  const int MAX = 15;
  myArray Array1(MAX, 1);
  myArray Array2(Array1);
  myArray Array3(MAX);

  for (int i = 0; i < MAX; i++) {
    Array2[i] *= (2 + i);
    Array3[i] = Array1[i] + Array2[i];
  }
```

(continued)

Listing 3-8 (continued)

```
Array1.show(MAX, "Array 1 is:\n"); cout << endl;
Array2.show(MAX, "Array 2 is:\n"); cout << endl;
Array3.show(MAX, "Array 3 is:\n"); cout << endl;

return 0;
}
```

Listing 3-8 declares the class myArray, which supports dynamic arrays of integers. The class declares protected and public members. The protected members are as follows:

✔ The int*-type data member m_pnArray, which is the pointer to the dynamic array of integers. The class uses this pointer to access the dynamic array of integers.

✔ The int-type data member m_nMaxSize, which stores the number of elements in the dynamic array (accessed by data member m_pnArray).

The class myArray has the following public members:

✔ The default constructor, which creates an array of integers containing nMaxSize elements. The second parameter of the constructor, nInitVal, specifies the initial value of the array elements. The two parameters have default arguments, enabling the constructor to double up as a default constructor.

✔ The copy constructor, which creates a new class instance using the instance specified by the parameter anArray.

✔ The destructor, which deletes the dynamic array accessed by the data member m_pnArray.

✔ The operator [], which accesses the elements of the dynamic array. The operator has the parameter nIndex, which specifies the index of the sought element.

✔ The member function show() which displays the first nNumElems elements in the dynamic array.

The definitions of the two class constructors use the operator new to allocate the space for the dynamic array. Each constructor displays a message to trace its execution. The definition of the destructor uses the operator delete to remove the dynamic array from memory. The destructor displays a message to trace its execution.

The function `main()` declares the constant `MAX` and the objects `Array1`, `Array2`, and `Array3` as instances of class `myArray`. The function creates the object `Array1` (using the custom constructor) to have `MAX` elements and the initial value of 1. The function creates the object `Array2` as a copy of the object `Array1` using the copy constructor. The function creates the object `Array3` (using the custom constructor) to have `MAX` elements and the initial value of 0 (the default argument). The function `main()` then performs the following tasks:

✔ Updates the values in the object `Array2` and calculates the values in the object `Array3` using the values in the objects `Array1` and `Array2`. This task uses a `for` loop to update the elements in the various objects. In addition, the loop statements use the `operator []` to access the individual array elements in the three objects.

✔ Displays the elements in the objects `Array1`, `Array2`, and `Array3` by sending the C++ message `show()` to each object. The argument for each message is the constant `MAX` and a string literal that identifies the array object.

Working (9 to 5) with Objects

C++ enables you to manipulate an object by sending it a message. Earlier programs in this chapter create class instances and send them messages. Consider, for example, the function `main()` in Listing 3-6. This function manipulates the object `Box1` (an instance of the class `Box`) by sending it various messages, as shown in the following code:

```
cout << "Box 1 has the following dimensions:\n"
     << "Length    = " << Box1.getLength() << endl
     << "Width     = " << Box1.getWidth() << endl
     << "Height    = " << Box1.getHeight() << endl
     << "Base area = " << Box1.getBaseArea() << endl
     << "Volume    = " << Box1.getVolume() << endl;
```

This output statement contains five C++ messages sent to the object `Box1`. The C++ message `getLength()` invokes the member function `Box::getLength()` and returns the length of the object `Box1`. The C++ message `getWidth()` invokes the member function `Box::getWidth()` and returns the width of the object `Box1`, and so on.

In Listing 3-7, the function main() creates the objects RN1, RN2, and RN3 as instances of the class Random. The function uses these objects to generate random numbers by sending each object the C++ message getRandom().

In Listing 3-8, the function main() creates the objects Array1, Array2, and Array3 as instances of the class myArray. The function displays the value in each object by sending it the C++ message show(). Moreover, the listing shows a special kind of C++ message whose syntax is unique to C++. I am talking about the operator []. The function main() sends the C++ message [] to each object and includes an index as an argument.

Summary

This chapter shows you how to interact with objects. You've read about tracing the life of an object from its creation (using a constructor) until its destruction (using a destructor). You've also read about sending messages to an object to alter or query the information in that object.

Part II
Cruising at Comfortable Levels

The 5th Wave   **By Rich Tennant**

"Now, when someone rings my doorbell, the current goes to a scanner that digitizes the audio impulses and sends the image to the PC where it's converted to a Pict file. The image is then animated, compressed, and sent via high-speed modem to an automated phone service that sends an e-mail message back to tell me someone was at my door 40 minutes ago."

In this part. . .

*I*n Part II, you move on to the main OOP-related features in C++ such as constructors, single inheritance, multiple inheritance, containment, class design, class hierarchy design, static members, and virtual member functions. These topics place you at the heart of object-oriented programming with C++.

Chapter 4

Static Members:
A Class of Their Own?

● ●

In This Chapter

▶ Understanding static data members

▶ Understanding static member functions

▶ Understanding instance counting

▶ Managing common errors

▶ Sharing information

● ●

*S*ome OOP gurus (or fanatics, depending on how you look at it) regard a class as a special kind of object — one that creates other objects. In fact, these gurus regard invoking a constructor as a special message sent to the class telling it to create an instance. We can all argue about whether a class is a special object or just a category of objects. This chapter may tip the scale in favor of the latter notion. C++ allows classes to have static members that conceptually belong to the class itself and not to any particular instance. This chapter shows you how to declare static members, initialize static data members, and use static members.

Static Data Members: Class-Owned Members

When you create a class instance, that instance has its own copy of the data members of the class. This feature enables each instance to maintain its own information separate from other class instances. In some cases, you need data members to conceptually belong to the class and not to any particular instance. C++ meets this need by offering *static data members*. Thus, although you have as many copies of nonstatic data members as you have instances, you have *only one* copy of a static data member, regardless of the number of class instances. In fact, the static data members of a class exist and are accessible even if you have not yet created any instances of that class.

Figure 4-1 depicts the class `Rectangle` with a static data member and nonstatic data members. The figure shows that the class instances `Rect1` and `Rect2` have their own copies of the nonstatic data members `fX` and `fY`, but share the single copy of the static data member `m_nCount`.

Each class has one and only one copy of each static data member.

What good are static data members? Essentially, static data members serve classes whose instances can (for the sake of saving memory) or must share information. Here are a few cases in which you can use static data members in a class:

- ✔ Counting the number of class instances. You can use a static data member to keep track of the number of instances. The class's constructors must increment the value of the instance counter, and the destructor needs to decrement the value of the instance counter.

- ✔ Sharing information. The static data members in a class can support a miniature database that provides common information to the class instances (such as general constants shared by all class instances). Thus, using static data members can eliminate redundant information and save memory.

- ✔ Iterating through all the class instances. You can use a static data member that stores a linked list for all the class instances and then process all of these instances.

- ✔ Sharing error status. You can use static data members to consolidate the management of logical errors that occur while invoking member functions.

- ✔ Communicating among instances. The static data members of a class can support the interaction between two or more class instances.

Declaring static data members: static buildup!

You use the following general syntax for declaring a static data member:

```
static type memberName;
```

The declaration of a static data member starts with the keyword `static`, which is followed by the member's type and name. Here is an example of declaring a static data member:

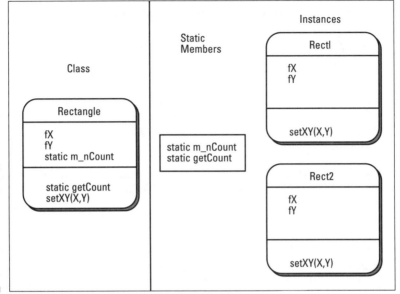

Figure 4-1:
A class with a static data member and nonstatic data members.

```
class Rectangle
{
 public:
  Rectangle()
     { m_nNumInstances++; }
  ~Rectangle()
     { m_nNumInstances--; }

  // other members

 protected:
  static int m_nNumInstances;
};
```

This example declares the class Rectangle, which contains the static data member m_nNumInstances. This data member counts the number of class instances. Thus, the constructor and the destructor increment and decrement, respectively, the value of the static data member.

Initializing static data members: zapping classes with static

In addition to showing how to declare a static data member, the preceding code snippet shows how the constructor and the destructor alter the values of that data member. You might have expected the constructor to initialize, rather than increment, the value of the static data member. However, if static data members exist regardless of the number of class instances, such an initialization is inappropriate (or even way out of line).

C++ requires that you initialize static data members *outside* the class declaration. You use the following general syntax for initializing a static data member:

```
type className::memberName = initialValue;
```

The member functions of a class access static data members just as they access nonstatic data members. Nonmember functions, such as the function main(), can access the public static data members by using the class name as a qualifier — that is, by using the following syntax:

```
className::staticMemberName
```

These nonmember functions can also access public static data members by using the name of any class instance.

The following example shows how you initialize a static data member:

```
class Rectangle
{
 public:
  Rectangle()
    { m_nNumInstances++; }
  ~Rectangle()
    { m_nNumInstances--; }

  // other members
protected:
  static int m_nNumInstances;
};
int Rectangle::m_nNumInstances = 0;
```

This example declares the class Rectangle, which contains the static data member m_nNumInstances. The last code line initializes the static data member outside the class declaration, as required by C++.

Static Member Functions: Static Guard!

C++ offers static member functions to access nonpublic static data members. You rarely declare static data members as public. Instead, classes typically declare static data members as protected and then access them using static member functions. The following general syntax declares a static member function:

```
static returnType functionName(parameterList);
```

The declaration of a static data member starts with the keyword `static`, which is followed by the function's return type, the function name, and an optional parameter list. C++ requires that static member functions cannot access nonstatic data members. Why? Because you can use static member functions when there are no class instances — that is, no copies of nonstatic data members are in memory.

A static member function should access static data members only. Nonstatic data members are off limits!

Here is an example of declaring a static member function:

```
class Rectangle
{
 public:
  Rectangle()
    { m_nNumInstances++; }
  ~Rectangle()
    { m_nNumInstances--; }
  static int getNumInstances()
    { return m_nNumInstances; }
  // other members

 protected:
  static int m_nNumInstances;
};
int Rectangle::m_nNumInstances = 0;
```

This example declares the class `Rectangle`, which contains the static data member `m_nNumInstances` and the static member function `getNumInstances()`. The static member function returns the value of the static data member.

Instance Counting: Go Figure!

The next example uses static members to count the number of class instances. The basic approach you use for an instance-counting class involves the following tasks:

- ✔ The class declares a nonpublic static data member that keeps track of the number of class instances.
- ✔ The class declares a static member function to return the value of the instance-counting static data member.
- ✔ The source code initializes the static data member outside the class declaration.
- ✔ The class constructors increment the value of the instance-counting static data member.
- ✔ The class destructor decrements the value of the instance-counting static data member.

The class constructors and the destructor should (directly or indirectly by calling auxiliary member functions) increment and decrement, respectively, the number of class instances.

The following example presents a special version of the class Box. This new version has an instance-counting static data member. The STATIC1.CPP program creates instances of the class Box in the function main() using two nested blocks. The main block creates the first instance, the first nested block creates a second instance, and the second nested block creates an array of instances. The program displays the current number of class instances before creating any instance and before and after the nested blocks.

Here is the output from the STATIC1.CPP program:

```
Before declaring an object
There are 0 instances of class Box

After declaring the Box1 object
There is 1 instance of class Box

Inside first nested block
There are 2 instances of class Box

Inside second nested block
There are 12 instances of class Box
```

```
After exiting second nested block
There are 2 instances of class Box

After exiting first nested block
There is 1 instance of class Box
```

Listing 4-1 shows the source code for the STATIC1.CPP program.

Listing 4-1	STATIC1.CPP

```cpp
// A C++ program that counts instances
// using static members

#include <iostream.h>
#include <iomanip.h>

class Box
{
  public:
    Box(double fLength = 0, double fWidth = 0, double fHeight⊃
    = 0);
    ~Box();

    // declare static member function to access
    // static data member
    static int getNumberOfInstances()
      { return m_nNumInstances; }
    void initialize(double fLength = 0,
                    double fWidth = 0,
                    double fHeight = 0);
    void setLength(double fLength)
      { m_fLength = fLength; }
    void setWidth(double fWidth)
      { m_fWidth = fWidth; }
    void setHeight(double fHeight)
      { m_fHeight = fHeight; }

    double getLength()
      { return m_fLength; }
    double getWidth()
      { return m_fWidth; }
    double getHeight()
      { return m_fHeight; }
```

(continued)

Listing 4-1 *(continued)*

```cpp
    double getBaseArea()
       { return m_fLength * m_fWidth; }
    double getVolume()
       { return m_fHeight * getBaseArea(); }

  protected:
    double m_fLength; // length of box
    double m_fWidth;  // width of box
    double m_fHeight; // height of box

    static int m_nNumInstances; // number of class instances
};
// initialize the static data member
int Box::m_nNumInstances = 0;

Box::Box(double fLength, double fWidth, double fHeight)
{
  initialize(fLength, fWidth, fHeight);
  // increase the number of instances
  m_nNumInstances++;
}
Box::~Box()
{
  // decrease the number of instances
  m_nNumInstances--;
}
void Box::initialize(double fLength,
                     double fWidth,
                     double fHeight)
{
  m_fLength = fLength;
  m_fWidth = fWidth;
  m_fHeight = fHeight;
}
main()
{
  cout << "Before declaring an object\n";

  cout << "There are " << Box::getNumberOfInstances()
       << " instances of class Box\n";
```

```
  Box Box1(10.5, 34.5, 12.3);

  cout << "\nAfter declaring the Box1 object\n";
  cout << "There is " << Box1.getNumberOfInstances()
       << " instance of class Box\n";
  {
    Box Box2(1.9, 3.4, 5.6);

    cout << "\nInside first nested block\n";
    cout << "There are " << Box2.getNumberOfInstances()
         << " instances of class Box\n";

    {
      const int MAX_BOXES = 10;
      // declare an array
      Box BoxArray[MAX_BOXES];

      cout << "\nInside second nested block\n";
      cout << "There are " <<⮎
      BoxArray[0].getNumberOfInstances()
           << " instances of class Box\n";
    }
    cout << "\nAfter exiting second nested block\n";
    cout << "There are " << Box2.getNumberOfInstances()
         << " instances of class Box\n";

  }
  cout << "\nAfter exiting first nested block\n";
  cout << "There is " << Box1.getNumberOfInstances()
       << " instance of class Box\n";

  return 0;
}
```

The special version of the class Box shown in Listing 4-1 has the following relevant members:

- ✔ The protected int-type static data member m_nNumInstances. This data member stores the current number of class instances.

- ✔ The public static member function getNumberOfInstances(), which returns the value in the static data member m_nNumInstances.

✔ The custom constructor, which also doubles up as the default constructor. This member initializes the nonstatic data members and increments the value of the static data member m_nNumInstances. Thus, each time you create a class instance, the run-time system invokes the constructor and therefore increments the value in the static data member.

✔ The destructor, which decrements the value in the static data member m_nNumInstances. Thus, each time a class instance reaches the end of its scope, the run-time system invokes the destructor to update the value in the static data member m_nNumInstances.

Notice that the listing initializes the static data member m_nNumInstances outside the class declaration and in the manner I describe in the section, "Initializing static data members: zapping classes with static." The initializing statement assigns 0 to the static data member.

The function main() performs the following tasks:

✔ Displays the initial number of instances of the class Box (which, of course, is 0). To obtain the number of class instances, this task involves using the expression Box::getNumberOfInstances(). Notice that this statement uses a reference to the class itself and not to a class instance (because the function has not yet created any instance).

✔ Creates the object Box1 as an instance of the class Box using arbitrary dimensions.

✔ Displays the current number of class instances (which is 1) by sending the C++ message getNumberOfInstances() to the object Box1. I could use the expression Box::getNumberOfInstances() to obtain the same result.

✔ Starts the first nested block.

✔ Declares the object Box2 as an instance of the class Box using arbitrary dimensions.

✔ Displays the current number of class instances (which is 2) by sending the C++ message getNumberOfInstances() to the object Box2. I could obtain the same result using the expression Box::getNumberOfInstances() or Box1.getNumberOfInstances().

✔ Starts the second nested block.

✔ Declares the array of objects BoxArray as instances of the class Box. This array contains ten elements.

✔ Displays the current number of class instances (which is 12) by sending the C++ message getNumberOfInstances() to the object BoxArray[0]. I could obtain the same result using the expressions Box::getNumberOfInstances(), Box1.getNumberOfInstances(), Box2.getNumberOfInstances(),BoxArray[1].getNumberOfInstances(), and so on.

✔ Ends the second nested block. The run-time system removes the array of objects `BoxArray`.

✔ Displays the current number of class instances (which is 2) by sending the C++ message `getNumberOfInstances()` to the object `Box2`. I could obtain the same result using the expressions `Box::getNumberOfInstances()` or `Box1.getNumberOfInstances()`.

✔ Ends the first nested block. The run-time system removes the object `Box2`.

✔ Displays the current number of class instances (which is 1) by sending the C++ message `getNumberOfInstances()` to the object `Box1`. I could obtain the same result using the expression `Box::getNumberOfInstances()`.

The program illustrates how the constructor and the destructor keep track of the correct number of instances. Every time the program creates a class instance, the constructor increments the value of the static data member `m_nNumInstances`. Likewise, every time the program removes a class instance, the destructor decrements the value of the static data member `m_nNumInstances`.

Common Error Management: Something's Rotten in Denmark

This section shows how a class uses a static data member to flag an error in any one of its instances. The basic concept behind using static data members in this manner is that it doesn't matter which is the offending instance. What's important is whether an error occurs when a class instance responds to a message.

The basic approach you use for an error-managing class involves the following tasks:

✔ The class declares a nonpublic static data member that keeps track of the error state.

✔ The class declares a static member function that returns the error state stored in the static data member and resets the value of that member.

✔ The source code initializes the static data member outside the class declaration.

✔ One or more member functions set an appropriate error value for the error-tracking static data member.

Enumerated types are ideal for modeling the state of an error. The simplest form of error has a Boolean nature — either an error has occurred or it hasn't. More sophisticated errors may possess several states, such as minor, critical, and fatal. You decide how much you want your class to panic.

The STATIC2.CPP program provides an example of a class that uses a static data member to track a common error state. This program declares a new version of the class myArray that I first presented in Listing 3-8 in Chapter 3. As you may remember, the class myArray supports dynamic arrays of integers. The class has the operator [] that allows you to access array elements. The version of the class myArray in Listing 3-8 does not check the arguments for the indices. Thus, the operator [] in Listing 3-8 is vulnerable to out-of-range indices (and all the horrors that follow such indices).

The STATIC2.CPP program presents a version of the class myArray that remedies this problem. The new class verifies the argument for the indices. In the case of an out-of-range index, the operator returns the reference to a new int-type data member m_nDummy. This new data member provides a dummy storage location for out-of-range indices.

Where does the error-tracking static data member fit in all this? The class myArray uses such a data member in dealing with out-of-range indices. When the operator [] detects a bad index, it sets the error-tracking static data member. The class has a static member function that reports (and resets) the current state of the error-tracking static data member.

The program creates three instances of the class myArray with varying sizes. The program attempts to process these arrays by using the sizes of the small, medium, and large arrays. The manipulation using the small array size is successful. In contrast, the manipulation using the medium and large array sizes sets the error flag. The program displays the values in the array when there is no error. Otherwise, the program displays an error message.

Here is the output from the STATIC2.CPP program:

```
Processing 15 array elements
Array 1 is:
1 1 1 1 1 1 1 1 1 1 1 1 1 1 1
Array 2 is:
2 2 2 2 2 2 2 2 2 2 2 2 2 2 2
Array 3 is:
3 3 3 3 3 3 3 3 3 3 3 3 3 3 3
Processing 20 array elements
Last array operation had an access error
Processing 30 array elements
Last array operation had an access error
```

Listing 4-2 shows the source code for the STATIC2.CPP program.

Listing 4-2 **STATIC2.CPP**

```cpp
// A C++ program that manages common errors
// using static members

#include <iostream.h>
#include <iomanip.h>

const int DUMMY_VAL = -32768;
const int MINIMUM_SIZE = 10;

enum Logical { FALSE, TRUE };

class myArray
{
  public:
   myArray(int nMaxSize = MINIMUM_SIZE, int nInitVal = 0);
   ~myArray();

   // declare static member function
   static Logical getAccessError();

   int& operator[](int nIndex);
   void show(int nNumElems, const char* pszMsg = "");

  protected:
   int* m_pnArray;
   int m_nMaxSize;
   int m_nDummy;

   // declare static data member
   static Logical m_bAccessError;
};
// initialize the static data member
Logical myArray::m_bAccessError = FALSE;

myArray::myArray(int nMaxSize, int nInitVal)
{
  m_nMaxSize = (nMaxSize < MINIMUM_SIZE) ?
               MINIMUM_SIZE : nMaxSize;
  m_pnArray = new int[m_nMaxSize];
  for (int i = 0; i < m_nMaxSize; i++)
```

(continued)

Listing 4-2 *(continued)*

```
    m_pnArray[i] = nInitVal;
    m_nDummy = DUMMY_VAL;
}
myArray::~myArray()
{
  // delete array
  delete [] m_pnArray;
}
Logical myArray::getAccessError()
{
  Logical bResult = m_bAccessError;
  m_bAccessError = FALSE; // reset access error
  return bResult;
}
int& myArray::operator[](int nIndex)
{
  if (nIndex >= 0 && nIndex < m_nMaxSize)
    return m_pnArray[nIndex];
  else {
    m_bAccessError = TRUE;
    return m_nDummy;
  }
}
void myArray::show(int nNumElems, const char* pszMsg)
{
  cout << pszMsg;
  for (int i = 0; i < nNumElems; i++)
    cout << m_pnArray[i] << ' ';
  cout << endl;
}
main()
{
  const int SIZE1 = 15;
  const int SIZE2 = 20;
  const int SIZE3 = 30;
  int nNumElems;
  myArray Array1(SIZE1, 1);
  myArray Array2(SIZE2, 2);
  myArray Array3(SIZE3);
```

```
  for (int i = 0; i < 3; i++) {
    switch (i) {
      case 0:
        nNumElems = SIZE1;
        break;

      case 1:
        nNumElems = SIZE2;
        break;

      case 2:
        nNumElems = SIZE3;
        break;
    }
    cout << "Processing " << nNumElems << " array⊃
    elements\n";
    for (int i = 0; i < nNumElems; i++)
      Array3[i] = Array1[i] + Array2[i];

    if (!myArray::getAccessError()) {
      Array1.show(nNumElems, "Array 1 is:\n");
      Array2.show(nNumElems, "Array 2 is:\n");
      Array3.show(nNumElems, "Array 3 is:\n");
    }
    else
      cout << "Last array operation had an access error\n";
  }
  return 0;
}
```

Listing 4-2 declares the global constants DUMMY_VAL and MINIMUM_SIZE, the enumerated type Logical, the class myArray, and the function main(). The constants DUMMY_VAL and MINIMUM_SIZE represent the dummy value obtained for the out-of-range indices and the minimum array size, respectively. The class myArray declares a number of protected and public members. This class declares the following protected members:

✔ The int* pointer m_pnArray, which accesses the dynamic array of integers.

✔ The int-type data member m_nMaxSize, which stores the maximum number of elements in the dynamic array.

✔ The int-type data member m_nDummy, which stores the dummy value returned by operator [] for out-of-range indices.

✔ The static `Logical` data member `m_bAccessError`, which stores the error state. The program uses this member to flag an out-of-range error in any class instance that uses the `operator []`.

The class `myArray` declares the following public members:

✔ The constructor, which creates a dynamic array whose size is defined by the parameter `nMaxSize`. The constructor also initializes the array elements using the argument for the parameter `nInitVal`.

✔ The destructor, which removes the dynamic array (accessed by the data member `m_pnArray`) when a class instance reaches the end of its scope.

✔ The static member function `getAccessError()`, which returns the value in the static data member `m_bAccessError` and sets that data member to `FALSE`.

✔ The `operator []`, which returns the reference for an array element in index `nIndex`. If the argument for this parameter is out of range, the function assigns `TRUE` to the static data member `m_bAccessError` and returns the reference of data member `m_nDummy`.

✔ The member function `show()`, which displays the elements of the dynamic array.

The listing initializes the static data member `m_bAccessError` outside the class declaration by assigning the value `FALSE` to that data member.

The function `main()` declares constants, variables, and objects. The constants `SIZE1`, `SIZE2`, and `SIZE3` specify the number of array elements used in creating instances of the class `myArray`. The variable `nNumElems` stores the number of elements in any class instance. The function `main()` declares the objects `Array1`, `Array2`, and `Array3` as instances of the class `myArray`. The objects `Array1`, `Array2`, and `Array3` have `SIZE1`, `SIZE2`, and `SIZE3` elements, respectively, and their elements have the initial values of 1, 2, and 0 (the default argument), respectively.

The function `main()` uses a `for` loop to process different numbers of elements in the three array objects. The loop processes `SIZE1`, `SIZE2`, and `SIZE3` elements in that sequence. Each iteration performs the following tasks:

1. Each iteration assigns the value of one of the constants to the variable `nNumElems` by using a `switch` statement.

2. Each iteration displays the number of elements to process.

3. Each iteration adds the `nNumElems` elements of the objects `Array1` and `Array2` and stores the result in the object `Array3`. This task uses a `for` loop that accesses the elements in the three objects using the `operator []`. (You also can say that each loop iteration accesses the elements of these objects by sending them the C++ message `operator []`.)

4. Each iteration determines whether the preceding step experienced an error by examining the result of the expression `!myArray::getAccessError()`. Notice that this expression uses the class name `myArray` (instead of the name of the `Array1` object) to qualify invoking the static member function `getAccessError()`. If the tested condition is true, the loop displays the elements in the three array objects. Otherwise, the program displays an error message.

The output indicates that only the first loop iteration goes without a hitch. The second and third loop iterations experience technical difficulties (that is, they bomb out). In the second loop iteration, the inner loop supplies the object `Array1[i]` with out-of-range indices. In the third loop iteration, the inner loop supplies the objects `Array1[i]` and `Array2[i]` with out-of-range indices.

Shared Information: Sharing Is Caring!

The next example shows how a class uses a static data member to share common information among class instances. This use of static data members reduces the amount of memory required because it eliminates redundant data.

The basic approach you use for a shared-information class involves the following tasks:

✔ The class declares a nonpublic static data member that stores the common data.

✔ The class declares a static member function to update and return the common information if such an operation is applicable.

✔ The source code initializes the static data member outside the class declaration.

The STATIC3.CPP program provides an example of a class that uses a static data member to manage common information. This program manages character sets by using arrays of bits to store the character set membership. The program declares the class `CharacterSet`, which stores and manipulates character sets. This manipulation includes adding, removing, querying, and displaying character sets. The program declares five character sets and manipulates them to test the various member functions of the class `CharacterSet`. What's really cool about this program is that you can cut and paste the class `CharacterSet` into your own code.

Here is the output from the STATIC3.CPP program:

```
Character set 1 has the range of:
[ABCDEF]
Character set 2 has the range of:
[LMNOP]
Adding set 2 to set 1 yields:
[ABCDEFLMNOP]
Character set 3 has the range of:
[CDEFGHIJKLMNOPQRSTUVWXY]
Members of set 3 are NOT in set 1
Character set 4 has the range of:
[NO]
After removing set 4 from set 1, set 1 is:
[ABCDEFLMP]
Character set 3 has the range of:
[CDEFGHIJKLMNOPQRSTUVWXY]
Members of set 3 are NOT in set 1
Character set 5 has the range of:
[BCDEF]
Members of set 5 are in set 1
```

Listing 4-3 shows the source code for the STATIC3.CPP program.

Listing 4-3	STATIC3.CPP

```
// A C++ program that illustrates shared information
// between objects using static members

#include <iostream.h>
#include <iomanip.h>


enum Logical { FALSE, TRUE };

typedef unsigned char Byte;
typedef unsigned char UChar;

const unsigned char NULL_CHAR = '\0';
const unsigned MAX_CHARS = 256;
const unsigned CHAR_SIZE = 8;
const unsigned CHAR_ARRAY_SIZE = MAX_CHARS / CHAR_SIZE;

class CharacterSet
{
    public:
      CharacterSet()
        { Clear(); }
```

```
    CharacterSet(UChar cFirst, UChar cLast);
    unsigned char GetSetSize()
      { return m_uSetSize; }
    CharacterSet& Clear();
    Logical IsMember(CharacterSet& cs);
    CharacterSet& Add(CharacterSet& cs);
    CharacterSet& Remove(CharacterSet& cs);
    void Show(const char* pszMsg = "");

  protected:
    UChar m_cSet[CHAR_ARRAY_SIZE];
    Byte m_uSetSize;

  private:
    void SetBit(Byte uBitNumber);
    void ClearBit(Byte uBitNumber);
    Logical IsBitSet(Byte uBitNumber);

    // declare static data member
    static UChar m_uBitValues[CHAR_ARRAY_SIZE];
};

UChar CharacterSet::m_uBitValues[CHAR_ARRAY_SIZE] =
               { 1, 2, 4, 8, 16, 32, 64, 128 };

CharacterSet::CharacterSet(UChar cFirst, UChar cLast)
{
    UChar c;

    Clear();
    // need to swap parameters cFirst and cLast?
    if (cFirst > cLast) {
       c = cFirst;
       cFirst = cLast;
       cLast = c;
    }
    m_uSetSize = cLast - cFirst + 1;
    for (c = cFirst; c <= cLast; c++)
        SetBit(c);
}
CharacterSet& CharacterSet::Clear()
{
```

(continued)

Listing 4-3 *(continued)*

```
  for (UChar i = 0; i < CHAR_ARRAY_SIZE; i++)
      m_cSet[i] = 0;
   m_uSetSize = 0;
   return *this;
}
void CharacterSet::SetBit(Byte uBitNumber)
{
  m_cSet[uBitNumber / CHAR_SIZE] |=
      m_uBitValues[uBitNumber % CHAR_SIZE];
}
void CharacterSet::ClearBit(Byte uBitNumber)
{
  m_cSet[uBitNumber / CHAR_SIZE] ^=
      m_uBitValues[uBitNumber % CHAR_SIZE];
}
Logical CharacterSet::IsBitSet(Byte uBitNumber)
{
   return ((m_cSet[uBitNumber / CHAR_SIZE] &
          m_uBitValues[uBitNumber % CHAR_SIZE]) > 0) ?
                                  TRUE : FALSE;
}
Logical CharacterSet::IsMember(CharacterSet& cs)
{
   int i;
   unsigned uBit = 0;
   // loop to test the members of cs
   do {
      // is character ASCII "uBit" a member of cs set?
      i = cs.IsBitSet((UChar)uBit);
      if (i) {
         // is member of cs not a member of this set?
         if (!IsBitSet((UChar)uBit))
            // cs is not equivalent or a subset of this set
            return FALSE;
      }
      uBit++;
   } while (uBit <= MAX_CHARS);
   // Every member of cs is also a member of this set
   return TRUE;
}
CharacterSet& CharacterSet::Add(CharacterSet& cs)
{
  // exit if set cs is empty
```

```
    if (cs.m_uSetSize == 0)
      return *this;
    // bitwize OR the m_cSet members of this set and set cs
    for (unsigned i = 0; i < CHAR_ARRAY_SIZE; i++)
      m_cSet[i] |= cs.m_cSet[i];
    // reset the set size
    m_uSetSize = 0;
    // scan the members of this set to recalculate m_uSetSize
    for (i = 0; i < MAX_CHARS; i++)
      // is ASCII i a member of this set?
      if (IsBitSet((UChar)i))
        m_uSetSize++; // increment the set size
    return *this;
}
CharacterSet& CharacterSet::Remove(CharacterSet& cs)
{
  // exit if the set cs is empty
  if (cs.m_uSetSize == 0)
    return *this;

  // bitwize XOR to clear members of this set
  // that are also in set cs
  for (unsigned i = 0; i < CHAR_ARRAY_SIZE; i++)
    m_cSet[i] ^= cs.m_cSet[i];
  // reset the set size
  m_uSetSize = 0;
  // scan the bits of this set to recalculate the new set
  size
  for (i = 0; i <= MAX_CHARS; i++)
    // is ASCII i a member of this set?
    if (IsBitSet((UChar)i))
      m_uSetSize++;
  return *this;
}
void CharacterSet::Show(const char* pszMsg)
{
  cout << pszMsg << "[";

  if (m_uSetSize == 0) {
    cout << "]\n";
    return;
  }
```

(continued)

Listing 4-3 *(continued)*

```
for (unsigned i = 0; i < MAX_CHARS; i++)
    if (IsBitSet((UChar)i))
        cout << UChar(i);

  cout << "]\n";
}
main()
{
  CharacterSet CharSet1('A', 'F');
  CharacterSet CharSet2('L', 'P');
  CharacterSet CharSet3('C', 'Y');
  CharacterSet CharSet4('N', 'O');
  CharacterSet CharSet5('B', 'F');

  CharSet1.Show("Character set 1 has the range of:\n");
  CharSet2.Show("Character set 2 has the range of:\n");

  // add characters of set 2 to set 1
  CharSet1.Add(CharSet2);
  CharSet1.Show("Adding set 2 to set 1 yields:\n");

  CharSet3.Show("Character set 3 has the range of:\n");
  if (CharSet1.IsMember(CharSet3))
    cout << "Members of set 3 are in set 1\n";
  else
    cout << "Members of set 3 are NOT in set 1\n";

  // remove the characters of set 4 from set 1
  CharSet1.Remove(CharSet4);
  CharSet4.Show("Character set 4 has the range of:\n");
  CharSet1.Show("After removing set 4 from set 1, set 1⊃
  is:\n");

  CharSet3.Show("Character set 3 has the range of:\n");
  if (CharSet1.IsMember(CharSet3))
    cout << "Members of set 3 are in set 1\n";
  else
    cout << "Members of set 3 are NOT in set 1\n";

  CharSet5.Show("Character set 5 has the range of:\n");
```

```
  if (CharSet1.IsMember(CharSet5))
    cout << "Members of set 5 are in set 1\n";
  else
    cout << "Members of set 5 are NOT in set 1\n";

  return 0;
}
```

Listing 4-3 uses `typedef` statements to declare the types `Byte` and `UChar`, which represent bytes and unsigned characters, respectively. The listing also declares the following constants:

- ✔ `NULL_CHAR`, which represents the null character.
- ✔ `MAX_CHARS`, which specifies the maximum number of characters.
- ✔ `CHAR_SIZE`, which defines the number of bits per byte.
- ✔ `CHAR_ARRAY_SIZE`, which defines the number of bytes needed to store `MAX_CHARS` bits.

The listing declares the class `CharacterSet`, which supports character sets using the private, protected, and public members described in the following sections.

The private members

The class `CharacterSet` declares the following private members:

- ✔ The static array of `UChar`-type `m_uBitValues`. This member has `CHAR_ARRAY_SIZE` elements that store powers of 2 (that is 1, 2, 4, 8, and so on) represented by bits 0 through 7.
- ✔ The member function `SetBit()`, which sets the bit number specified by the `Byte`-type parameter `uBitNumber`.
- ✔ The member function `ClearBit()`, which clears the bit number specified by the `Byte`-type parameter `uBitNumber`.
- ✔ The `Logical` member function `IsBitSet()`, which queries the state of the bit number specified by the `Byte`-type parameter `uBitNumber`.

The implementation of these member functions involves low-level bit manipulation that uses the static data member `m_uBitValues`. You can say that these member functions work strictly with bits and don't give a hoot as to what they represent. That's why I declared them private and set them aside from the character set manipulation functions.

The protected members

The class CharacterSet declares the following protected members:

- ✔ The UChar-type data member m_cSet, which stores an entire character set in CHAR_ARRAY_SIZE elements.
- ✔ The Byte-type data member m_uSetSize, which stores the number of elements in a set.

The public members

The class CharacterSet declares the following public members:

- ✔ The default constructor, which creates an empty set of characters.
- ✔ The custom constructor, which uses the parameters cFirst and cLast to create a character set by defining the range of the first and last characters.
- ✔ The member function GetSetSize(), which returns the number of set members stored in the data member m_uSetSize.
- ✔ The member function Clear(), which clears the bits in the data member m_cSet and assigns 0 to the data member m_uSetSize.
- ✔ The Logical member function IsMember(), which determines whether the members of the character set in parameter cs are members of the referenced instance — the one receiving the C++ message Clear().
- ✔ The member function Add(), which adds the members of the character set in the parameter cs to the members of the referenced instance.
- ✔ The member function Remove(), which removes the members of the character set in the parameter cs from the members of the referenced instance.
- ✔ The member function Show(), which displays the character set enclosed in a pair of square brackets.

The implementations of these member functions use the private member functions IsBitSet(), SetBit(), and ClearBit() to manipulate and query the bits that represent the characters.

The function main()

The function main() declares the following instances of the class CharacterSet:

✔ The object `CharSet1`, which has characters in the range of A to F.

✔ The object `CharSet2`, which has characters in the range of L to P.

✔ The object `CharSet3`, which has characters in the range of C to Y.

✔ The object `CharSet4`, which has characters in the range of N to O.

✔ The object `CharSet5`, which has characters in the range of B to F.

The function `main()` performs the following tasks:

✔ Displays character set 1 by sending the C++ message `Show()` to the object `CharSet1`.

✔ Displays character set 2 by sending the C++ message `Show()` to the object `CharSet2`.

✔ Adds the characters of set 2 to set 1 by sending the C++ message `Add()` to the object `CharSet1`. The argument for this message is the object `CharSet2`.

✔ Displays the updated character set 1 by sending the C++ message `Show()` to the object `CharSet1`.

✔ Displays character set 3 by sending the C++ message `Show()` to the object `CharSet3`.

✔ Determines whether all the members of set 3 are in set 1 by sending the C++ message `IsMember()` to the object `CharSet1`. The argument for this message is the object `CharSet3`. The function `main()` displays a message that reflects the result of sending the `IsMember()` message.

✔ Removes the members of set 4 from set 1 by sending the C++ message `Remove()` to the object `CharSet1`.

✔ Displays the updated character set 1 by sending the C++ message `Show()` to the object `CharSet1`.

✔ Displays character set 4 by sending the C++ message `Show()` to the object `CharSet4`.

✔ Displays character set 3 by sending the C++ message `Show()` to the object `CharSet3`.

✔ Determines whether all the members of set 3 are in the updated set 1 by sending the C++ message `IsMember()` to the object `CharSet1`. The argument for this message is the object `CharSet3`. The function `main()` displays a message that reflects the result of sending the `IsMember()` message.

✔ Displays character set 5 by sending the C++ message Show( ) to the object CharSet5.

✔ Determines whether all the members of set 5 are in set 1 by sending the C++ message IsMember( ) to the object CharSet1. The argument for this message is the object CharSet5. The function main( ) displays a message that reflects the result of sending the IsMember( ) message.

Summary

You've learned in this chapter that static members support special class-related information and not object-related data. In fact, without static data members, coding some classes becomes cumbersome if not impossible. The examples in this chapter show you how static data members support special shared information that is vital to the class instances (in the case of instance counting) and memory-saving as in the case of shared information.

Chapter 5

Class Design: The Good, the Bad, and the Ugly

- -

In This Chapter

▶ Analyzing objects before designing classes

▶ Following guidelines to create well designed classes

▶ Aiming for good cohesion

▶ Using coupling to connect functions

▶ Learning lessons from an ill designed class

▶ Revising the poorly designed class to improve it

- -

A significant part of software development involves analysis and planning. Programs designed with little forethought and vision end up serving few users, if any. This chapter covers the design of classes, focusing mostly on two main design criteria for member functions: cohesion and coupling. You read about designing robust and well-connected member functions, and you look at simple examples of an ill-designed class and its improved counterpart.

Analyzing Objects: How Was Your Relationship with Your Parent Class?

As programming environments (such as Windows 95) and applications (such as Word for Windows) become more slick and advanced, the need for better planned software increases. Gone are the days when you could cowboy your way into programming an application. Now, you must do a great deal of analysis before you start coding. The need to play Sigmund Freud before beginning to program an application arose long before the advent of object-oriented programming, but object-oriented programming has increased the need for analysis (of the task to be performed — and maybe of some programmers).

The main rule in creating a robust application is to build it by using robust components that correctly interact with each other. This rule also holds true for the computer you use, the car you drive, the appliances you use, and so on. In other words, a system is as strong as its weakest components. If you write an application that includes several weakly designed classes, don't be surprised when the results are mediocre!

With regard to C++ classes, the quality of a class's design depends on how well you define the class before you start coding. To define a class, you need to look at the attributes and the operations of the object that you are modeling. Chapter 2 discusses how to select the data members and the member functions of a class. The next section looks at this process with an analytical eye.

First-Class Class Design

In general, selecting the data members of a class is easier than selecting the member functions. It's easier because you can use various combinations of member functions to manipulate data in the same set of data members — some combinations of member functions are more efficient and easier to update than others. The degree of *cohesion* and *coupling* are two criteria for determining whether a member function is well designed or ill designed.

The following discussion about cohesion and coupling applies to both member functions and *ordinary functions* (that is, functions that are not member functions).

Cohesion: discipline in a function!

Cohesion answers the question "How closely do the operations of a member function (or an ordinary function) relate to each other?" In other words, cohesion determines whether a member function is highly focused or is a jack-of-all-trades. Highly cohesive member functions are very reliable; conversely, low-cohesion member functions are not very reliable.

Some kinds of cohesion are good, and some are poor. In the following sections, you look at the different flavors of cohesion as well as some examples of cohesion.

Functional cohesion

The best kind of cohesion is *functional cohesion*. Functional cohesion occurs in member functions that are very focused in what they do — in other words, they perform one and only one task. The following example shows a member function that exhibits functional cohesion:

```
class myClass
{
  public:
    // declaration of public members

  protected:
    double m_fCurrentValue;

    // declaration of other members

    double SquareCurrentValue()
       { return m_fCurrentValue * m_fCurrentValue; }
};
```

The member function SquareCurrentValue() performs one and only one
task: It returns the square of the value in data member m_fCurrentValue. The
member function is highly reliable (granted, it has only one simple statement)
because it performs only one task.

Here is an example of another member function that shows functional cohesion:

```
class NCSstring
{
  public:
    // declaration of public members
    int getLength()
      {
        int nLen = 0;
        while (m_pszString[nLen] != '\0')
             nLen++;
        return nLen;
      }

  protected:
    char* m_pszString;
    // declaration of other members
};
```

The member function getLength() performs only one task: It returns the
number of characters in the ASCIIZ string (a C-style string) accessed by the data
member m_pszString. The member function declares and initializes the local
variable nLen, uses a while loop to locate the null terminator of the ASCIIZ
string, and returns the value in the local variable nLen.

The member functions `SquareCurrentValue()` and `getLength()` provide examples of member functions whose statements perform one task and perform it reliably. The number of statements in a member function that has functional cohesion is not an issue — as long as these statements are truly contributing to a single task. Although the number of statements isn't an issue, functional cohesion tends to become questionable as the number of statements increases.

Sequential cohesion

Sequential cohesion takes place when the following occurs:

- ✔ A member function performs operations that must be carried out in a specific order.
- ✔ The operations share the same data.

Because the member functions of a class have access to all data members, sequential cohesion concerns nondata members. An example of a member function that exhibits sequential cohesion is one that prompts the user to enter a positive floating-point number, validates the input, and returns the square root. Here is the code for such a member function:

```
#include <math.h>

class myClass
{
   public:
   double getSquareRoot(const char* pszMessage);
};

double myClass::getSquareRoot(const char* pszMessage)
{
   double fX;

   do {
     // step 1: prompt for input
     cout << pszMessage;
     // step 2: get input
     cin >> fX;
     // step 3: validate
   while (fX <= 0.0);

   // step 4: calculate square root and return its value
   return sqrt(fX);
}
```

The definition of the member function getSquareRoot() shows the four tasks that the statements perform. In the case of a member function with multiple statements per task, you may be able to move the tasks into separate member functions — the new member functions would exhibit functional cohesion. In the example code, you can live with the sequential cohesion of the member function getSquareRoot().

Communicational cohesion

Communicational cohesion is a weaker version (or spin-off, if you prefer) of sequential cohesion. In communicational cohesion, the member function contains statements that perform tasks that merely share data. The tasks themselves are not related.

Like sequential cohesion, communicational cohesion mainly occurs in member functions that handle nondata members. This kind of cohesion is (barely) acceptable because it is practical — after all, we all write real-world applications every now and then, and we need to keep the end-user happy.

Here is an example of a member function that shows communicational cohesion. The following class includes the member function InvokeCalculator(), which supports a simple four-function calculator. (To simplify the code a bit, I didn't write statements that check for the sacrilege of dividing by zero.)

```
class myClass
{
   public:
    void InvokeCalculator();
   // declaration of other members
};

void myClass::InvokeCalculator()
{
   double fX, fY, fZ;
   char cOperation;

   cout << "Enter the first operand : ";
   cin >> fX;

   cout << "Enter the operation : ";
   cin >> cOperation;

   cout << "Enter the second operand : ";
   cin >> fY;
```

(continued)

(continued)

```
switch (cOperation) {
    case '+':
        fZ = fX + fY;
        break;

    case '-':
        fZ = fX - fY;
        break;

    case '*':
        fZ = fX * fY;
        break;

    case '/':
        fZ = fX / fY;
        break;

    default:
        cout << "Invalid operator";
        return;
    }

    // display operands, operation, and results
    cout << fX << ' ' << cOperation << ' '  << fY << " = " <<↩
fZ << "\n";
}
```

The member function `InvokeCalculator()` performs the following tasks:

1. Prompts you to enter the first operand

2. Prompts you to enter an operation

3. Prompts you to enter the second operand

4. Performs the operation (if valid)

5. Displays the operand, the operator, and the result

These five tasks share the local variables `fX`, `fY`, `fZ`, and `cOperation`. You could move some of the statements from the member function `InvokeCalculator()` into new member functions that prompt you for input and perform the calculations.

Temporal cohesion

Temporal cohesion takes place when a member function performs several tasks. Constructors and destructors are excellent examples of member functions that exhibit temporal cohesion. Other good examples are member functions that initialize (and reinitialize) and deinitialize class instances. In fact, you can have a constructor invoke the instance-initializing member function. Likewise, you can have the destructor invoke the instance-deinitializing member function. Temporal cohesion is acceptable for practical reasons.

Here is an example of a constructor and a destructor that exhibit temporal cohesion:

```
class myArray
{
  friend class myMatrix;

  public:
    myArray(int nMaxElems);
    ~myArray()
      { delete [] m_pfArray; }
    // declare other members

  protected:
    int m_nMaxElems;
    double* m_pfArray;

};

myArray::myArray(int nMaxElems)
{
  m_nMaxElems = (nMaxElems < 10) ? 10 : nMaxElems;
  m_pfArray = new double[nMaxElems];
  for (int i = 0; i< m_nMaxElems; i++)
    m_pfArray[i] = 0.0;
}

myArray::~myArray()
{
  delete [] m_pfArray;
}
```

This code snippet shows the definition of the constructor and the destructor of the class `myArray`. The constructor initializes the data members (a task that includes allocating dynamic memory) and then initializes the elements of the dynamic array. The tasks of initializing the data members are somewhat more related to each other than they are to the task of initializing the elements of the dynamic array. For example, the constructor could have called a member function `FillArray()` to perform the latter task. As for the destructor, it carries out the sole task of freeing the dynamic memory associated with the instance.

Procedural cohesion

Procedural cohesion takes place when the tasks of a member function are done in a specific sequence. However, these tasks do not share data, as is the case with communicational cohesion. This kind of cohesion is generally not acceptable. The solution for member functions with procedural cohesion is to create separate member functions (that are more cohesive) for the individual tasks. This approach turns the original member function into a kind of dispatcher.

Here is an example of a member function that exhibits procedural cohesion:

```
class myClass
{
  public:
    void Translate(const char* pszSourceFile,
               const char* pszTargetFile,
               const char* pszDictionaryFile);
    // declare other members
};

void myClass::Translate(const char* pszSourceFile,
                const char* pszTargetFile,
                const char* pszDictionaryFile)
{
  // declare variables for source file
  // declare variables for target file
  // declare variables for dictionary file

  // statements to open file pszSourceFile

  // statements to open, read, and close file
        pszDictionaryFile

  // statements to open file pszTargetFile

  // statements to translate lines from source file and write
    to the target file

  // statements to close source and target files
}
```

This code snippet shows the member function `Translate()`, which translates the text in a source file and writes the result to a target file. I placed comments in the definition instead of actual statements; the comments tell you the sequence of tasks. The member function reads the sequence of the search and replacement words from a dictionary file. The member function declares variables to contain data related to the source, target, and dictionary files. Thus, the member function `Translate()` contains three groups of unrelated variables and performs a sequence of tasks.

Logical cohesion

Logical cohesion takes place when a member function performs one or many tasks depending on the value of a switch parameter. Typically, the member function contains either a `switch` statement or a multiple-alternative `if-else` statement to select which tasks to perform. This type of cohesion is not acceptable. The solution to logical cohesion is the same as in the procedural cohesion.

Here is an example of a member function that shows logical cohesion:

```
enum Operation { addInt, addDbl, addLong };

class myClass
{
  public:
    void Add(Operation eOp);
    // declare other members

  protected:
    int m_nX;
    int m_nY;
    int m_nZ;
    double m_fX;
    double m_fY;
    double m_fZ;
    long m_lX;
    long m_lY;
    long m_lZ;
};

void myClass::Add(Operation eOp)
{
    switch(eOp) {
        case addInt:
```

(continued)

(continued)

```
                m_nZ = m_nX + m_nY;
                break;

        case addDbl:
                m_fZ = m_fX + m_fY;
                break;

        case addLong:
                m_lZ = m_lX + m_lY;
                break;
    }
}
```

This code snippet shows the member function Add(), which adds data members that have the types int, double, or long. The member function uses the enumerated type parameter eOp to select which set of data members it uses.

You can remedy this source code by replacing the addition statements with calls to new member functions that perform the various types of addition. Here is a better code version:

```
enum Operation { addInt, addDbl, addLong };

class myClass
{
  public:
    void Add(Operation eOp);
    // declare other members

  protected:
    int m_nX;
    int m_nY;
    int m_nZ;
    double m_fX;
    double m_fY;
    double m_fZ;
    long m_lX;
    long m_lY;
    long m_lZ;

    void AddInt()
        { m_nZ = m_nX + m_nY; }
    void AddDbl()
        { m_fZ = m_fX + m_fY; }
```

```
        void AddLong()
            { m_lZ = m_lX + m_lY; }

};

void myClass::Add(Operation eOp)
{
    switch(eOp) {
        case addInt:
            AddInt();
            break;

        case addDbl:
            AddDbl();
            break;

        case addLong:
            AddLong();
            break;
    }
}
```

This code snippet uses the member functions `AddInt()`, `AddDbl()`, and `AddLong()`, which exhibit functional cohesion (Yeah!). The new version of the member function `Add()` plays the role of a dispatcher, which is quite acceptable.

Coincidental cohesion

Coincidental cohesion takes place when statements that execute various tasks are just thrown together in a member function. In other words, the member function acts as a refuge for poorly organized statements. This kind of cohesion might get a programmer fired. This kind of cohesion is so bad that I don't even want to show you an example (which would make us all stoop down very low).

Cohesion is not sacred!

The various kinds of cohesion are not sacred, especially to a C++ compiler (or to any other compiler). In fact, the compiler will work with member functions that have any type of cohesion, as long as the syntax and the statements in that member function are correct. I discuss the various kinds of cohesion to make you more aware of the different kinds of coding and to encourage you to write member functions that are more focused in their tasks.

Coupling: the functional connection

C++ (like its parent language C) is a programming language that relies on functions to execute statements. Execution of a program starts with the function main(). This function can call a whole slew of other functions (which in turn call yet another set of functions) to perform the program's tasks. *Coupling* is a term that indicates the strength of the connection between two functions. While cohesion describes what a function does (and how well it does it), coupling describes how two functions relate to each other. Coupling complements cohesion.

Good coupling (also known as *loose coupling*) parallels the way two ice skaters perform. Each skater maintains his or her individuality, yet they interact splendidly with each other. Bad coupling (also known as *tight coupling*) parallels two skaters who are joined at the hip. Their movements are limited if not cumbersome! Thus, loose coupling translates into an easy connection between functions that are minimally dependent on each other. In contrast, tight coupling involves functions that are heavily dependent on each other. Loose coupling generates functions that are much more reusable than the ones generated by tight coupling.

Defining coupling

How do you evaluate coupling? Here are some general criteria for evaluating coupling between functions:

- The number of *connections* (mostly parameters) between two functions. The fewer the connections, the looser (that is, the better) the coupling. The number of connections is also called the *size*.

- The *intimacy* between the functions. A better connection between functions is based on more intimacy. Remember that member functions in a class can connect with each other using global data, data members, parameters, dynamic data, and file-stored information. Parameters pass data directly from one member function to another and thus offer better intimacy than relying on data members (although relying on data members isn't all that horrible). The other extreme is when member functions rely on global data (boo, hiss!) to pass data back and forth.

- The *visibility* factor. Visibility is a measure of the degree to which member functions (and ordinary functions) publicly and clearly define how they are to be supplied with data and how they will obtain data. For example, using global data to transfer data makes a member function far less visible than using parameters, because you can't readily tell which piece of global data is used.

Levels of coupling

What are the various levels of coupling? How do functions connect with each other? Here are the common levels of coupling:

- ✔ **Simple-data coupling** (also called *normal coupling*). This kind of coupling connects functions by using a parameter list of simple (nonstructured and nonclass-related) data types.

- ✔ **Data-structured coupling.** This sort of coupling connects functions by using a parameter list of structured and class-related data types.

- ✔ **Control coupling.** This kind of coupling has one function: to pass a parameter to another function that tells the latter what to do (the undesirable logical cohesion comes into play here).

- ✔ **Pathological coupling.** This type of coupling takes place when two functions modify each other's internal data.

- ✔ **Data-member coupling.** This sort of coupling happens when two member functions use data members to connect with each other.

- ✔ **Global-data coupling.** This genre of coupling occurs when functions use the same global data.

An Example of an Ill Designed Class: A Real Loser?

In this section, you look at a rather poor class design. The DESIGN1.CPP program declares the class myArray, which supports a dynamic array of integers. The class supports the following operations:

- ✔ Storing and recalling the array elements

- ✔ Displaying the array elements

- ✔ Searching for a value in the array elements, with the option of sorting the array elements

Here is the output from the DESIGN1.CPP program:

```
Unordered array is:
33 54 98 47 15 81 78 36 63 83
Searching for 83 : found at index 9
Searching for 63 : found at index 8
Searching for 36 : found at index 7
Searching for 78 : found at index 6
```

(continued)

(continued)

```
Searching for 81 : found at index 5
Searching for 15 : found at index 4
Searching for 47 : found at index 3
Searching for 98 : found at index 2
Searching for 54 : found at index 1
Searching for 33 : found at index 0

Ordered array is:
15 33 36 47 54 63 78 81 83 98
Searching for 83 : found at index 8
Searching for 63 : found at index 5
Searching for 36 : found at index 2
Searching for 78 : found at index 6
Searching for 81 : found at index 7
Searching for 15 : found at index 0
Searching for 47 : found at index 3
Searching for 98 : found at index 9
Searching for 54 : found at index 4
Searching for 33 : found at index 1
```

Listing 5-1 shows the source code for the DESIGN1.CPP program.

Listing 5-1	DESIGN1.CPP

```cpp
// A C++ program that illustrates
// a poor class design

#include <iostream.h>
#include <iomanip.h>

enum Logical { FALSE, TRUE };

const int ALL_ARRAY = -1;
const int NOT_FOUND = -1;
const int BAD_VALUE = -32768;

class myArray
{
  public:
    myArray(int nMaxElems, int nInitVal = 0);
    ~myArray();
    Logical Recall(int& nVal, int nIndex);
    Logical Store(int nVal, int nIndex);
```

```
      void Show(const char* pszMsg = "",
              const int nNumElems = ALL_ARRAY,
              const Logical bOneLine = TRUE);
    int Search(int nSearchVal, int nFirst = 0,
              Logical bSort = FALSE);

  protected:
    int m_nMaxElems;
    int m_nWorkSize;
    Logical m_bIsSorted;
    int* m_pnArray;
};

myArray::myArray(int nMaxElems, int nInitVal)
{
  m_nMaxElems = (nMaxElems < 1) ? 1 : nMaxElems;
  m_nWorkSize = 0;
  m_bIsSorted = FALSE;
  m_pnArray = new int[m_nMaxElems];
  for (int i = 0; i < m_nMaxElems; i++)
    m_pnArray[i] = nInitVal;
}


myArray::~myArray()
{
  delete [] m_pnArray;
}


Logical myArray::Recall(int& nVal, int nIndex)
{
  if (nIndex >= 0 && nIndex < m_nWorkSize) {
    nVal = m_pnArray[nIndex];
    return TRUE;
  }
  else
    return FALSE;
}


Logical myArray::Store(int nVal, int nIndex)
{
  if (nIndex < 0 || nIndex >= m_nMaxElems)
    return FALSE;
```

(continued)

Listing 5-1 *(continued)*

```
if (nIndex >= m_nWorkSize)
   m_nWorkSize = nIndex + 1;

 m_pnArray[nIndex] = nVal;
 m_bIsSorted = FALSE;
 return TRUE;
}

void myArray::Show(const char* pszMsg,
             const int nNumElems,
             const Logical bOneLine)
{
  int nCount;

  cout << pszMsg << endl;
  nCount = (nNumElems == ALL_ARRAY) ? m_nWorkSize :nNumElems;
  if (bOneLine) {
    for (int i = 0; i < nCount; i++)
      cout << m_pnArray[i] << ' ';
    cout << endl;

  }
  else {
    for (int i = 0; i < nCount; i++)
      cout << m_pnArray[i] << ' ';
    cout << endl;
  }
}

int myArray::Search(int nSearchVal, int nFirst, LogicalbSort)
{
  // sort the array?
  if (!m_bIsSorted && bSort) {
    // sort the array
    int nOffset = m_nWorkSize;
    int nElemI, nElemJ;

    do {
      nOffset = (nOffset * 8) / 11;
      nOffset = (nOffset < 1) ? 1 : nOffset;
      m_bIsSorted = TRUE; // set sorted flag
      // compare elements
      for (int i = 0, j = nOffset;
```

```
              i < (m_nWorkSize - nOffset);
              i++, j++) {
       nElemI = m_pnArray[i];
       nElemJ = m_pnArray[j];
       if (nElemI > nElemJ) {
          // swap elements
          m_pnArray[i] = nElemJ;
          m_pnArray[j] = nElemI;
          m_bIsSorted = FALSE; // clear sorted flag
       }
    }
  } while (!m_bIsSorted || nOffset != 1);
}

if (m_bIsSorted) {
  // search in the ordered array
  int nMedian;
  int nLast = m_nWorkSize - 1;

  // validate argument for parameter nFirst
  nFirst = (nFirst < 0 || nFirst >= m_nWorkSize) ?
                              0 : nFirst;

  do {
    nMedian = (nFirst + nLast) / 2;
    if (nSearchVal < m_pnArray[nMedian])
      nLast = nMedian - 1;
    else
      nFirst = nMedian + 1;
  } while (!(nSearchVal == m_pnArray[nMedian] ||
          nFirst > nLast));

  return (nSearchVal == m_pnArray[nMedian]) ?
                                nMedian : NOT_FOUND;
}
else {
  // search in unordered array
  for (int i = nFirst; i < m_nWorkSize; i++)
    if (m_pnArray[i] == nSearchVal)
      break;
  return (i < m_nWorkSize) ? i : NOT_FOUND;
}
```

(continued)

Listing 5-1 *(continued)*

```
}

main()
{
  const int MAX_ELEMS = 10;
  int nArr[MAX_ELEMS] = { 33, 54, 98, 47, 15,
                81, 78, 36, 63, 83 };
  myArray anArray(10);
  int k;

  // assign values to the object anArray
  for (int i = 0; i < MAX_ELEMS; i++)
    anArray.Store(nArr[i], i);

  // display unordered array
  anArray.Show("Unordered array is:");

  // search in unordered array
  for (i = MAX_ELEMS - 1; i >= 0; i--) {
    cout << "Searching for " << nArr[i] << " : ";
    k = anArray.Search(nArr[i]);
    if (k != NOT_FOUND)
      cout << "found at index " << k << endl;
    else
      cout << "no match found" << endl;
  }
  cout << endl;

  // sort the array using a dummy search
  anArray.Search(0, 0, TRUE);

  // display ordered array
  anArray.Show("Ordered array is:");

  // search in ordered array
  for (i = MAX_ELEMS - 1; i >= 0; i--) {
    cout << "Searching for " << nArr[i] << " : ";
    k = anArray.Search(nArr[i]);
    if (k != NOT_FOUND)
      cout << "found at index " << k << endl;
```

```
    else
      cout << "no match found" << endl;
  }

  return 0;
}
```

Listing 5-1 declares the class myArray, which contains public and protected members. Here are the protected members:

- The int-type data member m_nMaxElems, which stores the maximum number of array elements.

- The int-type data member m_nWorkSize, which stores the number of array elements that contain meaningful data (that is, they are not vacant).

- The Logical-type data member m_bIsSorted, which stores the ordered state of the array elements.

- The int*-type data member m_pnArray, which accesses the elements of the dynamic array.

The class declares the following public members:

- The constructor, which initializes the class instances by assigning values to the various data members and allocating memory to the dynamic array.

- The destructor, which frees the memory allocated to the dynamic array.

- The member function Recall(), which recalls the value of an array element specified by the index nIndex. The function returns the recalled value using the reference parameter nVal. The function validates the value of the parameter nIndex and yields TRUE if successful and FALSE if not.

- The member function Store(), which stores the value of the parameter nVal in an array element specified by the index nIndex. The function validates the value of the parameter nIndex and yields TRUE if successful and FALSE if not. If successful, the member function sets the data member m_bIsSorted to FALSE to clear the ordered state flag.

- The member function Show(), which displays the elements of the dynamic array in either one line or a column.

- The member function Search(), which searches for the value of the parameter nSearchVal in the array elements. The parameter nFirst specifies the index of the first array element to be searched. The Logical-type parameter bSort tells the member function whether to sort the array elements before searching. The member function returns the index of the matching element or yields the value of the constant BAD_RESULT if no match is found.

The definition of the member function Search() — the highlight of the bad class design — shows that the member function performs the following tasks:

- ✔ Sorts the array if the data member m_bIsSorted is FALSE and the argument of the parameter bSort is TRUE.

- ✔ Searches the array using the statements that implement the binary search method if the array elements are sorted. If the elements are not sorted, the member function uses statements that implement the linear search method.

Listing 5-1 shows that the class myArray contains the member function Search(), which is a jack-of-all-trades. The member function sorts and supports two searching methods. (All that's missing is for the member function to show multimedia clips!) As a result, the member function Search() exhibits procedural cohesion.

Overhauling Our Class Design: The Rolls Royce Version!

The class myArray in Listing 5-1 definitely needs fixing! The remedy involves creating separate member functions to sort, perform a linear search, and perform a binary search. As for the fate of the member function Search(), you can either eliminate it completely or keep it as a kind of dispatcher that invokes the linear or binary search member functions.

Listing 5-2 shows the source code for the DESIGN2.CPP program, which produces the same output as the program in Listing 5-1. Study the listing and observe that the new version of the class myArray has the new member functions Sort(), LinearSearch(), and BinarySearch().

Listing 5-2	DESIGN2.CPP

```
// A C++ program that illustrates
// a better class design

#include <iostream.h>
#include <iomanip.h>

enum Logical { FALSE, TRUE };

const int ALL_ARRAY = -1;
const int NOT_FOUND = -1;
const int BAD_VALUE = -32768;
```

```
class myArray
{
  public:
    myArray(int nMaxElems, int nInitVal = 0);
    ~myArray();
    Logical Recall(int& nVal, int nIndex);
    Logical Store(int nVal, int nIndex);
    void Show(const char* pszMsg = "",
              const int nNumElems = ALL_ARRAY,
              const Logical bOneLine = TRUE);
    void Sort();
    int Search(int nSearchVal, int nFirst = 0);

  protected:
    int m_nMaxElems;
    int m_nWorkSize;
    Logical m_bIsSorted;
    int* m_pnArray;

    int LinearSearch(int nSearchVal, int nFirst = 0);
    int BinarySearch(int nSearchVal, int nFirst = 0);

};

myArray::myArray(int nMaxElems, int nInitVal)
{
  m_nMaxElems = (nMaxElems < 1) ? 1 : nMaxElems;
  m_nWorkSize = 0;
  m_bIsSorted = FALSE;
  m_pnArray = new int[m_nMaxElems];
  for (int i = 0; i < m_nMaxElems; i++)
    m_pnArray[i] = nInitVal;
}

myArray::~myArray()
{
  delete [] m_pnArray;
}

Logical myArray::Recall(int& nVal, int nIndex)
{
```

(continued)

Listing 5-2 *(continued)*

```
if (nIndex >= 0 && nIndex < m_nWorkSize) {
    nVal = m_pnArray[nIndex];
    return TRUE;
  }
  else
    return FALSE;
}

Logical myArray::Store(int nVal, int nIndex)
{
  if (nIndex < 0 || nIndex >= m_nMaxElems)
    return FALSE;

  if (nIndex >= m_nWorkSize)
    m_nWorkSize = nIndex + 1;

  m_pnArray[nIndex] = nVal;
  m_bIsSorted = FALSE;
  return TRUE;
}

void myArray::Show(const char* pszMsg,
              const int nNumElems,
              const Logical bOneLine)
{
  int nCount;

  cout << pszMsg << endl;
  nCount = (nNumElems == ALL_ARRAY) ? m_nWorkSize :↲
  nNumElems;
  if (bOneLine) {
    for (int i = 0; i < nCount; i++)
      cout << m_pnArray[i] << ' ';
    cout << endl;

  }
  else {
    for (int i = 0; i < nCount; i++)
      cout << m_pnArray[i] << ' ';
    cout << endl;
  }
}
```

```
void myArray::Sort()
{
  if (m_bIsSorted)
    return; // exit if array is already sorted

  // sort the array
  int nOffset = m_nWorkSize;
  int nElemI, nElemJ;

  do {
    nOffset = (nOffset * 8) / 11;
    nOffset = (nOffset < 1) ? 1 : nOffset;
    m_bIsSorted = TRUE; // set sorted flag
    // compare elements
    for (int i = 0, j = nOffset;
         i < (m_nWorkSize - nOffset);
         i++, j++) {
      nElemI = m_pnArray[i];
      nElemJ = m_pnArray[j];
      if (nElemI > nElemJ) {
        // swap elements
        m_pnArray[i] = nElemJ;
        m_pnArray[j] = nElemI;
        m_bIsSorted = FALSE; // clear sorted flag
      }
    }
  } while (!m_bIsSorted || nOffset != 1);
}

int myArray::Search(int nSearchVal, int nFirst)
{
  return (m_bIsSorted) ? BinarySearch(nSearchVal, nFirst) :
                         LinearSearch(nSearchVal, nFirst);
}

int myArray::BinarySearch(int nSearchVal, int nFirst)
{
  // search in the ordered array
  int nMedian;
  int nLast = m_nWorkSize - 1;

  // validate argument for parameter nFirst
```

(continued)

Listing 5-2 *(continued)*

```
nFirst = (nFirst < 0 || nFirst >= m_nWorkSize) ?
                            0 : nFirst;

  do {
    nMedian = (nFirst + nLast) / 2;
    if (nSearchVal < m_pnArray[nMedian])
      nLast = nMedian - 1;
    else
      nFirst = nMedian + 1;
  } while (!(nSearchVal == m_pnArray[nMedian] ||
          nFirst > nLast));

  return (nSearchVal == m_pnArray[nMedian]) ?
                        nMedian : NOT_FOUND;
}

int myArray::LinearSearch(int nSearchVal, int nFirst)
{
  // search in unordered array
  for (int i = nFirst; i < m_nWorkSize; i++)
    if (m_pnArray[i] == nSearchVal)
      break;
  return (i < m_nWorkSize) ? i : NOT_FOUND;
}

main()
{
  const int MAX_ELEMS = 10;
  int nArr[MAX_ELEMS] = { 33, 54, 98, 47, 15,
                81, 78, 36, 63, 83 };
  myArray anArray(10);
  int k;

  // assign values to the object anArray
  for (int i = 0; i < MAX_ELEMS; i++)
    anArray.Store(nArr[i], i);

  // display unordered array
  anArray.Show("Unordered array is:");

  // search in unordered array
```

```
   for (i = MAX_ELEMS - 1; i >= 0; i--) {
     cout << "Searching for " << nArr[i] << " : ";
     k = anArray.Search(nArr[i]);
     if (k != NOT_FOUND)
       cout << "found at index " << k << endl;
     else
       cout << "no match found" << endl;
   }
   cout << endl;

   // sort the array
   anArray.Sort();

   // display ordered array
   anArray.Show("Ordered array is:");

   // search in ordered array
   for (i = MAX_ELEMS - 1; i >= 0; i--) {
     cout << "Searching for " << nArr[i] << " : ";
     k = anArray.Search(nArr[i]);
     if (k != NOT_FOUND)
       cout << "found at index " << k << endl;
     else
       cout << "no match found" << endl;
   }

   return 0;
}
```

Here are the relevant member functions in Listing 5-2:

- ✔ The member function Sort( ), which sorts the array elements.

- ✔ The member function LinearSearch( ), which performs the linear search on the array elements.

- ✔ The member function BinarySearch( ), which performs the binary search on the array elements.

- ✔ The member function Search( ), which invokes the member function BinarySearch( ) or LinearSearch( ) if the data member m_bIsSorted is TRUE or FALSE, respectively. In effect, the new version of the class myArray has a smart version of the member function Search( ) that knows which searching member function to invoke.

- ✔ The function main( ), which sorts the object anArray (an instance of the class myArray) by sending it the C++ message Sort( ). This message replaces (and it's a welcome and more readable replacement) the C++ message Search( ) found in Listing 5-1.

Listing 5-2 is a revision of Listing 5-1 that shows how you can split the tasks of a member function to create other member functions and make the class design more robust and more effective to use.

Summary

This chapter touches on the subject of class design. You've read about cohesion, which indicates how closely the operations of a member function relate to each other. You've also read about coupling, which indicates the strength of the connection between any two member functions. Although cohesion and coupling are not quantitative measures of how well the member functions of a class are designed, they do support a qualitative assessment of your design.

Chapter 6

Inheritance: A Touchy Subject among Child Classes

In This Chapter

▶ Learning about single and multiple inheritance

▶ Declaring a single-inheritance class hierarchy

▶ Using constructors for child classes

▶ Using descendant classes

▶ Working with nonpublic descendants

*I*nheritance, which is unique to object-oriented programming, is a form of software reuse that enables you to create new classes as descendants of existing classes. The descendant classes can extend the operations of their parent classes to offer more specialization. For example, you can create a small hierarchy of classes that supports generic files and text files. The base class represents generic files and supports general operations such as copying a file, deleting a file, and renaming a file. The descendant class represents text files. This class inherits the general file operations and adds new operations such as view, edit, find, and replace. Thus, inheritance in classes is like inheritance with humans; the descendant obtains the possessions of the parent, adding to the descendant's properties (which means more property tax to pay!).

This chapter introduces the single- and multiple-inheritance schemes supported by C++, but focuses on single inheritance. You find out how initializing and using descendant classes works in C++.

Single and Multiple Inheritance: An OOP Family Feud

As I mention in Chapter 1, object-oriented programming enables you to declare a new class as a descendant of another class. The descendant class (which is also called a *child class*) inherits the attributes and the operations of its parent class. The child class also defines new attributes and new operations, and it may override those inherited operations that are not suitable or appropriate for its purposes. Thus, inheritance enables you to reuse the code for parent classes and focus on writing new code for the child class.

Object-oriented programming languages vary in their support of inheritance schemes. The two main inheritance schemes are single inheritance and multiple inheritance. In *single inheritance,* a child class has one and only one parent class. When viewed in human terms, this inheritance scheme may sound weird and even somewhat unnatural. After all, each human being has two parents, and the idea that a human child could have only one parent sounds like something from a sci-fi book.

Multiple inheritance, on the other hand, enables you to declare a child class as a descendant of two or more parent classes. (Now things seem to be swinging to the other extreme!) C++ supports both inheritance schemes, whereas other OOP languages, such as SmallTalk, support only single inheritance.

The concept of multiple inheritance has sparked an extensive debate (which sometimes gets downright nasty) among OOP gurus. The gurus who oppose multiple inheritance say that it fosters bad design. (We humans seem to quarrel about *any* kind of inheritance!) The gurus who support multiple inheritance (the good guys in my book!) say that this inheritance scheme makes certain class designs possible — if not easy.

What is the main conceptual difference between single and multiple inheritance? Figures 6-1 and 6-2 can help you understand the two types. Figure 6-1 shows a hierarchy of classes modeling types of vehicles. The topmost class, which is called the *base class,* is Vehicle. This base class has the child class Automobile. Thus, the class Vehicle is the sole parent of the class Automobile. You can derive other classes from Vehicle, such as Planes, Trains, and Boats. Each of these classes will have the class Vehicle as the sole parent class.

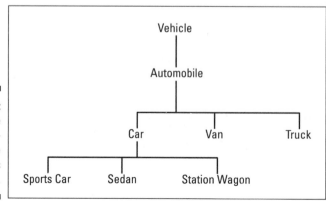

Figure 6-1:
An example
of a single-
inheritance
class
hierarchy.

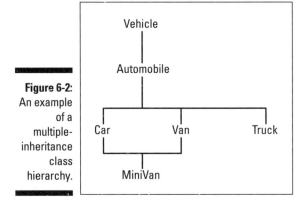

The child class Automobile has three child classes, namely, Car, Van, and Truck. Each of these classes has the class Automobile as the sole parent class. What's the relationship between these classes and the class Vehicle? The class Vehicle is said to be an ancestor class. (You see, *OOPese* does *not* use the term *grandparent* that is so endearing to humans.) Figure 6-1 also shows that the class Car is the single parent of the descendant classes Sedan, Sports Car, and Station Wagon.

Figure 6-1 shows a small four-level hierarchy of classes that uses only single inheritance to derive child classes. Each child class in this hierarchy has one and only one parent. The important concept behind this single-inheritance hierarchy is that all child classes relate to their parent classes through the "is-a" relationship. For example, a Car *is a* kind of Automobile. Likewise, a Sedan *is a* kind of Car. Thus, each child class represents a specialized version of its parent class; hence, the "is-a" relationship is central to single inheritance.

What about multiple inheritance? Figure 6-2 shows a sample multiple-inheritance class hierarchy. Although the hierarchy in this figure starts out like the one in Figure 6-1, notice the child class MiniVan. This class is a descendant of the classes Car and Van. In other words, a minivan is a cross between a car and a van. Multiple inheritance uses the concept of "has-a" to relate a child class with its parent classes. Thus, the class MiniVan has attributes and operations inherited from the classes Car and Van. In other words, a minivan is neither a kind of car nor a kind of van, but it has features from both.

The rest of this chapter focuses on single inheritance. Chapter 9 discusses multiple inheritance.

Declaring a Single-Inheritance Class Hierarchy: Single Parent Classes!

Under single inheritance, C++ supports the following general syntax for declaring a child class (the optional parts appear in italics and are enclosed in brackets which you don't type):

```
class className : [public] parentClassName
{
  public:
    // declarations of public members

  protected:
    // declarations of protected members

  private:
    // declarations of private members
};
```

Like its parent class, a child class may declare public, protected, and private sections. The same rules that I present in Chapter 2 about declaring base classes and their sections also apply here. You also need to follow these additional rules:

- ✔ The declaration of a child class must include the name of the parent class. This name appears after the name of the child class. A colon separates the two class names. The optional keyword `public` enables the instances of the child class to access the public members of the parent class. Otherwise, the public members of the parent class are hands-off! I present an example of this feature in the section, "Nonpublic Descendants: Silent Partners," later in this chapter.
- ✔ The member functions of the child class have access to the public and protected members of the parent class. The private members of the parent class are inaccessible to the member functions of the child class.
- ✔ The instances of the child class can access only the public members of the child class and those of the parent class.

The following simple code snippet shows a base class and its child class:

```
class Rectangle {
  public:
    Rectangle(double fLength = 0, double fWidth = 0);
```

```
      void setLength()(double fLength);
      double getLength();
      void setWidth(double fWidth);
      double getWidth();
      double getArea();

   protected:
      double m_fLength;
      double m_fWidth;
};

class Box : public Rectangle
{
   public:
      Box(double fLength = 0, double fWidth = 0, double⤴
      fHeight = 0);
      void setHeight(double fHeight);
      double getHeight();
      double getArea(); // overrides inherited member function
      double getVolume();

   protected:
      double m_fHeight;
};
```

The class Rectangle represents a rectangle. The class has the protected double-type data members m_fLength and m_fWidth. The class has a constructor and the member functions setLength(), getLength(), setWidth(), getWidth(), and getArea().

The code in this example declares the class Box as a public descendant of the class Rectangle. Thus, the class Box inherits all the members of the class Rectangle. The child class adds the double-type protected data member m_fHeight to support the height of the box. The class has a constructor and the member functions setHeight(), getHeight(), getArea(), and getVolume(). Notice that the class Box declares its own version of the member function getArea() to override the inherited member function Rectangle::getArea(). The member function Box::getArea() returns the surface area of the box object and not just the area of the base rectangle. Conceptually, you can say that the class Box *is a* kind of (three-dimensional) rectangle. This relationship connects the classes Box and Rectangle.

Constructors for Child Classes: Connecting with One's Heritage

You read in Chapter 3 that constructors are special members that automatically initialize class instances. In the case of a base class, the run-time system simply invokes the constructor of that class. In the case of descendant classes, you need to invoke the constructor of the parent class before you initialize the data members of the descendant class. When you apply this scheme in a multiple-class hierarchy, you end up invoking the constructor of the base class first and the constructor of the parent class last.

The general syntax for this cascaded constructor invocation is:

```
constructor(parameterList1) :
   constructorOfParentClass(parameterList2)
   {
     // initializing statements
   }
```

Here is an example of invoking the constructors of parent classes:

```
class A
{
  A()
   {
     // statements
   }
  // declarations of members
};

class B : public A
{
  B() : A()
   {
     // statements
   }
  // declarations of members
};

class C : public B
{
  C() : B()
   {
     // statements
```

```
    }
    // declarations of members
};
```

The code in this example shows a small class hierarchy that is made up of the classes A, B, and C. Class A is the base class, and classes B and C are descendant classes. The constructor of class B invokes the constructor of the parent class A before carrying out any further initialization. Likewise, the constructor of class C invokes the constructor of the parent class B (which in turn invokes the constructor of class A) before carrying out any additional initialization.

The following programming example illustrates the constructors of descendant classes. The CHILD1.CPP program declares the small hierarchy of trivial classes classA, classB, and classC, which store integers. The constructors of these classes store the integers and display a *tracer message* (that is, a message that tells you which member function the program is executing). Each class has a member function that displays the values of the integers stored in a class instance.

Here is the output from the CHILD1.CPP program (notice the sequence of tracer messages generated by the constructors of the classes classB and classC):

```
Invoking constructor of class classA
Object A stores 1

Invoking constructor of class classA
Invoking constructor of class classB
Object B stores 10, 20

Invoking constructor of class classA
Invoking constructor of class classB
Invoking constructor of class classC
Object C stores 100, 200, 300
```

Listing 6-1 shows the source code for the CHILD1.CPP program.

Listing 6-1	CHILD1.CPP

```
// A C++ program that illustrates
// invoking the constructors of parent classes
#include <iostream.h>
#include <iomanip.h>

class classA
{
  public:
```

(continued)

Listing 6-1 *(continued)*

```cpp
classA(int nA)
    { m_nA = nA;
      cout << "Invoking constructor of class classA\n";
    }
  void show(const char* pszMsg = "")
    { cout << pszMsg << m_nA << endl; }

  protected:
    int m_nA;
};

class classB : public classA
{
  public:
    classB(int nA, int nB)
      : classA(nA)
      { m_nB = nB;
        cout << "Invoking constructor of class classB\n";
      }
    void show(const char* pszMsg = "")
      { cout << pszMsg << m_nA
             << ", " << m_nB << endl;
      }

  protected:
    int m_nB;
};

class classC : public classB
{
  public:
    classC(int nA, int nB, int nC)
      : classB(nA, nB)
      { m_nC = nC;
        cout << "Invoking constructor of class classC\n";
      }
    void show(const char* pszMsg = "")
      { cout << pszMsg << m_nA
             << ", " << m_nB
             << ", " << m_nC
             << endl;
      }
```

```
   protected:
     int m_nC;
};

main()
{
   classA objectA(1);
   objectA.show("Object A stores ");
   cout << endl;
   classB objectB(10, 20);
   objectB.show("Object B stores ");
   cout << endl;
   classC objectC(100, 200, 300);
   objectC.show("Object C stores ");

   return 0;
}
```

Listing 6-1 declares the class classA, which has the protected int-type data member m_nA and the following public members:

- ✔ A constructor that assigns the value of the parameter nA to the data member m_nA and emits a tracer message.
- ✔ The member function show( ), which displays the value in the data member m_nA.

The listing also declares the class classB, which is a descendant of the class classA. This class has the protected int-type data member m_nB and the following public members:

- ✔ A constructor that invokes the constructor of the parent class (and passes the value of parameter nA to that constructor), assigns the value of parameter nB to the data member m_nB, and emits a tracer message.
- ✔ The member function show( ), which displays the value in the data members m_nA (inherited from the parent class) and m_nB.

The listing also declares the class classC, which is a descendant of the class classB. This class has the protected int-type data member m_nC and the following public members:

- ✔ A constructor that invokes the constructor of the parent class (and passes the values of the parameters nA and nB to that constructor), assigns the value of parameter nC to the data member m_nC, and emits a tracer message.
- ✔ The member function show( ), which displays the value in the data members m_nA, m_nB (both are inherited from the parent class), and m_nC.

The function `main()` performs the following tasks:

✔ Declares the object `objectA` as an instance of the class `classA`. This declaration initializes the class instance with the integer 1 and invokes the constructor of the class `classA`. This constructor assigns the integer 1 to data member `m_nA` and emits a tracer message.

✔ Displays the value in the object `objectA` by sending the C++ message `show()` to that object. The argument for this message is the string literal `"Object A stores "`.

✔ Declares the object `objectB` as an instance of the class `classB`. This declaration initializes the class instance with the integers 10 and 20 and invokes the constructor of the class `classB`. This constructor invokes the constructor of the parent class (and passes the integer 10 to it), assigns the integer 20 to data member `m_nB`, and emits a tracer message. Thus, the creation of the object `objectB` sends two tracer messages: one from the constructor of the class `classA` and the other from the constructor of the class `classB`.

✔ Displays the value in the object `objectB` by sending the C++ message `show()` to that object. The argument for this message is the string literal `"Object B stores "`.

✔ Declares the object `objectC` as an instance of the class `classC`. This declaration initializes the class instance with the integers 100, 200, and 300, and invokes the constructor of class `classC`. This constructor invokes the constructor of the parent class (and passes the integers 100 and 200 to it), assigns the character 300 to data member `m_nC` and emits a tracer message. Thus, creating object `objectC` ends up sending three tracer messages — one from each class constructor.

✔ Displays the value in the object `objectC` by sending the C++ message `show()` to that object. The argument for this message is the string literal `"Object C stores "`.

Using Descendant Classes: Inheriting and Displaying Family Traits

The next example builds on the classes `Rectangle` and `Box` that I presented earlier in this chapter, in the section "Declaring a Single-Inheritance Class Hierarchy: Single Parent Classes." The CHILD2.CPP program (which I created from the OBJECT2.CPP program found in Listing 3-2 in Chapter 3) contains the declaration of the classes `Rectangle` and `Box`, the definitions of their member functions, and the definition of the function `main()`. This function declares two instances of the class `Box`, called `myBox` and `yourBox`. The program performs the following tasks:

1. Prompts you to enter the dimensions of the object yourBox.

2. Assigns the dimensions of the object myBox.

3. Displays the dimensions, the base area, and the volume of the object yourBox.

4. Displays the dimensions, the base area, and the volume of the object myBox.

5. Determines whether the object yourBox fits inside the object myBox and displays a message if it does.

6. Determines whether the object myBox fits inside the object yourBox and displays a message if it does.

7. If neither box fits inside the other one, the program displays a message to that effect.

Here is the output from a sample session with the CHILD2.CPP program (the input is in boldface):

```
Enter the length of the box : 5
Enter the width of the box : 5
Enter the height of the box : 5
Your box has the following dimensions:
Length    = 5
Width     = 5
Height    = 5
Area      = 150
Volume    = 125

My box has the following dimensions:
Length    = 10
Width     = 10
Height    = 10
Area      = 600
Volume    = 1000
Your box can fit inside my box
```

Listing 6-2 shows the source code for the CHILD2.CPP program.

Listing 6-2	**CHILD2.CPP**

```cpp
// A C++ program that illustrates
// descendant classes

#include <iostream.h>
#include <iomanip.h>
```

(continued)

Listing 6-2 *(continued)*

```cpp
class Rectangle
{
  public:
    Rectangle(double fLength = 0, double fWidth = 0)
      { initialize(fLength, fWidth); }

    void initialize(double fLength = 0,
                    double fWidth = 0);
    void setLength(double fLength)
      { m_fLength = fLength; }
    void setWidth(double fWidth)
      { m_fWidth = fWidth; }
    double getLength()
      { return m_fLength; }
    double getWidth()
      { return m_fWidth; }
    double getArea()
      { return m_fLength * m_fWidth; }

  protected:
    double m_fLength; // length of rectangle
    double m_fWidth;  // width of rectangle
};

class Box : public Rectangle
{
  public:
    Box(double fLength = 0, double fWidth = 0, double⊃
    fHeight= 0)
      { initialize(fLength, fWidth, fHeight); }

    void initialize(double fLength = 0,
                    double fWidth = 0,
                    double fHeight = 0);
    void setHeight(double fHeight)
      { m_fHeight = fHeight; }
    double getHeight()
      { return m_fHeight; }
    double getArea()
      { return 2 * (Rectangle::getArea()  +
                    m_fLength * m_fHeight + .
                    m_fWidth * m_fHeight); }
```

```
   double getVolume()
     { return m_fHeight * m_fWidth * m_fHeight; }

  protected:
    double m_fHeight; // height of box
};

void Rectangle::initialize(double fLength,
                   double fWidth)
{
  m_fLength = fLength;
  m_fWidth = fWidth;
}

void Box::initialize(double fLength,
               double fWidth,
               double fHeight)
{
  // invoke inherited member function
  Rectangle::initialize(fLength, fWidth);
  m_fHeight = fHeight;
}

main()
{
  Box yourBox;
  Box myBox;
  double fX;

  // prompt the user to input the length
  do {
    cout << "Enter the length of the box : ";
    cin >> fX;
  } while (fX <= 0);
  // set the length of the box
  yourBox.setLength(fX);

  // prompt the user to input the width
  do {
    cout << "Enter the width of the box : ";
    cin >> fX;
  } while (fX <= 0);
```

(continued)

Listing 6-2 *(continued)*

```cpp
// set the width of the box
yourBox.setWidth(fX);

// prompt the user to input the height
do {
  cout << "Enter the height of the box : ";
  cin >> fX;
} while (fX <= 0);
// set the height of the box
yourBox.setHeight(fX);

myBox.initialize(10, 10, 10);

cout << "Your box has the following dimensions:\n"
     << "Length   = " << yourBox.getLength() << endl
     << "Width    = " << yourBox.getWidth()  << endl
     << "Height   = " << yourBox.getHeight() << endl
     << "Area     = " << yourBox.getArea()   << endl
     << "Volume   = " << yourBox.getVolume() << endl <<
     endl;

cout << "My box has the following dimensions:\n"
     << "Length   = " << myBox.getLength()   << endl
     << "Width    = " << myBox.getWidth()    << endl
     << "Height   = " << myBox.getHeight()   << endl
     << "Area     = " << myBox.getArea()     << endl
     << "Volume   = " << myBox.getVolume()   << endl;

if (myBox.getLength() < yourBox.getLength() &&
    myBox.getWidth() < yourBox.getWidth() &&
    myBox.getHeight() < yourBox.getHeight())
    cout << "My box can fit inside your box\n";
else if (myBox.getLength() > yourBox.getLength() &&
    myBox.getWidth() > yourBox.getWidth() &&
    myBox.getHeight() > yourBox.getHeight())
    cout << "Your box can fit inside my box\n";
else
    cout << "Neither box fits inside the other one\n";

return 0;
}
```

The code in this example declares the base class `Rectangle` and its descendant class `Box`. The class `Rectangle` declares the protected `double`-type data members `m_fLength` and `m_fWidth`, which store the length and the width, respectively, of a rectangle. The class declares the following public members:

- The constructor, which initializes the data members by calling the member function `initialize()`.

- The member function `initialize()`, which initializes the data members.

- The member function `setLength()`, which sets the new value for the data member `m_fLength`.

- The member function `getLength()`, which returns the value in the data member `m_fLength`.

- The member function `setWidth()`, which sets the new value for the data member `m_fWidth`.

- The member function `getWidth()`, which returns the value in the data member `m_fWidth`.

- The member function `getArea()`, which returns the area of the rectangle; the area is calculated using the data members.

The example also declares the class `Box` as a public descendant of the class `Rectangle`. The descendant class declares the protected `double`-type data member `m_fHeight`, which stores the height of the box. The class inherits the protected data members `m_fLength` and `m_fWidth` and ends up with three data members. The class `Box` also declares the following public members:

- The constructor, which initializes the data members.

- The member function `initialize()`, which assigns new values to the data members. This member function is a new version that assigns values to the inherited and declared data members. Notice that the implementation for this member function invokes the inherited member function, using the expression `Rectangle::initialize(fLength, fWidth)`.

- The member function `setHeight()`, which sets the new value of the data member `m_fHeight`.

- The member function `getHeight()`, which returns the value in the data member `m_fHeight`.

- The member function `getArea()`, which overrides the inherited version and calculates the total surface area. The implementation of this member function uses the expression `Rectangle::getArea()` to invoke the inherited version.

- The member function `getVolume()`, which returns the volume of the solid shape; the volume is calculated by using the data members `m_fLength`, `m_fWidth`, and `m_fHeight`.

The class `Box` inherits the member functions `setLength()`, `getLength()`, `setWidth()`, and `getWidth()`.

The function `main()` creates the objects `yourBox` and `myBox` as instances of the class `Box`. The function also declares the `double`-type variable `fX`. The function `main()` performs the following tasks:

- Prompts you to enter the length of the box. This task stores your input in the variable `fX` and uses a `do-while` loop to ensure that you enter a positive value.

- Assigns the length of the object `yourBox` by sending that object the C++ message `setLength()`. The argument for this message is the variable `fX`.

- Prompts you to enter the width of the box. This task stores your input in the variable `fX` and uses a `do-while` loop to ensure that you enter a positive value.

- Assigns the width of the object `yourBox` by sending that object the C++ message `setWidth`. The argument for this message is the variable `fX`.

- Prompts you to enter the height of the box. This task stores your input in the variable `fX` and uses a `do-while` loop to ensure that you enter a positive value.

- Assigns the height of the object `yourBox` by sending that object the C++ message `setHeight()`. The argument for this message is the variable `fX`.

- Assigns the length, the width, and the height of the object `myBox` by sending that object the C++ message `initialize()`. The arguments for this message are 10, 10, and 10, which represent the length, the width, and the height, respectively.

- Displays the dimensions, the area, and the volume of the object `yourBox`. This task obtains the length, the width, the height, the area, and the volume of the object `yourBox` by sending the C++ messages `getLength()`, `getWidth()`, `getHeight()`, `getArea()`, and `getVolume()`. None of these C++ messages has arguments.

- Displays the dimensions, the area, and the volume of the object `myBox`. This task obtains the length, the width, the height, the area, and the volume of the object `myBox` by sending the C++ messages `getLength()`, `getWidth()`, `getHeight()`, `getArea()`, and `getVolume()`. None of these C++ messages has arguments.

- Determines whether the object `myBox` can fit inside the object `yourBox`. This task determines whether the length, the width, and the height of the object `myBox` are each less than the corresponding dimensions of the object `yourBox`. If the dimensions are less, the function displays the string "My box can fit inside your box."

- If the tested conditions are not true, determines whether the object `yourBox` can fit inside the object `myBox`. This task determines whether the length, the width, and the height of the object `yourBox` are each less than the corresponding dimensions of the object `myBox`. If the dimensions are less, the function displays the string "Your box can fit inside my box."

- If these conditions are not true, the function `main()` displays the string "Neither box fits inside the other one."

Nonpublic Descendants: Silent Partners

The next example shows how to create a descendant class from a nonpublic class. In other words, the descendant supports a new kind of object that is based on the attributes and the operations of the parent class. Although the descendant class is still (technically speaking) a special version of the parent class, the descendant class uses the parent class mainly for basic support, like most college students. The following example illustrates how this concept works.

The CHILD3.CPP program creates a descendant class of a nonpublic class. The program declares the classes `myArray` and `myStack`. The class `myArray` supports a dynamic array of integers. The class `myStack`, which is a descendant of the class `myArray`, supports a fixed stack of integers. The number of array elements and the size of the stack are fixed at run time and not at compile time. This arrangement leaves some flexibility for sizing up the instances of both classes. The program creates an instance of the class `myStack` and performs the following tasks:

- ✔ Pushes integers into the stack.
- ✔ Displays the height of the stack.
- ✔ Pops the integers off the stack until the stack is empty.
- ✔ Displays the height of the stack (which should be 0).

Here is the output from the CHILD3.CPP program:

```
Pushing 23 into the stack
Pushing 45 into the stack
Pushing 89 into the stack
Pushing 74 into the stack
Pushing 51 into the stack

Stack has 5 elements

Popping 51 off the stack
Popping 74 off the stack
Popping 89 off the stack
Popping 45 off the stack
Popping 23 off the stack

Stack has 0 elements
```

Listing 6-3 shows the source code for the CHILD3.CPP program.

Listing 6-3	CHILD3.CPP

```cpp
// A C++ program that illustrates
// creating a new class as a nonpublic
// descendant of a parent class

#include <iostream.h>
#include <iomanip.h>

const int MAX_ELEMS = 5;
enum Logical { FALSE, TRUE };

class myArray
{
  public:
    myArray(int nNumElems = MAX_ELEMS, int fInitVal = 0);
    ~myArray()
      { delete [] m_pnArray; }
    int& operator[](int nIndex)
      { return m_pnArray[nIndex]; }
    void show(const char* pszMsg = "",
          const int nNumElems = MAX_ELEMS);

  protected:
    int* m_pnArray;
    int m_nNumElems;
};
class myStack : myArray
{
  public:
    myStack(int nMaxHeight = 10)
      : myArray(nMaxHeight, 0)
      { clear(); }
    Logical push(int nNum);
    Logical pop(int& nNum);
    int getHeight()
      { return m_nHeight; }
    void clear()
      { m_nHeight = 0; }

  protected:
    int m_nHeight;
};
```

```
myArray::myArray(int nNumElems, int fInitVal)
{
  m_nNumElems = (nNumElems > 0) ? nNumElems : 1;
  m_pnArray = new int[m_nNumElems];
  for (int i = 0; i < m_nNumElems; i++)
    m_pnArray[i] = fInitVal;
}

void myArray::show(const char* pszMsg,
            const int nNumElems)
{
  cout << pszMsg << endl;
  for (int i = 0; i < nNumElems; i++)
    cout << m_pnArray[i] << ' ';
  cout << endl;
}

Logical myStack::push(int nNum)
{
  if (m_nHeight < m_nNumElems) {
    m_pnArray[m_nHeight++] = nNum;
    return TRUE;
  }
  else
    return FALSE;
}

Logical myStack::pop(int& nNum)
{
  if (m_nHeight > 0) {
    nNum = m_pnArray[-m_nHeight];
    return TRUE;
  }
  else
    return FALSE;
}

main()
{
  int nArr[MAX_ELEMS] = { 23, 45, 89, 74, 51 };
  int nVal;
  myStack Stack(MAX_ELEMS);
```

(continued)

Listing 6-3 *(continued)*

```
for (int i = 0; i < MAX_ELEMS; i++) {
    cout << "Pushing " << nArr[i] << " into the stack\n";
    if (!Stack.push(nArr[i]))
      cout << "Stack overflow at i = " << i << endl;
  }

  cout << endl;
  cout << "Stack has " << Stack.getHeight() << " elements\n";
  cout << endl;

  while (Stack.pop(nVal))
    cout << "Popping " << nVal << " off the stack\n";

  cout << endl;
  cout << "Stack has " << Stack.getHeight() << " elements";

  return 0;
}
```

Listing 6-3 declares the classes myArray and myStack. The listing declares the class myStack as a nonpublic descendant of the class myArray. This means that the instances of the class myStack cannot access any member of the class myArray — not even the public members of the parent class.

The class myArray

The class myArray supports simple dynamic arrays of integers. The class declares protected and public members. The protected members are as follows:

✔ The int*-type data member m_pnArray, which accesses the dynamic array of integers.

✔ The int-type data member m_nNumElems, which stores the number of elements in the dynamic array.

The class declares the following public members:

✔ The constructor, which allocates the space for the dynamic array (using the operator new) and initializes the array elements by using the argument of the parameter fInitVal. The int-type parameter nNumElems specifies the number of elements in the dynamic array.

✔ The destructor, which deallocates the space for the dynamic array using the operator delete.

✔ The operator [], which accesses an element in the dynamic array.

✔ The member function show(), which displays the values in the dynamic array.

The statements that define the constructor, the operator [], and the member function show() access the array elements using the format m_pnArray [index].

The class myStack

The class myStack declares the protected data member m_nHeight to store the current stack height. The class declares the following public members:

✔ The constructor, which allocates the dynamic array of integers that supports the stack. The constructor also sets the data member m_nHeight to 0 by invoking the member function clear().

✔ The member function push(), which pushes the value of the parameter nNum into the stack. If the stack is not full, the member function stores the value of nNum in the next available element of the dynamic array, increments the stack height, and returns TRUE. In contrast, if the stack is full, the member function yields the enumerator FALSE and does not push the value of nNum into the stack.

✔ The member function pop() pops off the top of the stack and returns that value using the reference parameter nNum. The function yields TRUE if the stack is not empty and returns FALSE when it is empty. When the member function returns FALSE, the value returned by the parameter nNum is not relevant.

✔ The member function getHeight() returns the current height of the stack.

✔ The member function clear() resets the stack height to 0.

The statements that define the member functions push() and pop() access the supporting dynamic array using the inherited data member m_pnArray. The member function push() also uses the inherited data member m_nNumElems to determine whether the stack is full.

The function main() declares and initializes the C++ array nArr, declares the variable nVal, and declares the object Stack as an instance of the class myStack. The declaration of this object specifies a maximum stack size of MAX_ELEMS elements. The initialization of the object Stack creates a dynamic array with MAX_ELEMS elements. The function main() performs the following tasks:

✔ Pushes the values in the array nArr into the object Stack. This task uses a for loop to iterate over the elements of array nArr. Each loop iteration pushes the element nArr[i] into the object Stack by sending the C++ message push() to that object. The argument for this message is the array element nArr[i]. The loop displays a warning message in case the stack of the object Stack overflows.

✔ Displays the height of the stack in object Stack. This task involves sending the C++ message getHeight() to the object Stack.

✔ Pops off the elements from the object Stack. This task uses a while loop to pop off all the stack elements. The loop's condition is the result of sending the C++ message pop() to the object Stack. The argument for this message is the variable nVal, which obtains the popped value. The loop iteration displays the value in the variable nVal.

✔ Displays the height of the stack in the object Stack. This task involves sending the C++ message getHeight() to the object Stack. The program displays 0 because the while loop empties the stack.

Summary

This chapter presents single inheritance as a method for creating descendant classes that inherit the members of their parent classes. The chapter shows you how to create a class hierarchy with single-parent classes and how to initialize the descendant classes. You've also learned how to use nonpublic parent classes to support the special operations of the descendant classes.

The next chapter looks at polymorphism and how you apply it to C++ classes to support a uniform response in a class hierarchy.

Chapter 7

Polymorphism: Unified Response

- -

In This Chapter

▶ An overview of polymorphism

▶ Using virtual functions

▶ Using virtual destructors

▶ Knowing when to use virtual functions

- -

*T*his chapter focuses on polymorphism, which is one of the pillars of object-oriented programming. In Chapter 1, I describe how polymorphism empowers the members of a class hierarchy to support uniform behavior. In this chapter, I show you how C++ virtual member functions play a major role in supporting polymorphism. For example, consider a hierarchy of classes that support simple geometric shapes (points, lines, rectangles, circles, ellipses, and so on). The descendant classes support shapes that are more elaborate than those of the parent classes. So as you move down the hierarchy, the classes deal with more sophisticated shapes.

Polymorphism comes into play here with the member function that draws the shape supported by each class. For example, the class of lines has the member function Draw, the class of rectangles has the member function Draw, and so on. Each class can have its own version of the member function Draw to make sure that the program can draw the instances of that class.

Another example of polymorphism involves a class hierarchy that models cars. The base class supports generic cars, whereas the descendant classes support more refined cars (sports cars, luxury cars, and so on). You can imagine that each class in the hierarchy has the virtual member function Start that starts the car's engine, although on very cold days, some instances may not respond! Each class may have its own version of the virtual member function Start because different types of cars may well have different start-up mechanisms — I think! However, the virtual member function Start ensures a uniform response to a start-the-engine message. And if you believe this, I can sell you land on the Moon!

An Overview of Polymorphism: The Big OOP-Morphing Picture

In Chapter 1, I discuss polymorphism in general terms. The TV example in that chapter shows you how under polymorphism the members of a class hierarchy support uniform and consistent response. The TV example in Chapter 1 talks about the polymorphic behavior of the various TV models in responding to the on/off switch. This is a simple example of polymorphism.

Polymorphism is also associated with the notion of abstract behavior. When you turn on the power switch of a TV (or any other appliance or electronic device), you expect the TV to be powered up. Unless you are the designer of that TV set, you don't care about the details of the circuits that are attached to the power switch.

Polymorphic behavior also applies to human behavior. Often, you observe very similar behavior among family members. Although each family member is a unique person (akin to a distinct class), each person inherits polymorphic behavior (through the genes or as learned behavior) and responds in some situations in a manner that's similar to the response of other family members.

C++ supports polymorphism by using *virtual member functions*. Virtual member functions enable the various classes to offer consistent and proper responses. Without virtual member functions, C++ would not support polymorphism. Without polymorphism, the reuse of code in classes becomes rather limited.

Before I introduce you to virtual functions, look at a code snippet that illustrates what can go wrong if you don't use virtual functions:

```
class A
{
  public:
    int procA()
      { return procA1() * procA2(); }
    int procA1()
      { return 4; }
    int procA2()
      { return 5; }
};
class B : public A
{
  public:
    int procA1()
      { return 10; }
};
```

```
main()
{
  B objB;

  cout << objB.procA();

  return 0;
}
```

This example declares class A and its descendant, class B. Class A contains the member functions procA(), procA1(), and procA2(). The member function procA() returns a value that is the product of invoking the member functions procA1() and procA2(). Class B declares its own version of the member function procA1() and inherits the member functions procA() and procA2().

When the function main() sends the C++ message procA() to the object objB (an instance of class B), what value does that message yield? Because class B declares its own version of the member function procA2(), you expect the C++ message procA() to invoke the member functions B::procA1() and A::procA2(), yielding the value 50. However, the output statement in the function main() is 20! Why? Because the C++ message procA() ends up invoking the member functions A::procA1() and A::procA2(). In other words, the thick-headed compiler doesn't get the hint that you really want to invoke the member function B::procA1() when you send the C++ message procA() to the instances of class B.

The next section introduces virtual functions and shows you how to solve the problem in the preceding code snippet. So hang in there!

Virtual (Reality) Functions

The solution to the little nightmare in the preceding code snippet lies in using virtual member functions. C++ enables you to declare virtual member functions using the following general syntax:

```
virtual returnType functionName(parameterList);
```

The declaration starts with the keyword virtual and proceeds as with nonvirtual member functions. Applying this syntax to the classes A and B, I can write the following revised code, which works the way it should:

```
class A
{
  public:
    int procA()
      { return procA1() * procA2(); }
    virtual int procA1()
      { return 4; }
    int procA2()
      { return 5; }
};
class B : public A
{
  public:
    virtual int procA1()
      { return 10; }
};
main()
{
  B objB;

  cout << objB.procA();

  return 0;
}
```

Notice that this code snippet declares the member function procA1() as virtual in both class A and class B. When the function main() sends the C++ message procA() to the object objB, it invokes the member functions B::procA1() and A::procA2(), which yields the correct result of 50. Thanks to the virtual declaration of the member function procA1(), the compiler can make a better (or smarter, if you like) judgment about which member function to call. In this example, the compiler knows that member function procA1() is a virtual function. So when the compiler generates executable code for the C++ message objB.procA(), it performs the following general steps:

1. Examines the expression procA1() * procA2() and determines that it contains calls to two member functions.

2. Determines that the member function procA1() is virtual but that the member function procA2() is not.

3. Because the message is sent to an instance of class B, the compiler determines if class B declares its own virtual member function procA1(). In this case, the class B does declare its own virtual member function procA1().

4. Uses the member function B::procA1() to resolve the call to member function procA1() and uses the member function A::procA2() to resolve the call to member function procA2().

A Random Time Example: Does Anyone Have the Correct Time?

In the following programming example, the VIRTUAL1.CPP program declares the hierarchy of the classes `RandomTime1`, `RandomTime2`, and `RandomTime3`, which each generate random times. Each class has its own version of a function that generates random numbers. The program creates an instance of each class and then uses each instance to generate five random times.

Here is the output from the VIRTUAL1.CPP program:

```
Sequence of time generated by instance of class RandomTime1
         is:
15:48:41
01:00:09
04:09:40
13:44:57
01:17:16

Sequence of time generated by instance of class RandomTime2
         is:
19:04:37
11:49:30
21:36:27
00:06:05
00:40:43

Sequence of time generated by instance of class RandomTime3
         is:
15:08:40
05:38:38
12:11:48
02:15:13
05:14:41
```

Listing 7-1 shows the source code for the VIRTUAL1.CPP program.

Listing 7-1	VIRTUAL1.CPP

```cpp
// A C++ program that illustrates virtual functions

#include <iostream.h>
#include <iomanip.h>
```

(continued)

Listing 7-1 *(continued)*

```cpp
#include <math.h>

const double PI = 4 * atan(1);
const double INIT_SEED = 0.123456789;

void showPosInt(int nVal, char cTrail)
{
  // exit if nVal is not positive or zero
  if (nVal < 0)
    return;

  if (nVal < 10)
    cout << '0' << nVal;
  else
    cout << nVal;

  if (cTrail != '\0')
    cout << cTrail;
  else
    cout << endl;
}
void showTime(int nHour, int nMinute, int nSecond)
{
  showPosInt(nHour, ':');
  showPosInt(nMinute, ':');
  showPosInt(nSecond, '\0');
}
class RandomTime1
{
  public:
    RandomTime1()
      { m_fSeed = INIT_SEED; }
    void getTime(int& nHour, int& nMinute, int& nSecond);

  protected:
    double m_fSeed;

    virtual int random(int nMax);
    double sqr(double x)
      { return x * x; }
    double frac(double x)
      { return x - long(x); }
};
```

```
class RandomTime2 : public RandomTime1
{
  public:
    RandomTime2() : RandomTime1() {}

  protected:
    virtual int random(int nMax);
    double cube(double x)
      { return x * x * x; }
};
class RandomTime3 : public RandomTime2
{
  public:
    RandomTime3(): RandomTime2() {}

  protected:
    virtual int random(int nMax);
    double fourth(double x)
      { return sqr(x) * sqr(x); }
};
void RandomTime1::getTime(int& nHour, int& nMinute, int&⤵
nSecond)
{
  nHour = random(24);
  nMinute = random(60);
  nSecond = random(60);
}
int RandomTime1::random(int nMax)
{
  m_fSeed = nMax * frac(sqr(PI + m_fSeed));
  return int(m_fSeed);
}
int RandomTime2::random(int nMax)
{
  m_fSeed = nMax * frac(cube(PI + m_fSeed));
  return int(m_fSeed);
}
int RandomTime3::random(int nMax)
{
  m_fSeed = nMax * frac(fourth(PI + m_fSeed));
 return int(m_fSeed);
}
main()
```

(continued)

_____

Listing 7-1 *(continued)*
_____

```
{
  const int MAX = 5;

  int nHour, nMinute, nSecond;
  RandomTime1 RT1;
  RandomTime2 RT2;
  RandomTime3 RT3;

  cout << "Sequence of time generated by "
       << "instance of class RandomTime1 is:" << endl;
  for (int i = 0; i < MAX; i++) {
    RT1.getTime(nHour, nMinute, nSecond);
    showTime(nHour, nMinute, nSecond);
  }
  cout << endl;
  cout << "Sequence of time generated by "
       << "instance of class RandomTime2 is:" << endl;
  for (i = 0; i < MAX; i++) {
    RT2.getTime(nHour, nMinute, nSecond);
    showTime(nHour, nMinute, nSecond);
  }
  cout << endl;
  cout << "Sequence of time generated by "
       << "instance of class RandomTime3 is:" << endl;
  for (i = 0; i < MAX; i++) {
    RT3.getTime(nHour, nMinute, nSecond);
    showTime(nHour, nMinute, nSecond);
  }
  return 0;
}
```

Listing 7-1 declares the functions showPosInt() and showTime(), three classes, and the function main(). The function showPosInt() displays a positive integer with a leading 0 if that integer is less than 10. The function showTime() displays the time as supplied by its three int-type parameters, nHour, nMinute, and nSecond. The function displays the time using the popular hh:mm:ss 24-hour format (also known as the *military format*).

The next three sections discuss the three classes in Listing 7-1.

The class RandomTime1

The class RandomTime1 is the base class for the three-class hierarchy. This class declares protected and public members. Here are the protected members:

- The double-type data member m_fSeed, which stores the last random number generated. The class uses the value in this member to generate the next random number.
- The virtual member function random(), which returns a random number between 0 and (nMax - 1).
- The member function sqr(), which returns the squared value of a floating-point number.
- The member function frac(), which returns the fractional part of a floating-point number.

The class declares a public constructor and the public member function getTime(). This member function returns a random time value using the reference parameters nHour, nMinute, and nSecond. This member function invokes the virtual member function random() three times to return the hour, the minute, and the second.

The class RandomTime2

Listing 7-1 declares the class RandomTime2 as a public descendant of the class RandomTime1. The class RandomTime2 declares a constructor and the protected member functions random() and cube(). The member function cube() returns the cubed value of a floating-point number. The class declares the member function random() as virtual to override the inherited member function RandomTime1::random(). The new version of the member function random() uses a different method— using the member function cube()— for generating random numbers.

The class RandomTime3

Listing 7-1 declares the class RandomTime3 as a public descendant of the class RandomTime2. The class RandomTime3 declares a constructor and the protected member functions random() and fourth(). The member function fourth() returns the fourth power of its arguments. The class overrides the inherited member function RandomTime2::random(), declaring the member function random() as virtual. The new version of the member function random() uses a different method—using the member function fourth()— for generating random numbers.

The function `main()`

The function `main()` declares the local constant `MAX`, which defines the number of random times to generate for each class instance; the `int`-type variables `nHour`, `nMinute`, and `nSecond`; and the objects `RT1`, `RT2`, and `RT3`, which are instances of the classes `RandomTime1`, `RandomTime2`, and `RandomTime3`, respectively. The function `main()` performs the following relevant tasks:

- ✔ Generates and displays random times using the object `RT1`. This task uses a `for` loop that sends the C++ message `getTime()` to the object `RT1`. The arguments for this message are the variables `nHour`, `nMinute`, and `nSecond`. The program executes the message `getTime()` by invoking the member function `getTime()`, which in turn calls the member function `RandomTime1::random()`. The loop also invokes the function `showTime()` to display the time specified by the variables `nHour`, `nMinute`, and `nSecond`.

- ✔ Generates and displays random times using the object `RT2`. This task uses a `for` loop that sends the C++ message `getTime()` to the object `RT2`. The program executes the message `getTime()` by invoking the member function `getTime()`, which in turn calls the member function `RandomTime2::random()`—and not member function `RandomTime1::random()`. The arguments for this message are the variables `nHour`, `nMinute`, and `nSecond`. The loop also invokes the function `showTime()` to display the time specified by the variables `nHour`, `nMinute`, and `nSecond`.

- ✔ Generates and displays random times using the object `RT3`. This task uses a `for` loop that sends the C++ message `getTime()` to the object `RT3`. The arguments for this message are the variables `nHour`, `nMinute`, and `nSecond`. The program executes the message `getTime()` by invoking the member function `getTime()`, which in turn calls the member function `RandomTime3::random()`. The loop also invokes the function `showTime()` to display the time specified by the variables `nHour`, `nMinute`, and `nSecond`.

A Numeric Input Example: Get Real!

The VIRTUAL2.CPP program provides another simple example of classes that use virtual functions. This example illustrates using virtual functions to refine the input of floating-point numbers. The VIRTUAL2.CPP program has the class `InputReal` and its descendant `InputPositiveReal`. The instances of the base class prompt you for a floating-point number. The instances of the descendant class prompt you for a positive floating-point number (the refined feature brought by the descendant class). The program uses an instance of the class `InputPositiveReal` to prompt you for the distance and speed of a moving object. The program then displays the speed of that object.

Here is a sample session with the VIRTUAL2.CPP program (input is in boldface):

```
Enter distance (feet) : -5.0
Enter a positive value : 5.0
Enter elapsed time (sec) : -2.5
Enter a positive value : 2.5
Speed = 2 ft/sec
```

Listing 7-2 shows the source code for the VIRTUAL2.CPP program.

Listing 7-2	VIRTUAL2.CPP

```cpp
// Another C++ program that illustrates virtual functions

#include <iostream.h>
#include <iomanip.h>
#include <math.h>

class InputReal
{
  public:
    double getReal(const char* pszMsg);

  protected:
    void prompt(const char* pszMsg);
    virtual double getInput();
};
class InputPositiveReal : public InputReal
{
  protected:
    virtual double getInput();
};
double InputReal::getReal(const char* pszMsg)
{
  prompt(pszMsg);
  return getInput();
}
void InputReal::prompt(const char* pszMsg)
{
  cout << pszMsg;
}
double InputReal::getInput()
{
  double x;
```

(continued)

Listing 7-2 *(continued)*

```
    cin >> x;
    return x;
}

double InputPositiveReal::getInput()
{
    double x;

    do {
        cin >> x;
        if (x <= 0.0)
            cout << "Enter a positive value : ";
    } while (x <= 0.0);
    return x;
}
main()
{
    InputPositiveReal Real;
    double x, y;

    x = Real.getReal("Enter distance (feet) : ");
    y = Real.getReal("Enter elapsed time (sec) : ");
    cout << "Speed = " << (x/y) << " ft/sec\n";

    return 0;
}
```

Listing 7-2 declares the class InputReal and its descendant InputPositiveReal. The class InputReal contains public and protected members. Here are the protected members:

- ✔ The member function prompt(), which prompts you with the message found in the ASCIIZ string parameter pszMsg.

- ✔ The double-type virtual member function getInput(), which obtains the floating-point number from the input stream object (cin) and returns that input.

The class declares the public member function getReal(), which invokes the protected member functions prompt() and getInput().

The listing declares the class InputPositiveReal as a public descendant of the class InputReal. The descendant class merely declares the protected virtual member function getInput(). This version overrides the inherited function to support validated input — which the member function InputReal::getInput() does not support. Consequently, the member function InputPositiveReal::getInput() reprompts (a nice way to say *pesters*) you to enter a positive number until you do so.

The function main() declares the object Real as an instance of the class InputPositiveReal. The function also declares the double-type variables x and y. The function main() performs the following tasks:

- ✔ Prompts you to enter a distance. This task involves sending the C++ message getReal() to the object Real. The program executes the member function InputReal::getReal(), which in turn invokes the member function InputReal::prompt() and the virtual member function InputPositiveReal::getInput(). This task stores the input in the variable x.

- ✔ Prompts you to enter an elapsed time. This task involves sending the C++ message getReal() to the object Real. The program executes the member function InputReal::getReal(), which in turn invokes the member function InputReal::prompt() and the virtual member function InputPositiveReal::getInput(). This task stores the input in the variable y.

- ✔ Displays the speed, which main() calculates by dividing the value stored in the variable x (the distance) by the value stored in the variable y (the elapsed time).

When to Use Virtual Functions: The $64,000 Question

Although virtual functions seem to support the cool feature of polymorphism, using these functions has its price: Virtual functions are slower than nonvirtual member functions. So don't go around typing the keyword virtual ahead of each member function in a class. Hold your horses and ask yourself the following questions:

- ✔ Which member functions are called by other member functions?
- ✔ Are the called member functions overridden in descendant classes?

If the answer to both of these questions is yes, then you need to declare those member functions as virtual. The member function procA1() in classes A and B (in the code snippet in the section "Virtual (Reality) Functions," earlier in this chapter) qualifies as virtual, because it is called by another member function — A::procA() — and is overridden in the descendant class B.

Remember that the execution of a virtual member function is slower than that of a nonvirtual member function. Therefore, don't declare member functions as virtual unless they need to support polymorphic behavior. In other words, systematically declaring member functions as virtual is not refined programming. One of the OOP gurus, Polly Morphic (sorry, I couldn't help naming names) says "littering a class with virtual member functions turns it into a turtle!"

Virtual Destructors: Real or Virtual Damage?

Although C++ enables you to inherit destructors, many C++ programmers strongly recommend that you declare destructors as virtual. This kind of declaration ensures that you properly dispose of each class instance. A virtual destructor of a descendant class invokes the destructors of the parent class.

The following example demonstrates the use of virtual destructors:

```
class City
{
  public:
    City();
    virtual ~City();
    // declarations of other members
};
class State : public City
{
  public:
    State();
    virtual ~State();
    // declarations of other members
};
class Country : public State
{
  public:
    Country();
    virtual ~Country();
    // declarations of other members
};
```

This example declares the classes `City`, `State`, and `Country` as a miniature class hierarchy. The example declares the destructor of each class as virtual to ensure that the instances of these classes are properly removed. Thus, the destructor of the class `Country` also invokes the destructors of the classes `State` and `City`.

The VIRTUAL3.CPP program provides an example of the use of virtual destructors. This program has a two-class hierarchy that creates, removes, and manipulates dynamic integers. The destructors of the classes are virtual.

The output from the VIRTUAL3.CPP program is as follows:

```
Integer in Int1 is 1
Integer 1 in Int2 is 100
Integer 2 in Int2 is 200
Invoking destructor ~TwoInts
Invoking destructor ~OneInt
Invoking destructor ~OneInt
```

Listing 7-3 shows the source code for the VIRTUAL3.CPP program.

Listing 7-3	VIRTUAL3.CPP

```cpp
// A C++ program that illustrates
// declaring virtual destructors

#include <iostream.h>
#include <iomanip.h>

class OneInt
{
  public:
    OneInt()
      { m_pnInt1 = new int; }
    virtual ~OneInt()
      {
        delete m_pnInt1;
        cout << "Invoking destructor ~OneInt\n";
      }
    void setInt1(int nInt)
      { *m_pnInt1 = nInt; }
    int getInt1()
      { return *m_pnInt1; }
```

(continued)

_____

Listing 7-3 *(continued)*

_____

```
protected:
    int* m_pnInt1;
};
class TwoInts : public OneInt
{
  public:
    TwoInts() : OneInt()
      { m_pnInt2 = new int; }
    virtual ~TwoInts()
      {
        delete m_pnInt2;
        cout << "Invoking destructor ~TwoInts\n";
      }
    void setInt2(int nInt)
      { *m_pnInt2 = nInt; }
    int getInt2()
      { return *m_pnInt2; }

  protected:
    int* m_pnInt2;
};
main()
{
  OneInt Int1;
  TwoInts Int2;

  Int1.setInt1(1);
  Int2.setInt1(100);
  Int2.setInt2(200);

  cout << "Integer in Int1 is " << Int1.getInt1() << endl;
  cout << "Integer 1 in Int2 is " << Int2.getInt1() << endl;
  cout << "Integer 2 in Int2 is " << Int2.getInt2() << endl;

  return 0;
}
```

Listing 7-3 declares the class OneInt and its public descendant TwoInts. The class OneInt declares the protected data member m_pnInt1. This class has a constructor, a virtual destructor, and the member functions setInt1() and getInt1(). The constructor creates a dynamic integer and assigns its address to the data member m_pnInt1. The destructor deallocates the space for the dynamic integer.

The listing declares the class TwoInts as a descendant of the class OneInt. The class TwoInts declares the protected data member m_pnInt2. This class has a constructor, a virtual destructor, and the member functions setInt2() and getInt2(). The descendant class inherits the members of the class OneInt. The constructor creates the dynamic integers and assigns their addresses to the data members m_pnInt1 and m_pnInt2. The virtual destructor deallocates the space for the second dynamic integer and then invokes the destructor of the parent class to deallocate the space for the first dynamic integer.

The function main() creates the objects Int1 and Int2 as instances of the classes OneInt and TwoInts. For our purposes, the relevant part of this program is when the objects are out of scope. In the case of the object Int1, the program invokes the virtual destructor ~OneInt. In the case of the object Int2, the program invokes the destructor ~TwoInts (to deallocate the second dynamic integer) and then the destructor ~OneInt (to deallocate the first dynamic integer).

Rules for Using Virtual Functions: Regulating Relationships

Now that you've seen virtual functions at work, you can focus on the rules governing their use:

✔ A virtual member function can override a nonvirtual member function (with the same name, of course) inherited from a parent class.

✔ You can override a virtual member function only by using another virtual member function in a descendant class. (This rule is sometimes called "Once virtual, always virtual.") The overriding member function *must have* the same parameter list and return type as the one that is being overridden. In other words, if you play fast and loose with the parameter list of an overriding virtual function, you will mess up the uniform response of the descendant class.

✔ You may overload a virtual member function with a nonvirtual member function in a class. However, the descendants of that class can then inherit only the virtual member function! The remaining nonvirtual functions are not inherited by descendant classes.

Summary

This chapter shows you how to use virtual member functions and destructors to allow classes in a hierarchy to offer a uniform response. This uniform response makes classes in a hierarchy not only reusable but adaptable.

Chapter 8

Class Hierarchy Design:
Classification Mania

In This Chapter

▶ Following guidelines for designing class hierarchies

▶ Looking at an example of an inefficient class hierarchy

▶ Learning from an example of an efficient class hierarchy

*T*his chapter discusses (very briefly) the basics of class design. The main purpose of this chapter is to alert you that a good class hierarchy doesn't happen without effective planning and forethought. The chapter discusses a few class design rules that are helpful guidelines for planning your class hierarchy designs. The chapter also contains examples showing an inefficient class design and an efficient class design. The two examples deal with a small class hierarchy that supports integer arrays.

Designing Class Hierarchies: Guidelines for Creating a Class Act!

How do you design a good class hierarchy? The answer is "By experience." In other words, you need not shy away from redesigning a class hierarchy to improve it.

Are there concrete rules for designing good class hierarchies? No, but here are some helpful guidelines for planning your class hierarchy designs:

- ✔ Use abstract classes for the first few levels of classes (including the base class, of course) to create robust (that is, sturdy) hierarchies that can be reused for several designs. (See Chapter 11 for more details about abstract classes.)

- ✔ Use an abstract class in the middle of a class hierarchy to support common operations shared by the descendants of that abstract class.

✔ Create a template class as the base class for several related classes that each support a different data type. For example, declare a template class as the parent of a group of classes that model arrays using different data types. (See Chapter 12 for more details about template classes.)

✔ Build the class hierarchy by adding an appropriate set of operations to each descendant class. In other words, avoid using fewer classes which each have a rich set of operations when you can spread those operations over a greater number of descendant classes. This rule is really an OOP version of the general rule (in life, politics, programming, and so on) of divide-and-conquer.

✔ Use multiple inheritance very carefully and only as a last resort. Don't be trigger-happy with multiple inheritance!

✔ Use virtual member functions sparingly (that is, only when they really make sense), because they slow down the program's execution. Don't go around pasting `virtual` in the declaration of each member function.

The rule of thumb for planning and designing efficient classes is as follows: Create a class hierarchy such that no one class monopolizes the supported features. Thus, following this rule, let the upper-level classes in the hierarchy support more of the fundamental operations. Conversely, let the deep-level descendants support more sophisticated features. My OOP guru pal V. R. Sams summarizes this rule by saying, "Share the wealth among the different classes." Confucius says: "Efficient (and enlightened) class design comes after a lot of practice."

An Inefficient Class Hierarchy: The Array That Couldn't Shoot Straight

The HDESIGN1.CPP program provides an example of a two-class hierarchy with a weak design. The program declares the class myArray and its descendant class myOrderedArray. These classes support unordered and ordered dynamic arrays of integers, respectively. I created the HDESIGN1.CPP program by modifying the file DESIGN2.CPP (see Listing 5-2 in Chapter 5).

Here is the output from the HDESIGN1.CPP program:

```
Unordered array is:
33 54 98 47 15 81 78 36 63 83
Searching for 83 : found at index 9
Searching for 63 : found at index 8
Searching for 36 : found at index 7
Searching for 78 : found at index 6
```

```
Searching for 81 : found at index 5
Searching for 15 : found at index 4
Searching for 47 : found at index 3
Searching for 98 : found at index 2
Searching for 54 : found at index 1
Searching for 33 : found at index 0

Ordered array is:
15 33 36 47 54 63 78 81 83 98
Searching for 83 : found at index 8
Searching for 63 : found at index 5
Searching for 36 : found at index 2
Searching for 78 : found at index 6
Searching for 81 : found at index 7
Searching for 15 : found at index 0
Searching for 47 : found at index 3
Searching for 98 : found at index 9
Searching for 54 : found at index 4
Searching for 33 : found at index 1
```

Listing 8-1 presents the source code for the HDESIGN1.CPP program.

Listing 8-1	HDESIGN1.CPP

```
// A C++ program that illustrates
// a poor class hierarchy design

#include <iostream.h>
#include <iomanip.h>

enum Logical { FALSE, TRUE };

const int ALL_ARRAY = -1;
const int NOT_FOUND = -1;
const int BAD_VALUE = -32768;

class myArray
{
  public:
    myArray(int nMaxElems, int nInitVal = 0);
    ~myArray();
```

(continued)

Listing 8-1 *(continued)*

```cpp
    virtual Logical Recall(int& nVal, int nIndex);
    virtual Logical Store(int nVal, int nIndex);
    void Show(const char* pszMsg = "",
              const int nNumElems = ALL_ARRAY,
              const Logical bOneLine = TRUE);

  protected:
    int m_nMaxElems;
    int m_nWorkSize;
    int* m_pnArray;
};

class myOrderedArray : public myArray
{
  public:
    myOrderedArray(int nMaxElems, int nInitVal = 0) :
      myArray(nMaxElems, nInitVal) { m_bIsSorted = FALSE; }
    virtual Logical Store(int nVal, int nIndex);
    void Sort();
    int Search(int nSearchVal, int nFirst = 0);

  protected:
    Logical m_bIsSorted;

    int LinearSearch(int nSearchVal, int nFirst = 0);
    int BinarySearch(int nSearchVal, int nFirst = 0);
};

//
// definition of member functions of class myArray
//

myArray::myArray(int nMaxElems, int nInitVal)
{
  m_nMaxElems = (nMaxElems < 1) ? 1 : nMaxElems;
  m_nWorkSize = 0;
  m_pnArray = new int[m_nMaxElems];
  for (int i = 0; i < m_nMaxElems; i++)
    m_pnArray[i] = nInitVal;
}
```

```
myArray::~myArray()
{
  delete [] m_pnArray;
}

Logical myArray::Recall(int& nVal, int nIndex)
{
  if (nIndex >= 0 && nIndex < m_nWorkSize) {
    nVal = m_pnArray[nIndex];
    return TRUE;
  }
  else
    return FALSE;
}

Logical myArray::Store(int nVal, int nIndex)
{
  if (nIndex < 0 || nIndex >= m_nMaxElems)
    return FALSE;

  if (nIndex >= m_nWorkSize)
    m_nWorkSize = nIndex + 1;

  m_pnArray[nIndex] = nVal;
  return TRUE;
}

void myArray::Show(const char* pszMsg,
                   const int nNumElems,
                   const Logical bOneLine)
{
  int nCount;

  cout << pszMsg << endl;
  nCount = (nNumElems == ALL_ARRAY) ? m_nWorkSize :
           nNumElems;
  if (bOneLine) {
    for (int i = 0; i < nCount; i++)
      cout << m_pnArray[i] << ' ';
    cout << endl;

  }
```

(continued)

Listing 8-1 *(continued)*

```
  else {
    for (int i = 0; i < nCount; i++)
      cout << m_pnArray[i] << ' ';
    cout << endl;
  }
}


//
// definition of member functions of class myOrderedArray
//

Logical myOrderedArray::Store(int nVal, int nIndex)
{
  Logical bResult = myArray::Store(nVal, nIndex);

  if (bResult)
    m_bIsSorted = FALSE;

  return bResult;
}

void myOrderedArray::Sort()
{
  if (m_bIsSorted)
    return; // exit if array is already sorted

  // sort the array
  int nOffset = m_nWorkSize;
  int nElemI, nElemJ;

  do {
    nOffset = (nOffset * 8) / 11;
    nOffset = (nOffset < 1) ? 1 : nOffset;
    m_bIsSorted = TRUE; // set sorted flag
    // compare elements
    for (int i = 0, j = nOffset;
         i < (m_nWorkSize - nOffset);
         i++, j++) {
      nElemI = m_pnArray[i];
      nElemJ = m_pnArray[j];
```

```
        if (nElemI > nElemJ) {
          // swap elements
          m_pnArray[i] = nElemJ;
          m_pnArray[j] = nElemI;
          m_bIsSorted = FALSE; // clear sorted flag
        }
      }
  } while (!m_bIsSorted || nOffset != 1);
}

int myOrderedArray::Search(int nSearchVal, int nFirst)
{
  return (m_bIsSorted) ? BinarySearch(nSearchVal, nFirst) :
                         LinearSearch(nSearchVal, nFirst);
}

int myOrderedArray::BinarySearch(int nSearchVal, int nFirst)
{
  // search in the ordered array
  int nMedian;
  int nLast = m_nWorkSize - 1;

  // validate argument for parameter nFirst
  nFirst = (nFirst < 0 || nFirst >= m_nWorkSize) ?
                                   0 : nFirst;

  do {
    nMedian = (nFirst + nLast) / 2;
    if (nSearchVal < m_pnArray[nMedian])
      nLast = nMedian - 1;
    else
      nFirst = nMedian + 1;
  } while (!(nSearchVal == m_pnArray[nMedian] ||
          nFirst > nLast));

  return (nSearchVal == m_pnArray[nMedian]) ?
                        nMedian : NOT_FOUND;
}

int myOrderedArray::LinearSearch(int nSearchVal, int nFirst)
{
```

(continued)

Listing 8-1 *(continued)*

```
// search in unordered array
  for (int i = nFirst; i < m_nWorkSize; i++)

    if (m_pnArray[i] == nSearchVal)
      break;
  return (i < m_nWorkSize) ? i : NOT_FOUND;
}

main()
{
  const int MAX_ELEMS = 10;
  int nArr[MAX_ELEMS] = { 33, 54, 98, 47, 15,
             81, 78, 36, 63, 83 };
  myOrderedArray anArray(10);
  int k;

  // assign values to the object anArray
  for (int i = 0; i < MAX_ELEMS; i++)
    anArray.Store(nArr[i], i);

  // display unordered array
  anArray.Show("Unordered array is:");

  // search in unordered array
  for (i = MAX_ELEMS - 1; i >= 0; i--) {
    cout << "Searching for " << nArr[i] << " : ";
    k = anArray.Search(nArr[i]);
    if (k != NOT_FOUND)
      cout << "found at index " << k << endl;
    else
      cout << "no match found" << endl;
  }
  cout << endl;

  // sort the array
  anArray.Sort();

  // display ordered array
  anArray.Show("Ordered array is:");
```

```
// search in ordered array
for (i = MAX_ELEMS - 1; i >= 0; i--) {
  cout << "Searching for " << nArr[i] << " : ";
  k = anArray.Search(nArr[i]);
  if (k != NOT_FOUND)
    cout << "found at index " << k << endl;
  else
    cout << "no match found" << endl;
}

return 0;
}
```

Listing 8-1 declares the class myArray, which contains public and protected members. Here are the protected members:

- ✔ The int-type data member m_nMaxElems, which stores the maximum number of array elements.

- ✔ The int-type data member m_nWorkSize, which stores the number of array elements that contain meaningful data (that is, they are not vacant).

- ✔ The int*-type data member m_pnArray, which accesses the elements of the dynamic array.

The class declares the following public members:

- ✔ The constructor, which initializes the class instances by assigning values to the various data members and allocating the memory for the dynamic array.

- ✔ The destructor, which frees the memory allocated to the dynamic array.

- ✔ The virtual member function Recall(), which recalls the value of an array element specified by the index nIndex. The function returns the recalled value using the reference parameter nVal. The function validates the value of the parameter nIndex and yields TRUE if successful and FALSE if not.

- ✔ The virtual member function Store(), which stores the value of the parameter nVal in an array element specified by the index nIndex. The function validates the value of the parameter nIndex and yields TRUE if successful and FALSE if not. If successful, the member function sets the data member m_bIsSorted to FALSE to clear the ordered state.

- ✔ The member function Show(), which displays the elements of the dynamic array in either one line or a column.

Listing 8-1 declares the class `myOrderedArray`, which contains public and protected members. The class declares the following protected members:

- ✔ The `Logical`-type data member `m_bIsSorted`, which stores the ordered state of the array elements.
- ✔ The member function `LinearSearch()`, which performs a linear search on the unordered array elements.
- ✔ The member function `BinarySearch()`, which performs a linear search on the ordered array elements.

The class declares the following public members:

- ✔ The constructor, which initializes the class instances by assigning values to the various data members and allocating the memory for the dynamic array.
- ✔ The destructor, which frees up the memory allocated to the dynamic array.
- ✔ The virtual member function `Store()`, which stores the value of the parameter `nVal` in an array element specified by the index `nIndex`. This member function invokes the inherited one and then assigns `FALSE` to the data member `m_bIsSorted`.
- ✔ The member function `Sort()`, which sorts the array elements.
- ✔ The member function `Search()`, which searches for the value of the parameter `nSearchVal` in the array elements. The member function uses the value in the data member `m_bIsSorted` to determine whether to invoke the member function `LinearSearch()` or the member function `BinarySearch()`.

What's wrong with the class in Listing 8-1? The next section presents a critique of that class and offers suggestions for making it more efficient.

An Efficient Class Hierarchy: Saving the Day!

Look at Listing 8-1 again. What do you notice about the classes `myArray` and `myOrderedArray`? The first class supports a basic dynamic array that has no searching and sorting capabilities. The class `myArray` does support displaying the array elements. The descendant class `myOrderedArray` adds linear searching, binary searching, and sorting — all in one swoop. In other words, it's either feast or famine as far as the features supported by these two classes.

What if you need a class that supports unsorted dynamic arrays of integers with (linear) searching capability? The hierarchy in Listing 8-1 does not meet this need.

Refining the hierarchy in Listing 8-1 involves creating at least one more class and rearranging the features supported by the new class(es). The new hierarchy design includes the following classes:

✔ A base class (call it `myBasicArray`) that supports the most basic operations: create, remove, store, and recall. That's all! We're really talking minimal here.

✔ A descendant of `myBasicArray` (call it `myArray`) that adds a linear search feature. The class may also support displaying the array elements, because this goes along with the search operation (kind of). If you don't agree with displaying the elements, then please bear with me.

✔ A descendant of `myArray` (call it `myOrderedArray`) that adds sorting and binary searching. Because this class inherits the linear search operation of its parent, it may include a member function that performs a *smart search* (that is, one that can cleverly decide the best way to search the array elements, based on the array order state).

The new (and cool) design appears in Listing 8-2, which shows the source code for the HDESIGN2.CPP program. The output from this program is identical to that of the program in Listing 8-1.

Listing 8-2	HDESIGN2.CPP

```
// A C++ program that illustrates
// a better class hierarchy design

#include <iostream.h>
#include <iomanip.h>

enum Logical { FALSE, TRUE };

const int ALL_ARRAY = -1;
const int NOT_FOUND = -1;
const int BAD_VALUE = -32768;

class myBasicArray
{
  public:
```

(continued)

Listing 8-2 *(continued)*

```
    myBasicArray(int nMaxElems, int nInitVal = 0);
    virtual ~myBasicArray()
      { delete [] m_pnArray; }
    virtual Logical Recall(int& nVal, int nIndex);
    virtual Logical Store(int nVal, int nIndex);

  protected:
    int m_nMaxElems;
    int m_nWorkSize;
    int* m_pnArray;
};

class myArray : public myBasicArray
{
  public:
    myArray(int nMaxElems, int nInitVal = 0) :
      myBasicArray(nMaxElems, nInitVal) {}
    virtual ~myArray()
      { delete [] m_pnArray; }

    void Show(const char* pszMsg = "",
              const int nNumElems = ALL_ARRAY,
              const Logical bOneLine = TRUE);
    int LinearSearch(int nSearchVal, int nFirst = 0);
};

class myOrderedArray : public myArray
{
  public:
    myOrderedArray(int nMaxElems, int nInitVal = 0) :
      myArray(nMaxElems, nInitVal)
      { m_bIsSorted = FALSE; }
    virtual ~myOrderedArray()
      { delete [] m_pnArray; }
    virtual Logical Store(int nVal, int nIndex);
    void Sort();
    int SmartSearch(int nSearchVal, int nFirst = 0);
    int BinarySearch(int nSearchVal, int nFirst = 0);
```

```
  protected:
    Logical m_bIsSorted;
};


//
// definition of member functions of class myBasicArray
//

myBasicArray::myBasicArray(int nMaxElems, int nInitVal)
{
  m_nMaxElems = (nMaxElems < 1) ? 1 : nMaxElems;
  m_nWorkSize = 0;
  m_pnArray = new int[m_nMaxElems];
  for (int i = 0; i < m_nMaxElems; i++)
    m_pnArray[i] = nInitVal;
}

Logical myBasicArray::Recall(int& nVal, int nIndex)
{
  if (nIndex >= 0 && nIndex < m_nWorkSize) {
    nVal = m_pnArray[nIndex];
    return TRUE;
  }
  else
    return FALSE;
}

Logical myBasicArray::Store(int nVal, int nIndex)
{
  if (nIndex < 0 || nIndex >= m_nMaxElems)
    return FALSE;

  if (nIndex >= m_nWorkSize)
    m_nWorkSize = nIndex + 1;

  m_pnArray[nIndex] = nVal;
  return TRUE;
}


//
```

(continued)

Listing 8-2 _(continued)_

```cpp
// definition of member functions of class myArray
//

void myArray::Show(const char* pszMsg,
                   const int nNumElems,
                   const Logical bOneLine)
{
  int nCount;

  cout << pszMsg << endl;
  nCount = (nNumElems == ALL_ARRAY) ? m_nWorkSize :
           nNumElems;
  if (bOneLine) {
    for (int i = 0; i < nCount; i++)
      cout << m_pnArray[i] << ' ';
    cout << endl;

  }
  else {
    for (int i = 0; i < nCount; i++)
      cout << m_pnArray[i] << ' ';
    cout << endl;
  }
}

int myArray::LinearSearch(int nSearchVal, int nFirst)
{
  // search in unordered array
  for (int i = nFirst; i < m_nWorkSize; i++)
    if (m_pnArray[i] == nSearchVal)
      break;
  return (i < m_nWorkSize) ? i : NOT_FOUND;
}

//
// definition of member functions of class myOrderedArray
//

Logical myOrderedArray::Store(int nVal, int nIndex)
{
```

```
    Logical bResult = myBasicArray::Store(nVal, nIndex);

  if (bResult)
    m_bIsSorted = FALSE;

  return bResult;
}

void myOrderedArray::Sort()
{
  if (m_bIsSorted)
    return; // exit if array is already sorted

  // sort the array
  int nOffset = m_nWorkSize;
  int nElemI, nElemJ;

  do {
    nOffset = (nOffset * 8) / 11;
    nOffset = (nOffset < 1) ? 1 : nOffset;
    m_bIsSorted = TRUE; // set sorted flag
    // compare elements
    for (int i = 0, j = nOffset;
         i < (m_nWorkSize - nOffset);
         i++, j++) {
      nElemI = m_pnArray[i];
      nElemJ = m_pnArray[j];
      if (nElemI > nElemJ) {
        // swap elements
        m_pnArray[i] = nElemJ;
        m_pnArray[j] = nElemI;
        m_bIsSorted = FALSE; // clear sorted flag
      }
    }
  } while (!m_bIsSorted || nOffset != 1);
}

int myOrderedArray::SmartSearch(int nSearchVal, int nFirst)
{
  return (m_bIsSorted) ? BinarySearch(nSearchVal, nFirst) :
                         LinearSearch(nSearchVal, nFirst);
}
```

(continued)

_____

Listing 8-2 (continued)

```
int myOrderedArray::BinarySearch(int nSearchVal, int nFirst)
{
  // search in the ordered array
  int nMedian;
  int nLast = m_nWorkSize - 1;

  // validate argument for parameter nFirst
  nFirst = (nFirst < 0 || nFirst >= m_nWorkSize) ?
                           0 : nFirst;

  do {
    nMedian = (nFirst + nLast) / 2;
    if (nSearchVal < m_pnArray[nMedian])
      nLast = nMedian - 1;
    else
      nFirst = nMedian + 1;
  } while (!(nSearchVal == m_pnArray[nMedian] ||
            nFirst > nLast));

  return (nSearchVal == m_pnArray[nMedian]) ?
                  nMedian : NOT_FOUND;
}

main()
{
  const int MAX_ELEMS = 10;
  int nArr[MAX_ELEMS] = { 33, 54, 98, 47, 15,
                          81, 78, 36, 63, 83 };
  myOrderedArray anArray(10);
  int k;

  // assign values to the object anArray
  for (int i = 0; i < MAX_ELEMS; i++)
    anArray.Store(nArr[i], i);

  // display unordered array
  anArray.Show("Unordered array is:");

  // search in unordered array
  for (i = MAX_ELEMS - 1; i >= 0; i--) {
    cout << "Searching for " << nArr[i] << " : ";
```

```
      k = anArray.SmartSearch(nArr[i]);
      if (k != NOT_FOUND)
        cout << "found at index " << k << endl;
      else
        cout << "no match found" << endl;
    }
  cout << endl;

  // sort the array
  anArray.Sort();

  // display ordered array
  anArray.Show("Ordered array is:");

  // search in ordered array
  for (i = MAX_ELEMS - 1; i >= 0; i--) {
    cout << "Searching for " << nArr[i] << " : ";
    k = anArray.SmartSearch(nArr[i]);
    if (k != NOT_FOUND)
      cout << "found at index " << k << endl;
    else
      cout << "no match found" << endl;
  }

  return 0;
}
```

Listing 8-2 declares the classes myBasicArray, myArray, and myOrderedArray. You next look at the members of these classes.

The class myBasicArray

The class myBasicArray declares the data members m_nMaxElems, m_nWorkSize, and m_pnArray. The class also declares a constructor, a destructor, and the virtual member functions Store() and Recall().

The class myArray

The class myArray declares a constructor, a destructor, and the member functions LinearSearch() and Show().

The class myOrderedArray

The class myOrderedArray declares the data members m_bIsSorted, a constructor, a destructor, the virtual member function Store(), the member function BinarySearch(), the member function Sort(), and the member function SmartSearch(). SmartSearch() uses the value in the data member m_bIsSorted to determine whether to invoke the member function LinearSearch() or the member function BinarySearch().

The class hierarchy in Listing 8-2 spreads the operations of the integer arrays over three classes. Each successive class offers increasingly sophisticated operations. As I mentioned earlier in this section, the class myBasicArray supports very basic array operations. You can, for example, declare your own descendant to this class to support your own (more efficient) versions of sorting and searching. If the linear search operation is useful to you, then you may derive a class from myArray to inherit its operations and add new ones (such as file input and output to read and write the array elements). In other words, an efficient class hierarchy design offers different operations at different descendant levels. You select the class that offers just the right operations for supporting your applications or deriving classes.

Summary

This chapter presents basic guidelines for designing an efficient class hierarchy and offers two programming examples that demonstrate inefficient and efficient versions of the same hierarchy.

Chapter 9

Multiple Inheritance: OOP-Style Family Values

● ●

In This Chapter

▶ Declaring multiple inheritance classes

▶ Declaring descendants of distinct lineage

▶ Declaring descendants of common lineage

● ●

*T*his chapter focuses on multiple inheritance in C++ classes. The chapter shows you how to declare descendant classes under multiple inheritance and offers two examples. The first example shows a descendant class that has two parents that come from two different class hierarchies (or families, if you prefer). By contrast, the second example shows a descendant class that has two parents that are part of the same class hierarchy. Most OOP gurus agree that using multiple inheritance to create this kind of descendant class is not sound. The two examples show how having distinct and common class lineage affects the class declaration and design.

Declaring Multiple Inheritance Classes: OOP Potpourri!

Chapter 6 introduces you to the scheme of multiple inheritance. C++ allows you to declare a descendant class from multiple parent classes by using the following general syntax:

```
class className : [virtual] [public] parentClassName1,
                  [virtual] [public] parentClassName2,
                  [other classes]
{
public:
    // public constructors
    // public destructor
```

(continued)

(continued)

```
    // public data members
    // public member functions
protected:
    // protected constructors
    // protected destructor
    // protected data members
    // protected member functions
private:
    // private constructors
    // private destructor
    // private data members
    // private member functions
};
```

This declaration of a descendant class begins with the keyword class, which is followed by these items:

- The name of the class
- A colon
- The name of the first parent class preceded by the optional keywords virtual and public
- A comma
- The name of the second parent class preceded by the optional keywords virtual and public
- A comma
- The names of other parent classes, each preceded by the optional keywords virtual and public

Declaring virtual parent classes

The syntax you use for declaring a descendant class from multiple parent classes includes the optional keyword virtual, which tells the compiler that the descendant class has parent classes that share a common ancestor class. Thus, the keyword virtual permits the compiler to anticipate common class ancestry. Otherwise, the compiler will complain about such common ancestry! The keyword public allows the class instances to access the public members of the parent class. Without this keyword, only the member functions of the descendant class can access the parent's members. C++ allows you to declare the descendant class as a public or nonpublic descendant of the various parent classes.

Here is an example of declaring a descendant class from independent parent classes:

```
class Radio
{
   // declaration of members
};

class CDPlayer
{
   // declaration of members
};

class CassettePlayer
{
   // declaration of members
};

class BoomBox : public Radio, public CDPlayer, public
CassettePlayer
{
   // declaration of members
};
```

This example shows the skeleton declarations of four classes: Radio, CDPlayer, CassettePlayer, and BoomBox. The first three classes are nondescendant classes, whereas the class BoomBox is a public descendant of the classes Radio, CDPlayer, and CassettePlayer. Figure 9-1 shows the class hierarchy that involves the radio, the CD player, the cassette player, and the boom box.

Figure 9-1:
A class hierarchy involving multiple inheritance using distinct ancestors.

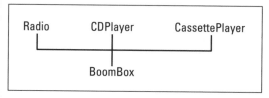

Suppose the classes `Radio`, `CDPlayer`, and `CassettePlayer` were descendants of some generic device class — call it `Device`. Figure 9-2 shows a diagram for the class hierarchy that involves the generic device, the radio, the CD player, the cassette player, and the boom box.

Figure 9-2:
The modified class hierarchy involves multiple inheritance using common ancestors.

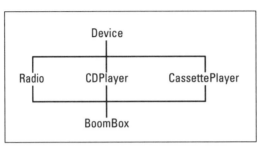

The declaration of these classes, which now share a common ancestor class, is as follows:

```
class Device
{
  // declaration of members
};

class Radio : virtual public Device
{
  // declaration of members
};

class CDPlayer : virtual public Device

{
  // declaration of members
};

class CassettePlayer : virtual public Device

{
  // declaration of members
```

```
};

class BoomBox : virtual public Radio, virtual public⊃
CDPlayer,
          virtual public CassettePlayer
{
  // declaration of members
};
```

These declarations use the keyword `virtual` in declaring all descendant classes, because these classes share the same base class, `Device`. If you do not use the keyword `virtual`, you rub the compiler the wrong way!

 Remember that you must use the keyword `virtual` when declaring every descendant class that is the product of a common ancestor or that will lead to other descendants that have a common ancestor! The latter case can be a problem if you did not design the class hierarchy to be involved in a multiple-inheritance scheme.

Next, you look at examples of creating descendant classes from multiple parent classes. In the first example, the parent classes do not share a common ancestor class. In contrast, the second example involves parent classes that share a common ancestor class.

Descendants of Distinct Lineage: Rescue 911!

The following example shows the creation of a descendant class from distinct parent classes. The sample program simulates searching for a lost person in a grid with X and Y coordinates ranging from 1 to 1,000.

The MI1.CPP program searches for the missing person in cycles. In each cycle, the program displays the distance between you and the missing person and displays the angle of the line joining your location with that of the lost person. The program prompts you to enter your move in the X and Y directions. If your final coordinates in a move are within a critical distance of the missing person's coordinates, you locate the person, and the simulation ends. If not, the program carries out another search cycle.

 I've included commented statements that you can uncomment to make the program even more interesting. If you uncomment these statements, the program makes the missing person move in each step, so you get to search for a moving target. Cool!

Sample output

Here is a sample session with the MI1.CPP program (the input is in boldface):

```
Current distance = 363.24
Current angle = 38.8381 degrees
Enter movement in X direction : 100
Enter movement in Y direction : 100
Current distance = 263.24
Current angle = 36.1699 degrees
Enter movement in X direction : 100
Enter movement in Y direction : 100
Current distance = 163.24
Current angle = 29.5248 degrees
Enter movement in X direction : 100
Enter movement in Y direction : 100
Current distance = 63.2395
Current angle = -6.80842 degrees
Enter movement in X direction : -7
Enter movement in Y direction : 60


Congratulations for the rescue!
```

Introducing you to the classes

The MI1.CPP program declares the following classes:

- ✔ The class Random, which generates random numbers between 0 and 1 (exclusive).

- ✔ The class Distance, which manages the coordinates of two points, calculates the distance between them, and calculates the angle of the line joining the two points.

- ✔ The class Rescue, a descendant of the classes Random and Distance, which simulates rescuing a person (this program is a real lifesaver!).

The source code for the MI1.CPP file is simply:

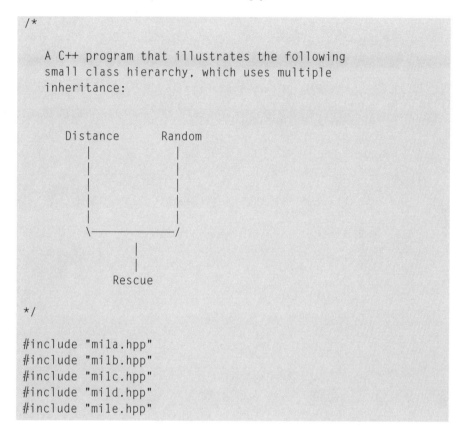

```
/*

    A C++ program that illustrates the following
    small class hierarchy, which uses multiple
    inheritance:


        Distance        Random
            |               |
            |               |
            |               |
            |               |
            |               |
            _____/
                    |
                    |
                 Rescue

*/

#include "mi1a.hpp"
#include "mi1b.hpp"
#include "mi1c.hpp"
#include "mi1d.hpp"
#include "mi1e.hpp"
```

In the following sections, I present the source code for the .HPP files that are included in the file MI1.CPP. I divide the source code into multiple included files to make it easier for me to present and for you to follow.

The globals

Listing 9-1 shows the source code for the included file MI1A.HPP, which declares a set of global constants that set the general parameters of the search simulation. The listing also declares the global functions `sqr()`, `cube()`, and `frac()` to return the square, cube, and fractional values of floating-point numbers, respectively.

Listing 9-1	MI1A.HPP

```cpp
#include <iostream.h>
#include <math.h>
#include <string.h>

const double PI = 4 * atan(1);
const double RAD2DEG = 180.0 / PI;
const double INIT_SEED = 113;
const double MIN_XY = 1.0;
const double MAX_XY = 1000.0;
const double CRITIC_DIST = 10.0;
const double EPSILON = 1.0e-8;
const double INFINITY = 1.0e+50;

enum Logical { FALSE, TRUE };

double sqr(double x)
{
  return x * x;
}

double cube(double x)
{
  return x * x * x;
}

double frac(double x)
{
  return x - (long)x;
}
```

The class Random

Listing 9-2 shows the source code for the included file MI1B.HPP, which declares the class Random. This class contains the protected double-type data member m_fSeed, which stores the last random number. The class uses this data member to generate the next random number. The class Random declares a constructor, which initializes the data member m_fSeed, and the member function getRandom(), which returns a random number between 0 and 1 (exclusive).

Listing 9-2	MI1B.HPP

```
class Random
{
  public:
    Random(double fSeed = INIT_SEED)
      { m_fSeed = fSeed; }

    double getRandom();

  protected:
    double m_fSeed;
};

double Random::getRandom()
{
  m_fSeed = frac(cube(m_fSeed + PI));
  return m_fSeed;
}
```

The class Distance

The class Distance manages the distance between the two points (that is, between your location and the location of the missing person) and declares protected and public members. This class declares the following protected members:

- The double-type data members m_fX1, m_fY1, m_fX2, and m_fY2, which store the coordinates of the two points.
- The double-type data members m_fDeltaX and m_fDeltaY, which store the differences in the X and Y coordinates of the two points.

The class Distance also declares the following public members:

- The constructor, which initializes the data members m_fX1, m_fY1, m_fX2, and m_fY2. These data members store the coordinates of the two points.
- The member functions setPoint1() and setPoint2(), which store new coordinates for the first and second point, respectively.
- The member function getDeltaX(), which returns the difference in the X coordinates.

✔ The member function getDeltaY(), which returns the difference in the Y coordinates.

✔ The member function getDistance(), which returns the distance between the two points.

✔ The member function getAngle(), which returns the angle (in degrees) of the line that connects the two points.

Listing 9-3 shows the source code for the included file MI1C.HPP, which declares and defines the class Distance.

Listing 9-3	MI1C.HPP

```
class Distance
{
  public:
    Distance(double fX1, double fY1,
         double fX2, double fY2);
    void setPoint1(double fX, double fY);
    void setPoint2(double fX, double fY);
    double getDeltaX()
      { return m_fX2 - m_fX1; }
    double getDeltaY()
      { return m_fY2 - m_fY1; }
    double getDistance()
      { return sqrt(sqr(m_fX2 - m_fX2) +
              sqr(m_fY2 - m_fY1)); }
    double getAngle();

  protected:
    double m_fX1;
    double m_fX2;
    double m_fY1;
    double m_fY2;
    double m_fDeltaX;
    double m_fDeltaY;
};
Distance::Distance(double fX1, double fY1,
            double fX2, double fY2)
{
  setPoint1(fX1, fY1);
  setPoint2(fX2, fY2);
```

```
}

void Distance::setPoint1(double fX, double fY)
{
  m_fX1 = fX;
  m_fY1 = fY;
}

void Distance::setPoint2(double fX, double fY)
{
  m_fX2 = fX;
  m_fY2 = fY;
}

double Distance::getAngle()
{
  double fDeltaY = m_fY2 - m_fY1;

  return (fabs(fDeltaY) > EPSILON) ?
    RAD2DEG * atan((m_fX2 - m_fX1) / fDeltaY) :
    INFINITY;
}
```

The class Rescue

The class Rescue is a public descendant of the classes Random and Distance. This descendant class declares protected and public members. The protected members are

- ✔ The double-type data members m_fMin and m_fMax, which define the range of the X and Y coordinates.

- ✔ The double-type data member m_fShift, which stores the maximum change in the X and Y coordinates for the lost person.

- ✔ The double-type data member m_fCriticalDistance, which stores the maximum distance considered for locating the lost person.

- ✔ The member function calcRandCoord(), which returns a random value for the X or Y coordinate for the location of the missing person.

- ✔ The member function calcRandShift(), which returns a random value for the shift in the X or Y coordinate for the location of the missing person.

- ✔ The member function checkCoord(), which verifies that the argument for the double-type parameter fX lies in the range of coordinates. If that argument is outside the defined range, the function returns the value of the expression m_fMin + m_fMax / 2.

The class `Rescue` declares the following public members:

- ✔ The constructor, which initializes the data members and invokes the member function `initRescue()`.
- ✔ The member function `initRescue()`, which sets up your initial coordinates and the coordinates of the lost person.
- ✔ The member function `searchMore()`, which determines whether you found the lost person or if you quit the search.
- ✔ The member function `getCoords()`, which displays and prompts for the various coordinates.

The definition of the member function `getCoords()` supports the following tasks:

- ✔ Displaying the current distance between you and the lost person.
- ✔ Displaying the angle of the line connecting your location with that of the lost person.
- ✔ Prompting you to enter a move in the X and Y directions. The member function verifies that your input is within the limit of `m_fShift`.
- ✔ Setting your new coordinates.

Listing 9-4 shows the source code for the included file MI1D.HPP, which declares and defines the class `Rescue`.

Listing 9-4	MI1D.HPP

```
class Rescue : public Random, public Distance
{
 public:
    Rescue(double fMin, double fMax,
        double fCriticalDistance);

    void initRescue();
    Logical searchMore();
    void getCoords();

 protected:
    double m_fMin;
    double m_fMax;
    double m_fShift;
    double m_fCriticalDistance;
```

```
      double calcRandCoord()
         { return getRandom() * m_fMax + m_fMin; }
      double calcRandShift()
         { return (0.5 - getRandom()) * m_fShift; }
      double checkCoord(double fX)
         { return (fX >= m_fMin && fX <= m_fMax) ?
                  fX : m_fMin + m_fMax / 2.; }
};

Rescue::Rescue(double fMin, double fMax,
            double fCriticalDistance)
         : Random(), Distance(0, 0, 0, 0)
{
  m_fMin = fMin;
  m_fMax = fMax;
  m_fShift = (fMax - fMin + 1) / 10.;
  m_fCriticalDistance = fCriticalDistance;
  initRescue();
}

void Rescue::initRescue()
{
  double fX = calcRandCoord();
  double fY = calcRandCoord();

  setPoint1((m_fMin + m_fMax) / 2, (m_fMin + m_fMax) / 2);
  setPoint2(fX, fY);
}

Logical Rescue::searchMore()
{
  if (fabs(m_fDeltaX) < 1.0 || fabs(m_fDeltaY) < 1.0 ||
        getDistance() < m_fCriticalDistance)
    return FALSE;
  else
    return TRUE;
}

void Rescue::getCoords()
{
```

(continued)

Listing 9-4 _(continued)_

```
cout << "Current distance = "
     << getDistance() << "\n"
     << "Current angle = "
     << getAngle() << " degrees\n";

// calculate the random movement of lost person
/// uncomment the next four lines to make the lost person
         move
///  m_fDeltaX = calcRandShift();
///  m_fDeltaY = calcRandShift();
///  setPoint2(checkCoord(m_fX2 + m_fDeltaX),
///            checkCoord(m_fY2 + m_fDeltaY));

// prompt for movement of rescuer
cout << "Enter movement in X direction : ";
cin >> m_fDeltaX;
if (m_fDeltaX > m_fShift) // verify limit
  m_fDeltaX = m_fShift;
cout << "Enter movement in Y direction : ";
cin >> m_fDeltaY;
if (m_fDeltaY > m_fShift) // verify limit
  m_fDeltaY = m_fShift;
setPoint1(checkCoord(m_fX1 + m_fDeltaX),
          checkCoord(m_fY1 + m_fDeltaY));
}
```

The function main()

The function main() declares the object R as an instance of the class Rescue. The function creates this instance using the constants MIN_XY, MAX_XY, and CRITIC_DIST to set the grid range and the critical distance. The function main() performs the following tasks:

- ✔ Displays the initial distance and angle and prompts you for your first move. This task involves sending the C++ message getCoords() to the object R.

- ✔ Performs the simulated search for the lost person using a while loop. The loop examines the Boolean value returned by sending the C++ message searchMore() to the object R. This message determines whether you found the lost person (or quit the search). Each loop iteration sends the C++ message getCoords() to the object R. This message displays the current distance and angle and prompts you for your next move.

✔ Determines whether you found the lost person or quit the search. This task involves sending the C++ message getDistance() to the object. The function uses an if statement to compare the result of the getDistance() message with the constant CRITIC_DIST. The function main() displays the message "Congratulations for the rescue!" if you find the person, or it dislays the message "Sorry you gave up!" if you stop searching.

Listing 9-5 shows the source code for the included file MI1E.HPP, which contains the function main().

Listing 9-5	**MI1E.HPP**

```
//
// test classes
//

main()
{
  Rescue R(MIN_XY, MAX_XY, CRITIC_DIST);

  R.getCoords();
  while (R.searchMore())
    R.getCoords();

  cout << "\n\n";
  if (R.getDistance() <= CRITIC_DIST)
    cout << "Congratulations for the rescue!";
  else
    cout << "Sorry you gave up!";

  return 0;
}
```

Descendants of Common Lineage: Cold and Calculating!

The next example shows a set of classes that share a common base class. Again, I divided this source code to make it easier to present. The classes in the MI2.CPP program model the computing engines of simple algebraic calculators. The base class of the hierarchy is the class NCScalc01 (the first three letters are my initials, revealing my deep desire to be a calculator manufacturer), which has the descendants NCScalc100, NCScalc120, and NCScalc200.

Figure 9-3 depicts the hierarchy of calculator classes.

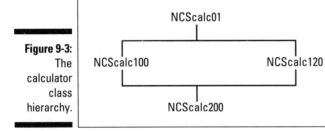

Figure 9-3:
The
calculator
class
hierarchy.

Here's the source code for the file MI2.CPP:

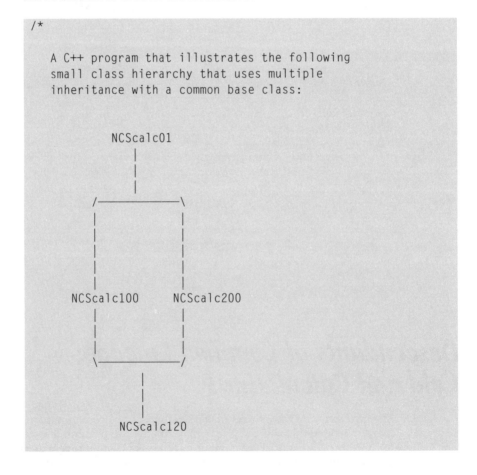

```
*/

#include "mi2a.hpp"
#include "mi2b.hpp"
#include "mi2c.hpp"
#include "mi2d.hpp"
#include "mi2e.hpp"
#include "mi2f.hpp"
```

The following section shows sample output from the MI2.CPP program. Then I present the source code for the .HPP files that are included in the file MI2.CPP.

Sample output

The output from the MI2.CPP program looks like this:

```
Testing class NCScalc120
55 + 13 = 68
123 - 55 = 68
0.55 * 13 = 7.15
355 / 113 = 3.14159
Sqrt(13) = 3.60555
Sqr(13) = 169
```

The globals

Listing 9-6 shows the source code for the included file MI2A.HPP, which declares the global double-type constants BAD_RESULT and EPSILON and the enumerated type Logical.

Listing 9-6	MI2A.HPP

```
#include <iostream.h>
#include <math.h>
#include <string.h>

const double BAD_RESULT = -1.0e+30;
const double EPSILON = 1.0e-50;

enum Logical { FALSE, TRUE };
```

The class NCScalc01

The class NCScalc01 represents the engine of a simple four-function calculator. This calculator engine contains the following components:

- The mathematical registers X and Y, which store the operands.
- The mathematical register Z, which stores the result of mathematical operations.
- The Boolean error flag register, which stores the error state of the last operation.
- The character-type register, which stores the single-character name of the last operation.

The calculator supports the following operations:

- Performing the four basic math operations.
- Assigning new values to the X and Y registers.
- Querying the value in the Z register.
- Querying the error state.
- Clearing the registers.
- Displaying the value in the Z register.
- Displaying the last operands, the operator, and the result.

Listing 9-7 shows the source code for the included file MI2B.HPP, which declares and defines the class NCScalc01.

Listing 9-7	MI2B.HPP

```
class NCScalc01
{
  public:
    NCScalc01(double fRegX = 0., double fRegY = 0.);

    // set new register values
    void setRegX(double fRegX)
      { m_fRegX = fRegX; }
    void setRegY(double fRegY)
      { m_fRegY = fRegY; }
    double getRegZ()
      { return m_fRegZ; }
    Logical getError();
```

```
   void add(Logical bShowResult = TRUE,
       const char* pszMsg = "");
   void sub(Logical bShowResult = TRUE,
       const char* pszMsg = "");
   void mult(Logical bShowResult = TRUE,
       const char* pszMsg = "");
   void div(Logical bShowResult = TRUE,
       const char* pszMsg = "");
   void showRegZ(const char* pszMsg = "");
   void showOperation(const char* pszMsg = "");
   void clearRegs();

 protected:
   double m_fRegX;
   double m_fRegY;
   double m_fRegZ;
   char m_cOp;
   Logical m_bErr;

};


//
// define member functions of class NCScalc01
//

NCScalc01::NCScalc01(double fRegX, double fRegY)
{
  m_fRegX = fRegX;
  m_fRegY = fRegY;
  m_fRegZ = 0.0;
  m_cOp = ' ';
  m_bErr = FALSE;
}

Logical NCScalc01::getError()
{
  Logical bTemp = m_bErr;
  m_bErr = FALSE;
  return bTemp;
}
```

(continued)

Listing 9-7 *(continued)*

```
void NCScalc01::add(Logical bShowResult, const char* pszMsg)
{
  m_fRegZ = m_fRegY + m_fRegX;
  m_cOp = '+';
  m_bErr = FALSE;
  if (bShowResult)
    cout << pszMsg << m_fRegZ;
}

void NCScalc01::sub(Logical bShowResult, const char* pszMsg)
{
  m_fRegZ = m_fRegY - m_fRegX;
  m_cOp = '-';
  m_bErr = FALSE;
  if (bShowResult)
    cout << pszMsg << m_fRegZ;
}

void NCScalc01::mult(Logical bShowResult, const char* pszMsg)
{
  m_fRegZ = m_fRegY * m_fRegX;
  m_cOp = '*';
  m_bErr = FALSE;
  if (bShowResult)
    cout << pszMsg << m_fRegZ;
}

void NCScalc01::div(Logical bShowResult, const char* pszMsg)
{
  if (fabs(m_fRegY) > EPSILON) {
    m_cOp = '/';
    m_bErr = FALSE;
    m_fRegZ = m_fRegY / m_fRegX;
    if (bShowResult)
      cout << pszMsg << m_fRegZ;
  }
  else {
    m_fRegZ = BAD_RESULT;
    m_cOp = ' ';
    m_bErr = TRUE;
```

```
    }
}

void NCScalc01::showRegZ(const char* pszMsg)
{
  cout << pszMsg << m_fRegZ;
}

void NCScalc01::showOperation(const char* pszMsg)
{
  cout << pszMsg << m_fRegY << " " << m_cOp << " "
       << m_fRegX << " = " << m_fRegZ << "\n";
}

void NCScalc01::clearRegs()
{
  m_fRegX = 0.0;
  m_fRegY = 0.0;
  m_fRegZ = 0.0;
  m_cOp = ' ';
  m_bErr = FALSE;
}
```

The class NCScalc01 declares public and protected members. The protected members are

- ✔ The double-type data members m_fRegX and m_fRegY, which emulate the registers X and Y in the calculator. These registers store the operands.

- ✔ The double-type data member m_fRegZ, which emulates the register Z in the calculator. This register stores the result of a mathematical operation.

- ✔ The char-type data member m_cOp, which stores a character that represents the last operation.

- ✔ The Logical-type data member m_bErr, which stores the error state for the last operation.

The class NCScalc01 declares the following public members:

- ✔ The constructor, which initializes the data members.

- ✔ The member functions setRegX() and setRegY(), which store new operands in the data members m_fRegX and m_fRegY, respectively.

- ✔ The member function getRegZ(), which returns the value in the data member m_fRegZ.

- ✔ The member function getError(), which returns (and resets) the value in the data member m_bErr.

- ✔ The member functions add(), sub(), mult(), and div(), which perform the addition, subtraction, multiplication, and division operations, respectively. These member functions use the operands in the data members m_fRegX and m_fRegY and store the result in the data member m_fRegZ. The functions reset the value in the data member m_bErr and assign the character that represents the operation in the data member m_cOp. The member function div() tests for division by zero. This member function sets the data member m_bErr to TRUE if the operation attempts to divide by a number whose absolute value is smaller than the value of the constant EPSILON.

- ✔ The member function showRegZ(), which displays the value in the data member m_fRegZ.

- ✔ The member function showOperation(), which displays the most recent operands, operation, and result.

- ✔ The member function clearRegs(), which resets the values in all the data members.

The class NCScalc100

The class NCScalc01 is the parent of the descendant classes NCScalc100 and NCScalc200. The class NCScalc100 supports the emulation of memory registers. The class instances enable you to specify the number of memory registers at run time. The class supports the following operations:

- ✔ Storing recall numbers in the memory registers, accessed by numeric indices.

- ✔ Recalling numbers from the memory registers.

- ✔ Clearing the contents of the memory registers by assigning zeros to them.

Listing 9-8 shows the source code for the included file MI2C.HPP, which declares and defines the class NCScalc100.

Listing 9-8	MI2C.HPP

```
class NCScalc100 : virtual public NCScalc01
{
  public:
    NCScalc100(int nMaxMem = 10,
```

```
                        double fRegX = 0.,
                        double fRegY = 0.);
     ~NCScalc100();
     void stoMem(int nIndex, double x);
     void rclMem(int nIndex, double& x);
     void clearMem();

   protected:
     double* m_pfMem;
     int m_nMaxMem;
};

//
// define member functions of class NCScalc100
//

NCScalc100::NCScalc100(int nMaxMem,
        double fRegX, double fRegY)
     : NCScalc01(fRegX, fRegY)
{
  m_pfMem = new double[m_nMaxMem = nMaxMem];
  for (int i = 0; i < m_nMaxMem; i++)
    m_pfMem[i] = 0.;
}

NCScalc100::~NCScalc100()
{
  delete [] m_pfMem;
}

void NCScalc100::stoMem(int nIndex, double x)
{
  if (nIndex >= 0 && nIndex < m_nMaxMem) {
    m_pfMem[nIndex] = x;
    m_bErr = FALSE;
  }
  else
    m_bErr = TRUE;
}
```

(continued)

Listing 9-8 *(continued)*

```
void NCScalc100::rclMem(int nIndex, double& x)
{
  if (nIndex >= 0 && nIndex < m_nMaxMem) {
    x = m_pfMem[nIndex];
    m_bErr = FALSE;
  }
  else
    m_bErr = TRUE;
}

void NCScalc100::clearMem()
{
  for (int i = 0; i < m_nMaxMem; i++)
    m_pfMem[i] = 0.;
}
```

The class NCScalc100 is a virtual descendant of the class NCScalc01. This class declares public and protected members to support the emulated memory registers feature. The class declares the following protected members:

✔ The data member m_pfMem, which is a pointer to the dynamic array of doubles. This array emulates the memory registers. The class instances use this member to access the elements of the dynamic array.

✔ The int-type data member m_nMaxMem, which contains the number of dynamic array elements.

The class declares the following public members:

✔ The constructor, which allows you to specify the number of memory registers (that is, the number of elements in the supporting dynamic array) and the initial values in the registers X and Y (that is, the inherited data members m_fRegX and m_fRegY).

✔ The member function stoMem( ), which stores the value of the parameter x at the memory register specified by the index nIndex. If you specify an out-of-range index, the function sets the inherited data member m_bErr to TRUE. The function uses the data member m_pfMem to access the targeted element of the dynamic array.

✔ The member function rclMem( ), which recalls the value of the memory register specified by the index nIndex. The reference parameter x passes the sought value. If you specify an out-of-range index, the function sets the inherited data member m_bErr to TRUE. The function uses the data member m_pfMem to access the targeted element of the dynamic array.

✔ The member function clearMem( ), which clears the memory registers by assigning zeros to the elements of the dynamic array.

The class NCScalc200

The class NCScalc200 is a child of the class NCScalc01. This class supports the following operations:

- ✔ A limited set of operations that calculate the square root and square functions. Feel free to extend the list of functions to include trigonometric, logarithmic, and hyperbolic functions (assuming that you have nothing better to do with your time). These operations make the class implement a limited scientific calculator.

- ✔ Displaying the last mathematical function evaluated, the argument of the function, and the result.

- ✔ Clearing the memory registers.

To display the last mathematical function executed, the class has a special data member that emulates a register and stores the name of the last function.

Listing 9-9 shows the source code for the included file MI2D.HPP, which declares and defines the class NCScalc200.

Listing 9-9	MI2D.HPP

```
class NCScalc200 : virtual public NCScalc01
{
  public:
    NCScalc200(double fRegX = 0., double fRegY = 0.)
      : NCScalc01(fRegX, fRegY)
    {
      strcpy(m_cFunc, "");
    }

    void Sqrt(Logical bShowResult = TRUE,
          const char* pszMsg = "");
    void Sqr(Logical bShowResult = TRUE,
          const char* pszMsg = "");
    void showFunction(const char* pszMsg = "");
    void clearRegs(); // override inherited function

  protected:
    char m_cFunc[10];
};
```

(continued)

Listing 9-9 (continued)

```
//
// define member functions of class NCScalc200
//

void NCScalc200::Sqrt(Logical bShowResult, const char*
            pszMsg)
{
  if (m_fRegX >= 0.) {
    m_fRegZ = sqrt(m_fRegX);
    m_bErr = FALSE;
    strcpy(m_cFunc, "Sqrt(");
    if (bShowResult)
      cout << m_fRegZ;
  }
  else {
    m_fRegZ = BAD_RESULT;
    m_bErr = TRUE;
    strcpy(m_cFunc, "");
  }
}

void NCScalc200::Sqr(Logical bShowResult, const char* pszMsg)
{
  m_fRegZ = m_fRegX * m_fRegX;
  m_bErr = FALSE;
  strcpy(m_cFunc, "Sqr(");
  if (bShowResult)
    cout << m_fRegZ;
}

void NCScalc200::showFunction(const char* pszMsg)
{
  cout << pszMsg << m_cFunc << m_fRegX
       << ") = " << m_fRegZ << "\n";
}

void NCScalc200::clearRegs()
{
  NCScalc01::clearRegs();
  strcpy(m_cFunc, "");
}
```

The class NCScalc200 is a virtual descendant of the class NCScalc01. The descendant class declares protected and public members. The class declares a single protected data member m_cFunc. This member stores the name of the last mathematical function evaluated.

The class declares the following public members:

- ✔ The constructor, which initializes the inherited data members (by invoking the constructor of the parent class) and initializes the data member m_cFunc with an empty string.

- ✔ The member functions Sqrt() and Sqr(), which evaluate the square root and the square, respectively. These functions use the value in the data member m_fRegX as the argument and store the result in the data member m_fRegZ. The square root function checks the value in the data member m_fRegX before evaluating the mathematical function.

- ✔ The member function showFunction(), which displays the name of the most recent mathematical function evaluated, its argument, and its result.

- ✔ The member function clearRegs(), which overrides the inherited member function. This function invokes the inherited member function and then resets the value in the data member m_cFunc.

The class NCScalc120

The class NCScalc120 is a descendant of the class NCScalc100 and the class NCScalc200. This class merely inherits the combined attributes and operations of its parent classes.

The highlight of the MI2.CPP program is the class NCScalc120, which shows the power of multiple inheritance.

Listing 9-10 shows the source code for the MI2E.HPP included file, which declares and defines the class NCScalc120. This class is a virtual descendant of the classes NCScalc100 and NCScalc200. This class supports the same operations as the classes NCScalc01, NCScalc100, and NCScalc200 combined. Declaring this class as a virtual descendant of multiple classes enables the compiler to resolve the redundancy in the lineage of the class NCScalc120.

Listing 9-10	**MI2E.HPP**

```
class NCScalc120 : virtual public NCScalc100,
          virtual public NCScalc200
{
  public:
    NCScalc120(int nMaxMem = 10, double fRegX = 0.,
        double fRegY = 0.)
      : NCScalc100(nMaxMem, fRegX, fRegY)
    {
      strcpy(m_cFunc, "");
    }
};
```

The function main()

Listing 9-11 shows source code for the included file MI2F.HPP, which contains the function main(). This function tests the class NCScalc120 (and all of its inherited member functions) using the object calculator (an instance of the class NCScalc120). The function tests the addition, subtraction, multiplication, division, square root, and square functions. The function main() performs these tasks by sending the C++ messages setRegX(), setRegY(), add(), sub(), mul(), div(), Sqrt(), Sqr(), showOperation(), and showFunction() to the object calculator.

Listing 9-11	**MI2F.HPP**

```
//
// test classes
//

main()
{
  NCScalc120 calculator;

  cout << "Testing class NCScalc120\n";

  // test addition
  calculator.setRegX(13.0);
  calculator.setRegY(55.0);
  calculator.add(FALSE);
  calculator.showOperation();
```

```
// test subtraction
calculator.setRegX(55.0);
calculator.setRegY(123.0);
calculator.sub(FALSE);
calculator.showOperation();

// test multiplication
calculator.setRegX(13.0);
calculator.setRegY(0.55);
calculator.mult(FALSE);
calculator.showOperation();

// test division
calculator.setRegX(113.0);
calculator.setRegY(355.0);
calculator.div(FALSE);
calculator.showOperation();

// test sqrt(x)
calculator.setRegX(13.0);
calculator.Sqrt(FALSE);
calculator.showFunction();

// test square function
calculator.Sqr(FALSE);
calculator.showFunction();
return 0;
}
```

Summary

This chapter describes using multiple inheritance to create descendant classes from multiple parent classes. You've learned about deriving descendant classes from parents with distinct class hierarchies. You've also learned about deriving classes from parents that are members of the same class hierarchy. If you must use multiple inheritance, avoid at all costs creating descendants from multiple parents that are members of the same class hierarchy. The examples in this chapter show you the power of multiple inheritance in combining the attributes and the operations of multiple classes.

Chapter 10

Containment: Better than Multiple Inheritance?

. . . .

In This Chapter

▶ What is containment?

▶ Understanding when to use containment

▶ Comparing containment and multiple inheritance

. . . .

*T*his chapter looks at containment, which is a special way of connecting classes that don't have the typical parent-child relationship. You find out what containment is and you read about how to enhance it by using the friend class feature. In this chapter, I show you an example of a program that uses containment without friend classes and another example that uses containment with friend classes.

Containment: Is It Related to Limiting Damage?

Containment is a programming technique that uses class instances or pointers to classes as data members of other classes. In other words, you declare a class that contains data members that are themselves instances of other classes or pointers to other classes. The contained classes need not be (and usually are not) related to the host class by common ancestor classes. Using containment gives the host class access to the public members of the contained classes. This point is important, because the contained classes must have access member functions that assist the host class.

Some C++ gurus prefer using containment rather than multiple inheritance, because initializing contained classes involves fewer possible ambiguities than initializing multiple-inheritance classes. Consider the following example of a class that represents a boom box. The boom box class contains data members that are instances of classes that represent the components of the boom box — that is, the radio, the cassette player, and the CD player. When you declare an instance of the boom box class, the run-time system automatically invokes the constructors of the data members that are instances of the radio, cassette player, and CD player classes (as well as the constructor of the boom box class).

Use pointers to classes as contained data members when these classes do not have default constructors or when you want to initialize these data members in a particular way. Don't forget to create and remove the dynamic class instances (accessed by the pointer-to-class data members) in the constructors and the destructor, respectively.

Here is an example of a class that contains other classes:

```
class Radio
{
  // declaration of members
};

class CDPlayer
{
  // declaration of members
};

class CassettePlayer
{
  // declaration of members
};
class BoomBox
{
  // declaration of public members

  protected:
    Radio* m_pRadio;
    CDPlayer* m_pCDPlayer;
    CassettePlayer* m_pCassettePlayer;

  // declaration of other protected members
};
```

This example declares the nondescendant classes Radio, CDPlayer, CassettePlayer, and BoomBox. The class BoomBox contains the data members m_pRadio, m_pCDPlayer, and m_pCassettePlayer, which are pointers to the classes Radio, CDPlayer, and CassettePlayer, respectively. The class BoomBox uses these special data members to create instances of the classes Radio, CDPlayer, and CassettePlayer and to access the public members of these classes. Figure 10-1 shows the "physical" containment of the classes. (In other words, you are looking at my fine drawing of a boom box.)

Figure 10-1:
The boom box containing the radio, the CD player, and the cassette player.

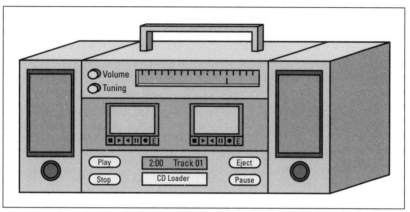

Guidelines for Using Contained Classes: Use 'em or Lose 'em!

Conceptually, containment is a special way of relating classes to each other *without* (and this is the key word) involving a parent-child relationship. Instead, the relationship between the host class and the contained classes is a "has-a" relationship, which resembles the relationship between parent and child classes in multiple inheritance.

For example, the code snippet in the preceding section shows you the "has-a" relationship between the classes BoomBox and Radio. You can say that a boom box *has a* radio. In OOP terms, the class BoomBox contains a data member that is a pointer to the class Radio.

Because the host class is not a child of the contained classes, the relationship between these classes is more formal, so to speak. This formality reflects the fact that the host class cannot automatically access nonpublic members of the contained classes (as is the case with a descendant class in a multiple inheritance scheme). Consequently, the contained classes should be well designed to provide the host class access to the members by using access member functions. Although such member functions add to the software overhead, some C++ gurus (bless their hearts) praise this feature as a blessing. Why? These gurus prefer a robust connection between contained classes and their host class to the treacherous ways of multiple inheritance (which should tell you how much these C++ gurus love multiple inheritance).

When you use containment, you need to follow a few general guidelines:

✔ Declare a data member as an instance of the contained class if that class has a default constructor.

✔ Declare a data member as a pointer to the contained class. This approach works well when the contained class has no default constructor or when using an existing custom constructor is more convenient. The constructor of the host class should create the dynamic instances of the contained classes. Likewise, the destructor of the host classes should remove the dynamic instances of the contained classes.

✔ Remember that the host class, by default, has access to only the public members of the contained classes.

✔ Declare the host class as a friend of the contained classes. This friendship gives the host class the privilege of accessing the nonpublic members of the contained classes. Use the friendship between classes to do away with the overhead of using access member functions.

The first two guidelines give you a choice of declaring data members as class instances or as pointers to classes. I recommend declaring them as pointers to classes because this method gives you more control over when to create the instances of the contained classes. Otherwise, Mr. Compiler decides where and when to create the nondynamic class instances (in accordance with the C++ rules). So my advice is: Use pointers to contained classes.

Revisiting the Rescue Example: Help Is on the Way!

To illustrate containment, I have modified the source code for the rescue programming example shown in Listings 9-1 through 9-5 in Chapter 9 (MI1A.HPP through MI1E.HPP). The new program, CONTAIN1.CPP, interacts with the user the same way that MI1.CPP does, but it uses containment instead of multiple inheritance.

Here is a sample session with the new version of the rescue program (input is in boldface):

```
Current distance = 466.337
Current angle = 38.8381 degrees
Enter movement in X direction : 100
Enter movement in Y direction : 100
Current distance = 326.086
Current angle = 36.1699 degrees
Enter movement in X direction : 100
Enter movement in Y direction : 100
Current distance = 187.601
Current angle = 29.5248 degrees
Enter movement in X direction : 100
Enter movement in Y direction : 100
Current distance = 63.6886
Current angle = -6.80842 degrees
Enter movement in X direction : -7
Enter movement in Y direction : 60


Congratulations for the rescue!
```

Here's the source code for the CONTAIN1.CPP file:

```
/*

    A C++ program that illustrates the following
    small class hierarchy which uses containment:

        Distance      Random
           |            |
           |            |
           |            |
         data members of
           |            |
         \———————/
              |
              |
            Rescue

*/
```

(continued)

(continued)

```
#include "contai1a.hpp"
#include "contai1b.hpp"
#include "contai1c.hpp"
#include "contai1d.hpp"
#include "contai1e.hpp"
```

In the following sections, I describe and list the source code for the included files of the CONTAIN1.CPP program.

The globals

Listing 10-1 shows the source code for the included file CONTAI1A.HPP, which declares a set of global constants that set the general parameters of the search simulation. The listing also declares the global functions sqr( ), cube( ), and frac( ), which return the square, cube, and fractional values, respectively, of floating-point numbers. The statements in the listing are identical to those of Listing 9-1 in Chapter 9.

Listing 10-1	CONTAI1A.HPP

```
#include <iostream.h>
#include <math.h>
#include <string.h>

const double PI = 4 * atan(1);
const double RAD2DEG = 180.0 / PI;
const double INIT_SEED = 113;
const double MIN_XY = 1.0;
const double MAX_XY = 1000.0;
const double CRITIC_DIST = 10.0;
const double EPSILON = 1.0e-8;
const double INFINITY = 1.0e+50;

enum Logical { FALSE, TRUE };

double sqr(double x)
{
  return x * x;
}
```

```
double cube(double x)
{
  return x * x * x;
}

double frac(double x)
{
  return x - (long)x;
}
```

The class Random

Listing 10-2 shows the source code for the included file CONTAI1B.HPP, which
declares the class Random. The source code for this included file is identical to
that in Listing 9-2. This class contains the protected double-type data member
m_fSeed, which stores the last random number. The class uses this data
member to generate the next random number. The class Random declares a
constructor that initializes the data member m_fSeed and the member function
getRandom( ), which returns a random number between 0 and 1 (exclusive).

Listing 10-2	CONTAI1B.HPP

```
class Random
{
  public:
    Random(double fSeed = INIT_SEED)
      { m_fSeed = fSeed; }

    double getRandom();

  protected:
    double m_fSeed;
};

double Random::getRandom()
{
  m_fSeed = frac(cube(m_fSeed + PI));
  return m_fSeed;
}
```

The class Distance

The class Distance manages the distance between two points and declares protected and public members. The protected members are as follows:

- ✔ The double-type data members m_fX1, m_fY1, m_fX2, and m_fY2, which store the coordinates of the two points.

- ✔ The double-type data members m_fDeltaX and m_fDeltaY, which store the differences in the X and Y coordinates of the two points.

The class Distance also declares the following public members:

- ✔ The constructor, which initializes the data members m_fX1, m_fY1, m_fX2, and m_fY2. These data members store the coordinates of the two points.

- ✔ The member functions setPoint1() and setPoint2(), which store new coordinates for the first and second points, respectively.

- ✔ The member function getDeltaX(), which returns the value in the data member m_fDeltaX.

- ✔ The member function getDeltaY(), which returns the value in the data member m_fDeltaY.

- ✔ The member function getDistance(), which returns the distance between the two points.

- ✔ The member function getAngle(), which returns the angle (in degrees) of the line that connects the two points.

- ✔ The member function setDeltaX(), which assigns a new value to the data member m_fDeltaX. I added this member function to the new version of the class Distance.

- ✔ The member function setDeltaY(), which assigns a new value to the data member m_fDeltaY. I added this member function to the new version of the class Distance.

- ✔ The member functions getX1(), getX2(), getY1(), and getY2(), which return the data members m_fX1, m_fY1, m_fX2, and m_fY2, respectively. These data members store the coordinates of the two points. I added these member functions to the new version of the class Distance.

Listing 10-3 shows the source code for the included file CONTAI1C.HPP, which declares and defines the class Distance.

Listing 10-3	CONTAI1C.HPP

```cpp
class Distance
{
  public:
    Distance(double fX1, double fY1,
             double fX2, double fY2);
    void setPoint1(double fX, double fY);
    void setPoint2(double fX, double fY);
    double getDeltaX()
      { return m_fDeltaX; }
    double getDeltaY()
      { return m_fDeltaY; }
    double getDistance()
      { return sqrt(sqr(m_fX2 - m_fX1) +
                    sqr(m_fY2 - m_fY1)); }
    double getAngle();
    void setDeltaX(double fDeltaX)
      { m_fDeltaX = fDeltaX; }
    void setDeltaY(double fDeltaY)
      { m_fDeltaY = fDeltaY; }
    double getX1()
      { return m_fX1; }
    double getX2()
      { return m_fX2; }
    double getY1()
      { return m_fY1; }
    double getY2()
      { return m_fY2; }

  protected:
    double m_fX1;
    double m_fX2;
    double m_fY1;
    double m_fY2;
    double m_fDeltaX;
    double m_fDeltaY;
};

Distance::Distance(double fX1, double fY1,
             double fX2, double fY2)
{
```

(continued)

Listing 10-3 *(continued)*

```
  setPoint1(fX1, fY1);
  setPoint2(fX2, fY2);
}

void Distance::setPoint1(double fX, double fY)
{
  m_fX1 = fX;
  m_fY1 = fY;
}

void Distance::setPoint2(double fX, double fY)
{
  m_fX2 = fX;
  m_fY2 = fY;
}

double Distance::getAngle()
{
  double fDeltaY = m_fY2 - m_fY1;

  return (fabs(fDeltaY) > EPSILON) ?
    RAD2DEG * atan((m_fX2 - m_fX1) / fDeltaY) :
    INFINITY;
}
```

The class Rescue

The class Rescue resembles the version of the class Rescue in Listing 9-4 in chapter 9. Notice the following differences in the new class version:

- ✔ The protected data member m_pDistance is a pointer to the class Distance.

- ✔ The protected data member m_pRandom is a pointer to the class Random.

- ✔ The constructor creates dynamic instances of the classes Random and Distance to be accessed by the data members m_pRandom and m_pDistance, respectively.

- ✔ The destructor removes the dynamic instances of the classes Random and Distance.

✔ The member functions `Rescue::searchMore()` and
   `Rescue::getCoords()` use the member functions `getDeltaX()`,
   `getDeltaY()`, `getX1()`, `getY1()`, `getX2()`, and `getY2()` to access the
   data members of the class `Distance`. Thus, you learn that a contained
   class should declare all the member functions needed by the host class.

Listing 10-4 shows the source code for the included file CONTAI1D.HPP, which
declares and defines the class `Rescue`.

Listing 10-4   **CONTAI1D.HPP**

```
class Rescue
{
  public:
    Rescue(double fMin, double fMax,
        double fCriticalDistance);
    ~Rescue();
    void initRescue();
    Logical searchMore();
    void getCoords();
    double getDistance()
      { return m_pDistance->getDistance(); }

  protected:
    double m_fMin;
    double m_fMax;
    double m_fShift;
    double m_fCriticalDistance;
    // declare pointers to contained classes
    Distance* m_pDistance;
    Random* m_pRandom;

    double calcRandCoord()
      { return m_pRandom->getRandom() * m_fMax + m_fMin; }
    double calcRandShift()
      { return (0.5 - m_pRandom->getRandom()) * m_fShift; }
    double checkCoord(double fX)
      { return (fX >= m_fMin && fX <= m_fMax) ?
              fX : m_fMin + m_fMax / 2.; }
};

Rescue::Rescue(double fMin, double fMax,
        double fCriticalDistance)
```

(continued)

Listing 10-4 *(continued)*

```
{
  m_fMin = fMin;
  m_fMax = fMax;
  m_fShift = (fMax - fMin + 1) / 10.;
  m_fCriticalDistance = fCriticalDistance;
  m_pDistance = new Distance(0, 0, 0, 0);
  m_pRandom = new Random;
  initRescue();
}

Rescue::~Rescue()
{
  delete m_pDistance;
  delete m_pRandom;
}

void Rescue::initRescue()
{
  double fX = calcRandCoord();
  double fY = calcRandCoord();

  m_pDistance->setPoint1((m_fMin + m_fMax) / 2,
                         (m_fMin + m_fMax) / 2);
  m_pDistance->setPoint2(fX, fY);
}

Logical Rescue::searchMore()
{
  if (fabs(m_pDistance->getDeltaX()) < 1.0 ||
      fabs(m_pDistance->getDeltaY()) < 1.0 ||
        m_pDistance->getDistance() < m_fCriticalDistance)
    return FALSE;
  else
    return TRUE;
}

void Rescue::getCoords()
{
  int fX, fY;
```

```
   cout << "Current distance = "
        << m_pDistance->getDistance() << "\n"
        << "Current angle = "
        << m_pDistance->getAngle() << " degrees\n";

  // calculate the random movement of lost person
/// uncomment the next 8 lines to make the lost person move
///   m_pDistance->setDeltaX(calcRandShift());
///   m_pDistance->setDeltaY(calcRandShift());
///   m_pDistance->setPoint2(
///       checkCoord(m_pDistance->getX2() +
///                   m_pDistance->getDeltaX()),
///       checkCoord(m_pDistance->getY2() +
///                   m_pDistance->getDeltaY())
///       );

// prompt for movement of rescuer
  cout << "Enter movement in X direction : ";
  cin >> fX;
  m_pDistance->setDeltaX(fX);
  if (m_pDistance->getDeltaX() > m_fShift) // verify limit
    m_pDistance->setDeltaX(m_fShift);
  cout << "Enter movement in Y direction : ";
  cin >> fY;
  m_pDistance->setDeltaY(fY);
  if (m_pDistance->getDeltaY() > m_fShift) // verify limit
    m_pDistance->setDeltaY(m_fShift);
  m_pDistance->setPoint1(
      checkCoord(m_pDistance->getX1() +
              m_pDistance->getDeltaX()),
      checkCoord(m_pDistance->getY1() +
              m_pDistance->getDeltaY())
      );
}
```

The function main()

The function main() declares the object R as an instance of the class Rescue. The function creates this instance by using the constants MIN_XY, MAX_XY, and CRITIC_DIST to set the grid range and the critical distance. The function main() performs the following tasks:

✔ Displays the initial distance and angle and prompts you for your first move. This task involves sending the C++ message getCoords() to the object R.

✔ Performs the simulated search for the lost person using a while loop. The loop examines the Boolean value returned by sending the C++ message searchMore() to the object R. This message determines whether you found the lost person (or quit the search). Each loop iteration sends the C++ message getCoords() to the object R. This message displays the current distance and angle and prompts you for your next move.

✔ Determines whether you found the lost person or quit the search. This task involves sending the C++ message getDistance() to the object. The function uses an if statement to compare the result of the getDistance() message with the constant CRITIC_DIST. The function main() displays the message "Congratulations for the rescue!" if you found the person or the message "Sorry you gave up!" if you stopped searching.

Listing 10-5 shows the source code for the included file CONTAI1E.HPP, which contains the function main().

Listing 10-5	CONTAI1E.HPP

```
//
// test classes
//

main()
{
  Rescue R(MIN_XY, MAX_XY, CRITIC_DIST);

  R.getCoords();
  while (R.searchMore())
    R.getCoords();

  cout << "\n\n";
  if (R.getDistance() <= CRITIC_DIST)
    cout << "Congratulations for the rescue!";
  else
    cout << "Sorry you gave up!";

  return 0;
}
```

Using Friend Classes in Containment: A Friend in Need Is a Friend Indeed

C++ has a special feature that allows one class to access the nonpublic members of another class that is not in the same class hierarchy. This feature is called *friendship* (how appropriate). Chapter 14 discusses friend classes, member functions, and operators in greater detail. Although I don't mean to jump the gun, I discuss friendship among classes here because it is related to containment and greatly benefits containment.

C++ offers the following statement to declare a class as a friend of another class:

```
friend class1, class2, ...
```

The keyword `friend` tells the compiler that the listed classes are friends to the class that contains the friendship declarations. Here is a simple example:

```
class Radio
{
   friend class BoomBox;
   // declaration of members
};

class CDPlayer
{
   friend class BoomBox;
   // declaration of members
};

class CassettePlayer
{
   friend class BoomBox;
   // declaration of members
};

class BoomBox
{
   // declaration of public members

   protected:
     Radio* m_pRadio;
```

(continued)

(continued)

```
    CDPlayer* m_pCDPlayer;
    CassettePlayer* m_pCassettePlayer;

  // declaration of other protected members
};
```

The classes `Radio`, `CDPlayer`, and `CassettePlayer` declare the class `BoomBox` as a friend class. Each one of the three classes contains the declaration `friend class BoomBox`. Thus, the host class `BoomBox` can access the nonpublic members of the classes `Radio`, `CDPlayer`, and `CassettePlayer` through their related dynamic instances (accessed by the data members `m_pRadio`, `m_pCDPlayer`, and `m_pCassettePlayer`).

Yet Another Rescue Program: Operation Friendship

If you're dying to find out how friend classes work with the version of the rescue program that you've been examining in this chapter, then the following sections should satisfy your curiosity! In these sections, I show you the source code for the included files for the CONTAIN2.CPP program.

The source code for the CONTAIN2.CPP file is:

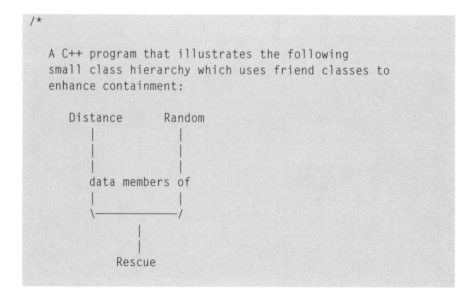

```
/*

    A C++ program that illustrates the following
    small class hierarchy which uses friend classes to
    enhance containment:

        Distance      Random
          |             |
          |             |
          |             |
        data members of
          |             |
        _____/
                |
                |
             Rescue
```

```
*/

#include "contai2a.hpp"
#include "contai2b.hpp"
#include "contai2c.hpp"
#include "contai2d.hpp"
#include "contai2e.hpp"
```

The globals

Listing 10-6 shows the source code for the included file CONTAI2A.HPP, which declares the global constants and the global functions used by the search simulation.

Listing 10-6	CONTAI2A.HPP

```
#include <iostream.h>
#include <math.h>
#include <string.h>

const double PI = 4 * atan(1);
const double RAD2DEG = 180.0 / PI;
const double INIT_SEED = 113;
const double MIN_XY = 1.0;
const double MAX_XY = 1000.0;
const double CRITIC_DIST = 10.0;
const double EPSILON = 1.0e-8;
const double INFINITY = 1.0e+50;

enum Logical { FALSE, TRUE };

double sqr(double x)
{
  return x * x;
}

double cube(double x)
{
  return x * x * x;
```

(continued)

Listing 10-6 *(continued)*

```
}

double frac(double x)
{
  return x - (long)x;
}
```

The class Random

Listing 10-7 shows the source code for the included file CONTAI2B.HPP, which declares and defines the class Random. Notice that this declaration contains the following statement:

```
friend class Rescue
```

This statement allows the class Rescue to access the protected data member m_fSeed, if necessary.

Listing 10-7   **CONTAI2B.HPP**

```
class Random
{
  friend class Rescue;

  public:
    Random(double fSeed = INIT_SEED)
      { m_fSeed = fSeed; }

    double getRandom();

  protected:
    double m_fSeed;
};

double Random::getRandom()
{
  m_fSeed = frac(cube(m_fSeed + PI));
  return m_fSeed;
}
```

The class Distance

Listing 10-8 shows the source code for the included file CONTAI2C.HPP, which contains the declaration of the class Distance. Notice that the declaration of this class has the following statement:

```
friend class Rescue
```

This statement plays a major role in reducing the overhead of accessing the protected data members by instances of the class Rescue. Consequently, notice that the class declaration in Listing 10-8 does not have (or need) the member functions getDeltaX(), getDeltaY(), setDeltaX(), setDeltaY(), getX1(), getX2(), getY1(), and getY2().

Listing 10-8	CONTAI2C.HPP

```
class Distance
{
  friend class Rescue;

  public:
    Distance(double fX1, double fY1,
          double fX2, double fY2);
    void setPoint1(double fX, double fY);
    void setPoint2(double fX, double fY);
    double getDistance()
      { return sqrt(sqr(m_fX2 - m_fX1) +
               sqr(m_fY2 - m_fY1)); }
    double getAngle();

  protected:
    double m_fX1;
    double m_fX2;
    double m_fY1;
    double m_fY2;
    double m_fDeltaX;
    double m_fDeltaY;
};

Distance::Distance(double fX1, double fY1,
          double fX2, double fY2)
{
```

(continued)

Listing 10-8 *(continued)*

```
    setPoint1(fX1, fY1);
    setPoint2(fX2, fY2);
}

void Distance::setPoint1(double fX, double fY)
{
  m_fX1 = fX;
  m_fY1 = fY;
}

void Distance::setPoint2(double fX, double fY)
{
  m_fX2 = fX;
  m_fY2 = fY;
}

double Distance::getAngle()
{
  double fDeltaY = m_fY2 - m_fY1;

  return (fabs(fDeltaY) > EPSILON) ?
    RAD2DEG * atan((m_fX2 - m_fX1) / fDeltaY) :
    INFINITY;
}
```

The class Rescue

Listing 10-9 shows the source code for the included file CONTAI2D.HPP, which declares and defines the class Rescue. This source code shows that the implementation of the member functions for the class Rescue directly accesses the data members of the class Distance using the data member m_pDistance. The source code does not need the access member functions to store and recall values in the protected data members of the class Distance. Consequently, the code is easier to read, thanks to the C++ friend class feature.

Listing 10-9   **CONTAI2D.HPP**

```
class Rescue
{
  public:
    Rescue(double fMin, double fMax,
           double fCriticalDistance);
```

```
    ~Rescue();
    void initRescue();
    Logical searchMore();
    void getCoords();
    double getDistance()
      { return m_pDistance->getDistance(); }

  protected:
    double m_fMin;
    double m_fMax;
    double m_fShift;
    double m_fCriticalDistance;
    // declare pointers to contained classes
    Distance* m_pDistance;
    Random* m_pRandom;

    double calcRandCoord()
      { return m_pRandom->getRandom() * m_fMax + m_fMin; }
    double calcRandShift()
      { return (0.5 - m_pRandom->getRandom()) * m_fShift; }
    double checkCoord(double fX)
      { return (fX >= m_fMin && fX <= m_fMax) ?
                 fX : m_fMin + m_fMax / 2.; }
};

Rescue::Rescue(double fMin, double fMax,
              double fCriticalDistance)
{
  m_fMin = fMin;
  m_fMax = fMax;
  m_fShift = (fMax - fMin + 1) / 10.;
  m_fCriticalDistance = fCriticalDistance;
  m_pDistance = new Distance(0, 0, 0, 0);
  m_pRandom = new Random;
  initRescue();
}

Rescue::~Rescue()
{
  delete m_pDistance;
  delete m_pRandom;
}
```

(continued)

Listing 10-9 *(continued)*

```
void Rescue::initRescue()
{
  double fX = calcRandCoord();
  double fY = calcRandCoord();

  m_pDistance->setPoint1((m_fMin + m_fMax) / 2,
              (m_fMin + m_fMax) / 2);
  m_pDistance->setPoint2(fX, fY);
}

Logical Rescue::searchMore()
{
  if (fabs(m_pDistance->m_fDeltaX) < 1.0 ||
      fabs(m_pDistance->m_fDeltaY) < 1.0 ||
       m_pDistance->getDistance() < m_fCriticalDistance)
    return FALSE;
  else
    return TRUE;
}

void Rescue::getCoords()
{
  int fX, fY;

  cout << "Current distance = "
       << m_pDistance->getDistance() << "\n"
       << "Current angle = "
       << m_pDistance->getAngle() << " degrees\n";

  // calculate the random movement of lost person
/// uncomment the next 8 lines to make the lost person move
///   m_pDistance->m_fDeltaX =calcRandShift());
///   m_pDistance->m_fDeltaY = calcRandShift());
///   m_pDistance->setPoint2(
///      checkCoord(m_pDistance->m_fX2 +
///            m_pDistance->m_fDeltaX),
///      checkCoord(m_pDistance->m_fY2 +
///            m_pDistance->m_fDeltaY)
///      );
```

```
  // prompt for movement of rescuer
  cout << "Enter movement in X direction : ";
  cin >> fX;
  m_pDistance->m_fDeltaX = fX;
  if (m_pDistance->m_fDeltaX > m_fShift) // verify limit
    m_pDistance->m_fDeltaX =m_fShift;
cout << "Enter movement in Y direction : ";
  cin >> fY;
  m_pDistance->m_fDeltaY = fY;
  if (m_pDistance->m_fDeltaY > m_fShift) // verify limit
    m_pDistance->m_fDeltaY = m_fShift;
  m_pDistance->setPoint1(
      checkCoord(m_pDistance->m_fX1 +
            m_pDistance->m_fDeltaX),
      checkCoord(m_pDistance->m_fY1 +
            m_pDistance->m_fDeltaY)
      );
}
```

The function `main()`

Listing 10-10 shows the source code for the included file CONTAI2E.HPP, which contains the function `main()`. Listings 10-5 and 10-10 contain identical source code. I include Listing 10-10 just to complete the source code for this new version of the sample program.

Listing 10-10	**CONTAI2E.HPP**

```
//
// test classes
//

main()
{
  Rescue R(MIN_XY, MAX_XY, CRITIC_DIST);

  R.getCoords();
  while (R.searchMore())
    R.getCoords();
```

(continued)

Listing 10-10 *(continued)*

```
cout << "\n\n";
if (R.getDistance() <= CRITIC_DIST)
  cout << "Congratulations for the rescue!";
else
  cout << "Sorry you gave up!";

return 0;
}
```

Summary

This chapter discusses containment, a programming technique that rivals multiple inheritance. You now know how to create classes that include data members that are themselves instances (or pointers of instances) of other classes. You also know that using the friend class feature can simplify class containment.

Part III
Advanced OOP Features

The 5th Wave   By Rich Tennant

WANDA HAD THE DISTINCT FEELING HER HUSBAND'S NEW SOFTWARE PROGRAM WAS ABOUT TO BECOME INTERACTIVE.

In this part. . .

The chapters in Part III get you on your way to becoming an OOP guru. You find out about advanced OOP-related topics such as abstract classes, class templates, exceptions, friend classes, and nested classes.

Chapter 11
Abstract Classes: The Trendsetters!

A good and robust design of a nontrivial class hierarchy often involves the use of abstract classes. Such classes set the tone of the class design, so to speak, by focusing on the general aspects of the operations that are common to all descendants of the abstract classes. This chapter discusses abstract classes in C++ and shows you how to declare them and use them in class hierarchies. You look at two examples: the first involves a hierarchy that has a single abstract class; the second shows a hierarchy that has multiple abstract classes.

Are Abstract Classes Just Another Sacred Buzzword?

Abstraction deals with generalities and overlooks specific issues. For example, if I say that I watched TV last night, I am talking in general terms. The term *TV* by itself is abstract and points to a device that receives sounds and images. The TV could be any kind of television set: black and white, color, cable-connected, and so on.

If I say that I turned on the TV set to watch the news, I am referring to the TV in an abstract fashion and to turning it on as an operation that is common to all TV sets. You still do not know a great deal about my TV set. In contrast, if I say that I turned on the TV to watch "CNN Headline News," you know that I'm talking about a cable-connected TV set. But you still have no way of knowing whether my TV has a built-in VCR or other features.

This discussion about my TV set demonstrates that you can have multiple levels of abstraction. I made a few statements about my TV. Some statements are more general than others. Likewise, in OOP thinking, some statements are more abstract than others.

Does C++ support abstract classes? The answer is yes. Not all C++ classes need to be *working* (that is, nonabstract) classes. Indeed, C++ supports abstract classes that mainly set the specifications for their descendant classes. The compiler does not allow you to create instances of an abstract class (just try!).

Where do you use abstract classes, you might ask? You can place abstract classes in the root of a class hierarchy as well as in the root of a subhierarchy. You also can build a class hierarchy using abstract classes as the base class and the first sibling descendant classes. In addition, you can use an abstract class as a parent class deep inside a hierarchy.

Abstract classes focus on the general specifications that are common to their descendant classes. Abstract classes can simplify the design of elaborate class hierarchies that contain many branches.

Declaring Abstract Classes: I Do Declare!

Does declaring an abstract class involve a big production? No. You need to declare at least one *pure* virtual member function using the following syntax:

```
virtual returnType functionName(parameterList) = 0;
```

This syntax declares a pure virtual member function and includes = 0 to signal to Mr. Compiler that this member function has no definition and is, therefore, a member of an abstract class. In other words, C++ doesn't require a special keyword that comes immediately before or after the keyword class in a class declaration.

Must all member functions of an abstract class lack definitions? Not necessarily. You can have an abstract class that defines some of its member functions to invoke the not-yet-defined member functions of its descendant classes. The descendant classes define the latter member functions and can, therefore, use the fully-defined member functions inherited from the abstract classes.

Abstract classes vary between being very general (perhaps too general) and somewhat specific. Highly abstract classes stick with the declaration of pure virtual member functions. Less abstract classes may define some member functions that use the pure virtual functions.

Here is a simple example of an abstract class and its nonabstract descendant class:

```
class AbstractIntStack
{
  public:
    virtual void Push(int nVal) = 0;
    virtual int Pop(int& nVal) = 0;
    void Clear();
};

class IntStack : public AbstractIntStack
{
  public:
    AbstractIntStack()
      { Clear(); }
    virtual void Push(int nVal);
    virtual int Pop(int& nVal);

  protected:
    int m_nHeight;
    int* m_pData;
};

void AbstractIntStack::Clear()
{
  int nVal;

  // the next loop uses the member function Pop
  while (Pop(nVal)
   // do nothing
     ;
}

void IntStack::Push(int nVal)
{
  // statements
}

 virtual int IntStack::Pop(int& nVal)
{
  // statements
}
```

This example shows the abstract class AbstractIntStack, which declares the virtual member functions Push() and Pop() and the member function Clear(). The declarations of the virtual member functions indicate that the class AbstractIntStack does not define these member functions. However, that class does define the member function Clear(). The example also shows the descendant class IntStack, which declares and defines the virtual member functions Push() and Pop(). The descendant class inherits the member function Clear().

Declaring a Simple Hierarchy with One Abstract Class: One Is a Lonely Number!

The ABSTRAC1.CPP program illustrates abstract classes that store floating-point numbers (using the predefined data type double). The program declares an abstract array class and two sibling descendant classes. The first descendant models arrays that store their data in memory. The second descendant models arrays that store their data in a binary data file (this kind of array is also called a *virtual array*). Figure 11-1 depicts this simple class hierarchy.

Figure 11-1:
The class hierarchy for the single-level abstract class example.

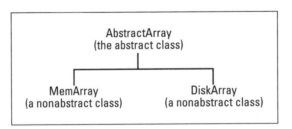

AbstractArray
(the abstract class)

MemArray
(a nonabstract class)

DiskArray
(a nonabstract class)

The program assigns values to the instances of the two kinds of nonabstract classes and then performs the following tasks on each instance:

- ✔ Displays the unsorted elements in that instance.
- ✔ Sorts the elements in that instance.
- ✔ Displays the sorted elements in that instance.

Here is the output from the ABSTRAC1.CPP program:

```
Unsorted array is:
33.4 54.1 98.2 47.5 15.6 81.2 78.7 36.7 63.3 83.9
Sorted array is:
15.6 33.4 36.7 47.5 54.1 63.3 78.7 81.2 83.9 98.2
Unsorted disk-based array is:
33.4 54.1 98.2 47.5 15.6 81.2 78.7 36.7 63.3 83.9
Sorted disk-based array is:
15.6 33.4 36.7 47.5 54.1 63.3 78.7 81.2 83.9 98.2
```

Listing 11-1 shows the source code for the ABSTRAC1.CPP program.

Listing 11-1	ABSTRAC1.CPP

```cpp
// A C++ program that illustrates
// a single-level abstract class

#include <fstream.h>
#include <iomanip.h>

enum Logical { FALSE, TRUE };

const int MAX_ELEMS = 10;

class AbstractArray
{
  public:
    virtual void Store(double fVal, int nIndex) = 0;
    virtual void Recall(double& fVal, int nIndex) = 0;

    void Show(const char* pszMsg = "",
              const int nNumElems = MAX_ELEMS,
              const int bOneLine = TRUE);
    void Sort(int nNumElems);
};

class MemArray : public AbstractArray
{
  public:
    MemArray(double fInitVal = 0);
    double& operator[](int nIndex)
      { return m_fArray[nIndex]; }
    virtual void Store(double fVal, int nIndex);
    virtual void Recall(double& fVal, int nIndex);
```

(continued)

Listing 11-1 *(continued)*

```cpp
protected:
    double m_fArray[MAX_ELEMS];
};

class DiskArray : public AbstractArray
{
  public:
    DiskArray(const char* pszFilename,
              int nMaxSize = MAX_ELEMS,
              double fInitVal = 0);
    ~DiskArray()
      { m_f.close(); }
    virtual void Store(double fVal, int nIndex);
    virtual void Recall(double& fVal, int nIndex);

  protected:
    fstream m_f;
    int m_nMaxSize;
};

void AbstractArray::Show(const char* pszMsg,
                         const int nNumElems,
                         const int bOneLine)
{
  double fVal;

  cout << pszMsg << endl;
  if (bOneLine) {
    for (int i = 0; i < nNumElems; i++) {
      Recall(fVal, i);
      cout << fVal << ' ';
    }
    cout << endl;

  }
  else {
    for (int i = 0; i < nNumElems; i++) {
      Recall(fVal, i);
      cout << fVal << endl;
    }
    cout << endl;
  }
```

```
}
void AbstractArray::Sort(int nNumElems)
{
  int nOffset = nNumElems;
  double nElemI, nElemJ;
  Logical bSorted;

  if (nNumElems < 2)
    return;

  do {
    nOffset = (nOffset * 8) / 11;
    nOffset = (nOffset < 1) ? 1 : nOffset;
    bSorted = TRUE; // set sorted flag
    // compare elements
    for (int i = 0, j = nOffset;
         i < (nNumElems - nOffset);
         i++, j++) {
      Recall(nElemI, i);
      Recall(nElemJ, j);
      if (nElemI > nElemJ) {
        // swap elements
        Store(nElemI, j);
        Store(nElemJ, i);
        bSorted = FALSE; // clear sorted flag
      }
    }
  } while (!bSorted || nOffset != 1);
}

MemArray::MemArray(double fInitVal)
{
  for (int i = 0; i < MAX_ELEMS; i++)
    m_fArray[i] = fInitVal;
}

void MemArray::Store(double fVal, int nIndex)
{
  if (nIndex >= 0 && nIndex < MAX_ELEMS)
    m_fArray[nIndex] = fVal;
}
```

(continued)

Listing 11-1 *(continued)*

```
void MemArray::Recall(double& fVal, int nIndex)
{
  if (nIndex >= 0 && nIndex < MAX_ELEMS)
    fVal = m_fArray[nIndex];
}

DiskArray::DiskArray(const char* pszFilename,
                     int nMaxSize,
                     double fInitVal)
{
  m_f.open(pszFilename, ios::in | ios::out | ios::binary);
  m_nMaxSize = nMaxSize;
  for (int i = 0; i < m_nMaxSize; i++)
    m_f.write((const char*)&fInitVal, sizeof(fInitVal));
}

void DiskArray::Store(double fVal, int nIndex)
{
  if (nIndex >= 0 && nIndex < m_nMaxSize) {
    m_f.seekg(nIndex * sizeof(fVal));
    m_f.write((const char*)&fVal, sizeof(fVal));
  }
}

void DiskArray::Recall(double& fVal, int nIndex)
{
  if (nIndex >= 0 && nIndex < m_nMaxSize) {
    m_f.seekg(nIndex * sizeof(fVal));
    m_f.read((char*)&fVal, sizeof(fVal));
  }
}

main()
{
  double fArr[MAX_ELEMS] = { 33.4, 54.1, 98.2, 47.5, 15.6,
                             81.2, 78.7, 36.7, 63.3, 83.9 };
  MemArray Array;
  DiskArray VirtArray("ARRDATA.DAT");
```

```
  // assign values to the memory-based array
  for (int i = 0; i < MAX_ELEMS; i++)
    Array.Store(fArr[i], i);
  // assign values to the disk-based array
  for (i = 0; i < MAX_ELEMS; i++)
    VirtArray.Store(fArr[i], i);

  Array.Show("Unsorted array is:");
  Array.Sort(MAX_ELEMS);
  Array.Show("Sorted array is:");

  VirtArray.Show("Unsorted disk-based array is:");
  VirtArray.Sort(MAX_ELEMS);
  VirtArray.Show("Sorted disk-based array is:");

  return 0;
}
```

Listing 11-1 declares the class AbstractArray and its descendant classes MemArray and DiskArray. In the following sections, I describe these classes and the function main().

The class AbstractArray

The class AbstractArray, as the name suggests, is an array that models abstract arrays. The class declares no data members (abstract classes can declare data members if they reflect general characteristics common to all descendants), but it declares the following member functions:

- ✔ The virtual member function Store(), which stores an array element. This member function is not defined in the class.

- ✔ The virtual member function Recall(), which recalls an array element. This member function is not defined in the class.

- ✔ The member function Show(), which displays the elements of an array. The definition of this function uses the virtual member function Recall().

- ✔ The member function Sort(), which sorts the array elements. The definition of this function uses the virtual member functions Store() and Recall().

The descendants of the class AbstractArray can use the member functions Show() and Sort() if the descendants define their own versions of the member functions Store() and Recall().

The class MemArray

Listing 11-1 declares the class MemArray as a public descendant of the class AbstractArray. MemArray supports fixed-size arrays that are stored in the protected data member m_fArray. MemArray declares a constructor, the operator [], and the virtual member functions Store() and Recall(). These virtual member functions access the elements in the data member m_fArray.

The class DiskArray

Listing 11-1 declares the class DiskArray as a public descendant of the class AbstractArray. The class declares the following protected data members:

- The data member m_f, which is a file stream object. This member accesses the elements stored in the supporting binary file.
- The int-type data member m_nMaxSize, which stores the maximum number of elements.

The class also declares the following public members:

- The constructor, which opens the file stream and associates it with the argument of the parameter pszFilename. The other parameters of the constructor specify the maximum number of elements and their initial value.
- The destructor, which closes the file stream object by sending it the C++ message close().
- The member function Store(), which stores an array element. The definition of this member function uses the stream member functions seekg() and write() with the data member m_f.
- The member function Recall(), which recalls an array element. The reference parameter nVal passes the recalled value back to the caller. The definition of this member function uses the stream member functions seekg() and read() with the data member m_f.

The function main()

The function main() declares and initializes the C++ array fArr. The function also declares the objects Array and VirtArray as instances of the classes MemArray and DiskArray, respectively. The function main() performs the following tasks:

✔ Copies the values from the array fArr to the elements of the object Array. This task uses a for loop to copy the elements. Each loop iteration sends the C++ message Store() to the object Array. The arguments for this message are the element fArr[i] and the loop control variable i.

✔ Copies the values from the array fArr to the elements of the object VirtArray. This task uses a for loop to copy the elements. Each loop iteration sends the C++ message Store() to the object VirtArray. The arguments for this message are the element fArr[i] and the loop control variable i.

✔ Displays the unsorted elements in the object Array by sending the C++ message Show() to that object. The argument for this message is the string literal "Unsorted array is:".

✔ Sorts the elements in the object Array by sending the C++ message Sort() to that object. The argument for this message is the constant MAX_ELEMS.

✔ Displays the sorted elements in the object Array by sending the C++ message Show() to that object. The argument for this message is the string literal "Sorted array is:".

✔ Displays the unsorted elements in the object VirtArray by sending the C++ message Show() to that object. The argument for this message is the string literal "Unsorted disk-based array is:".

✔ Sorts the elements in the object VirtArray by sending the C++ message Sort() to that object. The argument for this message is the constant MAX_ELEMS.

✔ Displays the sorted elements in the object VirtArray by sending the C++ message Show() to that object. The argument for this message is the string literal "Sorted disk-based array is:".

Declaring a Hierarchy with Multiple Abstract Classes: The More the Merrier

C++ allows you to declare abstract classes that are descendants of other abstract classes. You can set the number of abstract descendant classes to as many levels as are needed. The syntax for declaring abstract descendant classes is the same as the syntax for declaring nonabstract descendant classes:

```
class abstractClassName : [public] parentAbstractClassName
{
  public:
    // declarations of public members
```

(continued)

(continued)

```
    protected:
    // declarations of protected members

    private:
    // declarations of private members
};
```

How can the C++ compiler distinguish between an abstract descendant class and a nonabstract descendant class? Mr. Compiler considers a descendant class as abstract if it fulfills either of the following requirements:

- ✔ The descendant class declares additional pure virtual member functions.
- ✔ The descendant class declares member functions that use the inherited pure virtual member functions but does not define them.

The example program that I describe in this section contains multiple-level abstract classes. Recall that Listing 11-1 shows a single-level abstract class that supports arrays that store floating-point numbers. The abstract class AbstractArray in that listing defines the member functions Show() and Sort() to display and sort the array elements, respectively.

You can split the class AbstractArray in Listing 11-1 into two abstract classes, (the new) AbstractArray and its descendant OrderedAbstractArray. The member function Sort() is contained in the descendant abstract class OrderedAbstractArray and not in its parent class (AbstractArray).

Figure 11-2 shows the new class hierarchy. Notice that in this new hierarchy, the nonabstract class MemArray is a descendant of the class OrderedAbstractArray, whereas the nonabstract class DiskArray is a descendant of the class AbstractArray. This means that the instances of the class DiskArray cannot receive the C++ message Sort(), because the member function Sort() is no longer part of the class AbstractArray.

Figure 11-2:
The class hierarchy for the multiple-level abstract classes example.

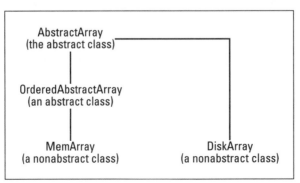

As this example demonstrates, you can create nonabstract descendant classes from the abstract classes in the class hierarchy. Note that you may not be able to create such classes if the upper-level abstract classes are just too abstract to create nonabstract descendant classes.

The ABSTRAC2.CPP program performs the following tasks with the instances of the classes `MemArray` and `DiskArray`:

✔ Displays the unsorted elements in the instance of the class `MemArray`

✔ Sorts elements in the instance of the class `MemArray`

✔ Displays the sorted elements in the instance of the class `MemArray`

✔ Displays the unsorted elements in the instance of the class `DiskArray`

Here is the output from the ABSTRAC2.CPP program:

```
Unsorted array is:
33.4 54.1 98.2 47.5 15.6 81.2 78.7 36.7 63.3 83.9
Sorted array is:
15.6 33.4 36.7 47.5 54.1 63.3 78.7 81.2 83.9 98.2
Disk-based array is:
33.4 54.1 98.2 47.5 15.6 81.2 78.7 36.7 63.3 83.9
```

Listing 11-2 shows the source code for the ABSTRAC2.CPP program.

Listing 11-1	ABSTRAC2.CPP

```
// A C++ program that illustrates
// multiple-level abstract classes

#include <fstream.h>
#include <iomanip.h>

enum Logical { FALSE, TRUE };

const int MAX_ELEMS = 10;

class AbstractArray
{
  public:
    virtual void Store(double fVal, int nIndex) = 0;
    virtual void Recall(double& fVal, int nIndex) = 0;
```

(continued)

Listing 11-2 *(continued)*

```
    void Show(const char* pszMsg = "",
              const int nNumElems = MAX_ELEMS,
              const int bOneLine = TRUE);
};

class OrderedAbstractArray : public AbstractArray
{
  public:
    void Sort(int nNumElems);
};

class MemArray : public OrderedAbstractArray
{
  public:
    MemArray(double fInitVal = 0);
    double& operator[](int nIndex)
      { return m_fArray[nIndex]; }
    virtual void Store(double fVal, int nIndex);
    virtual void Recall(double& fVal, int nIndex);

  protected:
    double m_fArray[MAX_ELEMS];
};

class DiskArray : public AbstractArray
{
  public:
    DiskArray(const char* pszFilename,
              int nMaxSize = MAX_ELEMS,
              double fInitVal = 0);
    ~DiskArray()
      { m_f.close(); }
    virtual void Store(double fVal, int nIndex);
    virtual void Recall(double& fVal, int nIndex);

  protected:
    fstream m_f;
    int m_nMaxSize;
};

void AbstractArray::Show(const char* pszMsg,
                         const int nNumElems,
                         const int bOneLine)
```

```
{
  double fVal;

  cout << pszMsg << endl;
  if (bOneLine) {
    for (int i = 0; i < nNumElems; i++) {
      Recall(fVal, i);
      cout << fVal << ' ';
    }
    cout << endl;

  }
  else {
    for (int i = 0; i < nNumElems; i++) {
      Recall(fVal, i);
      cout << fVal << endl;
    }
    cout << endl;
  }
}

void OrderedAbstractArray::Sort(int nNumElems)
{
  int nOffset = nNumElems;
  double nElemI, nElemJ;
  Logical bSorted;

  if (nNumElems < 2)
    return;

  do {
    nOffset = (nOffset * 8) / 11;
    nOffset = (nOffset < 1) ? 1 : nOffset;
    bSorted = TRUE; // set sorted flag
    // compare elements
    for (int i = 0, j = nOffset;
         i < (nNumElems - nOffset);
         i++, j++) {
      Recall(nElemI, i);
      Recall(nElemJ, j);
      if (nElemI > nElemJ) {
```

(continued)

Listing 11-2 *(continued)*

```
          // swap elements
          Store(nElemI, j);
          Store(nElemJ, i);
          bSorted = FALSE; // clear sorted flag
      }
    }
  } while (!bSorted || nOffset != 1);
}


MemArray::MemArray(double fInitVal)
{
  for (int i = 0; i < MAX_ELEMS; i++)
    m_fArray[i] = fInitVal;
}

void MemArray::Store(double fVal, int nIndex)
{
  if (nIndex >= 0 && nIndex < MAX_ELEMS)
    m_fArray[nIndex] = fVal;
}

void MemArray::Recall(double& fVal, int nIndex)
{
  if (nIndex >= 0 && nIndex < MAX_ELEMS)
    fVal = m_fArray[nIndex];
}

DiskArray::DiskArray(const char* pszFilename,
                     int nMaxSize,
                     double fInitVal)
{
  m_f.open(pszFilename, ios::in | ios::out | ios::binary);
  m_nMaxSize = nMaxSize;
  for (int i = 0; i < m_nMaxSize; i++)
    m_f.write((const char*)&fInitVal, sizeof(fInitVal));
}

void DiskArray::Store(double fVal, int nIndex)
{
  if (nIndex >= 0 && nIndex < m_nMaxSize) {
    m_f.seekg(nIndex * sizeof(fVal));
    m_f.write((const char*)&fVal, sizeof(fVal));
  }
```

```
}

void DiskArray::Recall(double& fVal, int nIndex)
{
  if (nIndex >= 0 && nIndex < m_nMaxSize) {
    m_f.seekg(nIndex * sizeof(fVal));
    m_f.read((char*)&fVal, sizeof(fVal));
  }
}

main()
{
  double fArr[MAX_ELEMS] = { 33.4, 54.1, 98.2, 47.5, 15.6,
                             81.2, 78.7, 36.7, 63.3, 83.9 };
  MemArray Array;
  DiskArray VirtArray("ARRDATA.DAT");

  // assign values to the memory-based array
  for (int i = 0; i < MAX_ELEMS; i++)
    Array.Store(fArr[i], i);
  // assign values to the disk-based array
  for (i = 0; i < MAX_ELEMS; i++)
    VirtArray.Store(fArr[i], i);

  Array.Show("Unsorted array is:");
  Array.Sort(MAX_ELEMS);
  Array.Show("Sorted array is:");

  VirtArray.Show("Disk-based array is:");

  return 0;
}
```

Because Listings 11-1 and 11-2 are very similar, I want to focus on the differences between the two listings:

- ✔ The class AbstractArray no longer declares the member function Sort().
- ✔ The class OrderedAbstractArray is a descendant of AbstractArray and is also an abstract class. This class declares only the member function Sort(). The compiler determines that this class is abstract, because the class does not define the member functions Store() and Recall().

✔ The class `MemArray` is a descendant of the class `OrderedAbstractArray`. This class defines the member functions `Store()` and `Recall()` and inherits the member functions `Show()` and `Sort()`.

✔ The class `DiskArray` is a descendant of the class `AbstractArray`. This class defines the member functions `Store()` and `Recall()` and inherits the member function `Show()`.

✔ The function `main()` does not sort the elements in the object `VirtArray`, because that instance cannot receive the C++ message `Sort()`.

✔ The function `main()` does not display the sorted elements of the object `VirtArray` because the object cannot be sorted (unless the function `main()` does the sorting).

Listing 11-2 shows you two levels of abstract classes: one that supports general arrays of integers and another that supports sorted arrays of integers. This example shows that the class hierarchy is more flexible with two abstract classes than with the one abstract class used in Listing 11-1.

Listing 11-2 declares a class of disk-based arrays that are not ordered. You can expand the class hierarchy to declare another class to support sorted disk-based arrays. In general terms, the more abstract classes you have in a hierarchy, the more choices you have for descendant classes. Consequently, the design shown in Listing 11-2 is more flexible than the one in Listing 11-1.

Summary

In this chapter, you've learned how to declare and use abstract classes in C++ class hierarchies. As the examples in this chapter demonstrate, the effective use of abstract classes can lend greater flexibility to the design of your class hierarchies.

Chapter 12

Templates: Class Factories

· ·

In This Chapter

▶ Understanding class templates

▶ Declaring class templates

▶ Defining the member functions of class templates

▶ Instantiating class templates

▶ Creating hierarchies of class templates

· ·

*T*he template feature was added to C++ just a few years ago. C++ supports the creation of function templates and class templates. These functions and classes are not tied to specific data types. Instead, they represent generic versions of functions and classes. When you declare a function template or a class template, you postpone declaring the one or more specific data types and instead use *general* template parameters. You can think of templates as sophisticated macros (C and C++ allow you to create macros using the #define directive that works by substituting text). In this chapter, you find out about class template declaration, class template implementation, class template instances, template parameters, class derivation, and template instantiation.

What Are Class Templates?

Sooner or later, you'll find yourself creating and recreating new versions of classes that accommodate new data types by using existing classes that support other data types. This process of cutting and pasting source code can really get out of control. For example, imagine having to create array classes that sort and search data for every predefined data type and every user-defined type that you work with! The nightmare part in this scenario comes when you want to update the code for a replicated function to make it more efficient. Horror of horrors!! You have to go back and edit every single version of that class to provide the improvement to all the supported data types. Duhh!! This kind of programming is not too smart.

And now the good news. C++ offers a solution to this problem — *templates*. Using this programming feature, you can create general-purpose (or *generic,* if you prefer) classes that are not tied to a specific data type. Instead, these templates use template parameters that represent general data types. When the compiler encounters a class template, it switches to a learning mode and mainly memorizes the template source code. To use a class template, you (and Mr. Compiler) *instantiate* (yet another new buzzword to learn) that template. This process involves associating the template parameters with defined data types. When the compiler instantiates a template, it generates code and then verifies that code. If you have not provided sufficient information — for example, if you did not define operators needed for the class that instantiates the template — the instantiation may cause the compiler to generate error messages indicating that it cannot instantiate the template.

Class templates empower you to write generic classes that handle various data types in a similar manner. The proposed C++ standard includes a Standard Template Library (STL) that supports popular data structures such as arrays, lists, queues, and stacks.

Declaring Class Templates: Setting the Specs

C++ allows you to declare class templates to represent objects whose exact data types are defined during instantiation. In other words, class templates are more abstract than ordinary classes. Class templates are commonly used to build generic data structures, such as arrays, stacks, queues, lists, trees, and hash tables— just to name a few.

You use the following general syntax for declaring a base class template:

```
template <class T [, other template parameters]>
class className
{
  // declarations of nested structures, enumerated types,
  // classes, and friend classes

  public:
    // public constructors
    // public destructor
    // public member functions
    // public data members
```

```
protected:
  // protected constructors
  // protected destructor
  // protected member functions
  // protected data members

private:
  // private constructors
  // private destructor
  // private member functions
  // private data members
};
```

This syntax shows that declaring a base class template is not very different from declaring an ordinary base class. Class templates have to follow the same rules as ordinary classes, plus some special rules for templates.

The syntax of the class template shows that its declaration starts with the keyword template, followed by the list of template parameters enclosed in angle brackets. The list of template classes enumerates one or more template parameters. You can use the keyword class or any predefined type with these template parameters. When you use the keyword class, you tell the compiler that you can instantiate the template class with user-defined classes, structures, and predefined types. In contrast, when you specify a predefined type, you specify that the argument for that template parameter must be a compatible type.

Most of the class templates you see or write yourself have one template parameter. Here is the skeleton declaration of a typical sample class template:

```
template <class T>
class myTemplateCoordinate
{
  // declarations of members
};
```

The class myTemplateCoordinate uses the single template parameter T. Here is the skeleton declaration of a sample class template that uses two template parameters:

```
template <class ValueType, class NodeType>
class myTemplateHashTable
{
  // declarations of members
};
```

The class myTemplateHashTable uses the template parameters Value Type and NodeType. Here is an example using class and nonclass template parameters:

```
template <class T, int arraySize>
class myArray
{
    // declarations of members
};
```

The class myArray uses the class T and int arraySize template parameters.

Defining the Member Functions of Class Templates

C++ requires the following syntax for defining the member functions of class templates:

```
template <class T, ...>
returnType classTemplate<T,
...>::memberFunction(parameterList)
{
    // statements
}
```

Notice the following aspects of this general syntax:

- ✓ The definition of the member function starts with the keyword template, followed by the angle brackets that contain the list of template parameters.

- ✓ The name of the class template is followed by the angle brackets that contain the list of template parameter identifiers. In fact, C++ requires that you use this syntax with all references to the class template.

Here is an example of a class template declaration and the definition of one of its member functions:

```
template <class T, int arraySize>
class myArray
{
    // declarations of members
    T& operator[](int nIndex);
    // declarations of other members
    T* m_pData;
};
```

```
template <class T, int arraySize>
T& myArray<T, arraySize>::operator [](int nIndex)
{
  return m_pData[nIndex];
}
```

The class myArray (which is the same class presented earlier in this section) declares the operator []. Notice that the definition of the operator starts with template <class T, int arraySize>. In addition, the definition uses the class name myArray<T, arraySize>:: and not just myArray::.

Instantiating Class Templates: A Class Is Born!

Instantiating class templates is easy in C++. You declare an instantiated class template by specifying the actual types for the template parameters. Here is an example:

```
class Circle
{
  // declarations
};

main()
{
  myArray<int, 20> intArray;
  myArray<double, 1000> dblArray;
  myArray<long, 20> longArray;
  myArray<char, 80> charArray;
  myArray<Circle, 20> CircleArray;

  // statements

  return 0;
}
```

This example instantiates the class myArray with the types int, double, long, char, and Circle. The first four types are predefined types, whereas the last type is a user-defined class.

The following programming example illustrates template classes. The TEMPLAT1.CPP program models a class template that supports generic arrays. The program declares the class template `myArray` and the class `myString`. The program uses the class template to create dynamic arrays of integers, characters, and strings (using the class `myString`) and to perform the following tasks for each kind of array:

- ✔ Assigning values to the array elements
- ✔ Displaying the unsorted array elements
- ✔ Sorting the elements of the array
- ✔ Displaying the sorted array elements

Here is the output from the TEMPLAT1.CPP program:

```
Unsorted array is:
89 34 32 47 15 81 78 36 63 83

Sorted array is:
15 32 34 36 47 63 78 81 83 89

Unsorted array is:
C W r Y k J X Z y s

Sorted array is:
C J W X Y Z k r s y

Unsorted array is:
London
Paris
Madrid
Rome
Athens
Bern
Lisbon
Warsaw
Berlin
Dublin

Sorted array is:
Athens
Berlin
```

```
Bern
Dublin
Lisbon
London
Madrid
Paris
Rome
Warsaw
```

Listing 12-1 shows the source code for the TEMPLAT1.CPP program.

Listing 12-1	**TEMPLAT1.CPP**

```
// A C++ program that illustrates
// template classes

#include <iostream.h>
#include <iomanip.h>
#include <string.h>

const int MIN_SIZE = 30;

enum Logical { FALSE, TRUE };

///
/// ---------- class myArray ----------
///

template <class T>
class myArray
{
  public:
    myArray(int nSize, T InitVal);
    ~myArray()
      { delete [] m_pArray; }
    T& operator[](int nIndex)
      { return m_pArray[nIndex]; }
    void Show(const int nNumElems,
          const char* pszMsg = "",
          const Logical bOneLine = TRUE);
    void Sort(int nNumElems);
```

(continued)

Listing 12-1 *(continued)*

```
   protected:
    T* m_pArray;
    int m_nSize;
};

template <class T>
myArray<T>::myArray(int nSize, T InitVal)
{
  m_nSize = (nSize > 1) ? nSize : 1;
  m_pArray = new T[m_nSize];
  for (int i = 0; i < m_nSize; i++)
    m_pArray[i] = InitVal;
}

template <class T>
void myArray<T>::Show(const int nNumElems,
            const char* pszMsg,
            const Logical bOneLine)
{
  cout << pszMsg << endl;
  if (bOneLine) {
    for (int i = 0; i < nNumElems; i++)
      cout << m_pArray[i] << ' ';
    cout << endl;
  }
  else {
    for (int i = 0; i < nNumElems; i++)
      cout << m_pArray[i] << endl;
    cout << endl;
  }
}

template <class T>
void myArray<T>::Sort(int nNumElems)
{
  int nOffset = nNumElems;
  Logical bSorted;

  // check argument of parameter nNumElems
  if (nNumElems < 2)
    return;

  do{
```

```
      nOffset = (nOffset * 8) / 11;
      nOffset = (nOffset < 1) ? 1 : nOffset;
      bSorted = TRUE; // set sorted flag
      // compare elements
      for (int i = 0, j = nOffset;
           i < (nNumElems - nOffset);
           i++, j++) {
        if (m_pArray[i] > m_pArray[j]) {
          // swap elements
          T nSwap = m_pArray[i];
          m_pArray[i] = m_pArray[j];
          m_pArray[j] = nSwap;
          bSorted = FALSE; // clear sorted flag
        }
      }
    } while (!bSorted || nOffset != 1);
}


///
/// ---------- class myString ----------
///

class myString
{
  public:
    myString(int nSize = MIN_SIZE)
      { m_pszString = new char[m_nSize = nSize]; }
    myString(myString& aString);
    myString(const char* pszString);
    myString(const char cChar);
    ~myString()
      { delete [] m_pszString; }
    int getLen()
      { return strlen(m_pszString); }
    int getMaxLen()
      { return m_nSize; }
    myString& operator =(myString& aString);
    myString& operator =(const char* pszString);
    myString& operator =(const char cChar);
    friend int operator >(myString& aString1, myString&↵
    aString2)
      { return (strcmp(aString1.m_pszString,
                  aString2.m_pszString) > 0) ? 1 : 0; }
```

(continued)

Listing 12-1 *(continued)*

```
      friend ostream& operator <<(ostream& os, myString&⊃
      aString);

  protected:
    char* m_pszString;
    int m_nSize;
};

myString::myString(myString& aString)
{
  m_pszString = new char[m_nSize = aString.m_nSize];
  strcpy(m_pszString, aString.m_pszString);
}

myString::myString(const char* pszString)
{
  m_pszString = new char[m_nSize = strlen(pszString) + 1];
  strcpy(m_pszString, pszString);
}

myString::myString(const char cChar)
{
  m_pszString = new char[m_nSize = MIN_SIZE];
  m_pszString[0] = cChar;
  m_pszString[1] = '\0';
}

myString& myString::operator =(myString& aString)
{
  // source string small enough to copy?
  if (strlen(aString.m_pszString) < unsigned(m_nSize))
    strcpy(m_pszString, aString.m_pszString);
  else
    // copy first m_nSize - 1 characters
    strncpy(m_pszString, aString.m_pszString, m_nSize - 1);
  return *this;
}

myString& myString::operator =(const char* pszString)
{
  // source string small enough to copy?
  if (strlen(pszString) < unsigned(m_nSize))
```

```
      strcpy(m_pszString, pszString);
    else
      // copy first m_nSize - 1 characters
      strncpy(m_pszString, pszString, m_nSize - 1);
    return *this;
}

myString& myString::operator =(const char cChar)
{
  if (m_nSize > 1) {
    m_pszString[0] = cChar;
    m_pszString[1] = '\0';
  }
  return *this;
}

ostream& operator <<(ostream& os, myString& aString)
{
  os << aString.m_pszString;
  return os;
}

main()
{
  const int MAX_ELEMS = 10;
  int nArr[MAX_ELEMS] = { 89, 34, 32, 47, 15,
              81, 78, 36, 63, 83 };
  int cArr[MAX_ELEMS] = { 'C', 'W', 'r', 'Y', 'k',
              'J', 'X', 'Z', 'y', 's' };

  myArray<int> IntegerArray(MAX_ELEMS, 0);
  myArray<char> CharArray(MAX_ELEMS, ' ');
  myArray<myString> StringArray(MAX_ELEMS, "");

  // assign integers to elements of array IntegerArray
  for (int i = 0; i < MAX_ELEMS; i++)
    IntegerArray[i] = nArr[i];
  // assign characters to elements of array CharArray
  for (i = 0; i < MAX_ELEMS; i++)
    CharArray[i] = cArr[i];
  // assign strings to elements of array stringArray
  StringArray[0] = "London";
```

(continued)

Listing 12-1 (continued)

```
    StringArray[1] = "Paris";
    StringArray[2] = "Madrid";
    StringArray[3] = "Rome";
    StringArray[4] = "Athens";
    StringArray[5] = "Bern";
    StringArray[6] = "Lisbon";
    StringArray[7] = "Warsaw";
    StringArray[8] = "Berlin";
    StringArray[9] = "Dublin";

    // test array IntegerArray
    IntegerArray.Show(MAX_ELEMS, "Unsorted array is:");
    IntegerArray.Sort(MAX_ELEMS);
    IntegerArray.Show(MAX_ELEMS, "Sorted array is:");
    cout << "\n\n";

    // test array CharArray
    CharArray.Show(MAX_ELEMS, "Unsorted array is:");
    CharArray.Sort(MAX_ELEMS);
    CharArray.Show(MAX_ELEMS, "Sorted array is:");
    cout << "\n\n";

    StringArray.Show(MAX_ELEMS, "Unsorted array is:", FALSE);
    StringArray.Sort(MAX_ELEMS);
    StringArray.Show(MAX_ELEMS, "Sorted array is:", FALSE);

    return 0;
}
```

Listing 12-1 declares the class template myArray, the class myString, and the function main(). The following sections discuss these program components in more detail.

The class template myArray

The listing declares the class template myArray to have the template parameter T that represents the type of each array element. The class template declares protected and public members. Here are the protected members:

- The data member m_pArray, which is a pointer to the template parameter T. This member accesses the dynamic array.

- The int-type data member m_nSize, which stores the number of elements in the dynamic array.

The class template declares the following public members:

- The constructor, which creates the dynamic array and initializes it using the T-type parameter InitVal.

- The destructor, which frees the memory allocated to the dynamic array.

- The operator [], which accesses the elements of the dynamic array. The operator returns a reference to the template parameter T.

- The member function Show(), which displays the elements of the dynamic array. This member function requires that you define the operator << for the instantiating data type.

- The member function Sort(), which sorts the elements of the dynamic array. Using this member function requires that you define the operators = and > for the instantiating data types.

The definition of each member function follows the general syntax that I mentioned in the section "Defining the Member Functions of Class Templates"— the definition starts with the keywords template <class T> and uses myArray<T>:: (instead of just myArray::) to qualify the name of the member function.

Using the class template myArray requires that you define the operators <<, >, and = for the instantiating data types.

The class myString

The listing declares the class myString, which models a string class that instantiates the class template myArray. The class myString declares constructors, a destructor, the member function getLen(), the member function getMaxLen(), the operator =, the friend operator >, and the friend operator <<. The class needs the last three operators to work with the member functions Sort() and Show() in the class template.

The function main()

The function main() declares and initializes the int-type array nArr and the char-type array cArr. The function also declares the following objects:

✔ The object `IntegerArray`, which instantiates the class template `myArray` with the predefined type `int`. The function creates `MAX_ELEMS` elements and initializes them with zeros.

✔ The object `CharArray`, which instantiates the class template `myArray` with the predefined type `char`. The function creates `MAX_ELEMS` elements and initializes them with the space character.

✔ The object `StringArray`, which instantiates the class template `myArray` with the class `myString`. The function creates `MAX_ELEMS` elements and initializes them with null strings.

The function `main()` performs the following tasks:

✔ Assigns integers to the elements of the array `IntegerArray`. This task uses a `for` loop to copy the elements of the array `nArr` into the elements of the array `IntegerArray`.

✔ Assigns characters to the elements of the array `CharArray`. This task uses a `for` loop to copy the elements of the array `cArr` into the elements of the array `CharArray`.

✔ Assigns string literals to the elements of the array `StringArray`. This task uses a set of assignment statements.

✔ Displays the unsorted elements in the object `IntegerArray` by sending the C++ message `Show()` to that object. The arguments for the message are the constant `MAX_ELEMS` and the string literal `"Unsorted array is:"`.

✔ Sorts the elements in the object `IntegerArray` by sending the C++ message `Sort()` to that object. The argument for the message is the constant `MAX_ELEMS`.

✔ Displays the sorted elements in the object `IntegerArray` by sending the C++ message `Show()` to that object. The arguments for the message are the constant `MAX_ELEMS` and the string literal `"Sorted array is:"`.

✔ Displays the unsorted elements in the object `CharArray` by sending the C++ message `Show()` to that object. The arguments for the message are the constant `MAX_ELEMS` and the string literal `"Unsorted array is:"`.

✔ Sorts the elements in the object `CharArray` by sending the C++ message `Sort()` to that object. The argument for the message is the constant `MAX_ELEMS`.

✔ Displays the sorted elements in the object `CharArray` by sending the C++ message `Show()` to that object. The arguments for the message are the constant `MAX_ELEMS` and the string literal `"Sorted array is:"`.

✔ Displays the unsorted elements in the object `StringArray` by sending the C++ message `Show()` to that object. The arguments for the message are the constant `MAX_ELEMS` and the string literal `"Unsorted array is:"`.

✔ Sorts the elements in the object `StringArray` by sending the C++ message `Sort()` to that object. The argument for the message is the constant `MAX_ELEMS`.

✔ Displays the sorted elements in the object `StringArray` by sending the C++ message `Show()` to that object. The arguments for the message are the constant `MAX_ELEMS` and the string literal `"Sorted array is:"`.

Declaring Hierarchies of Class Templates: When One Is Not Enough

C++ allows you to declare descendants of class templates. You use the following general syntax for declaring a descendant class template:

```
template <class T, ...>
class className : [public] parentClass [, otherParentClasses]
{
  // declarations of nested structures, enumerated types,
  // classes, and friend classes

  public:
    // public constructors
    // public destructor
    // public member functions
    // public data members

  protected:
    // protected constructors
    // protected destructor
    // protected member functions
    // protected data members

  private:
    // private constructors
    // private destructor
    // private member functions
    // private data members
};
```

C++ requires that when you use descendant class templates, you observe the same rules that apply for ordinary descendant classes. In fact, you can create an ordinary descendant class from a class template. You also can create abstract class templates. Thus, C++ allows you to implement powerful class templates that significantly reduce the number of classes that perform the same tasks on different data types.

Here is an example of a declaration of a descendant class template:

```
template <class T>
class myArray
{
  // declarations of members
};

template <class T>
class myRamArray : public myArray<T>
{
  // declarations of members
};
```

This example declares the class template myArray and its descendant class myRamArray. Notice that the reference to the parent class uses public myArray<T> instead of public myArray. This syntax conforms to the rule that requires stating the template parameter identifiers when referencing the class template.

The following programming example illustrates descendant class templates. The TEMPLAT2.CPP program declares the class templates myArray and mySortedArray. Notice that each class has not one, but two, template parameters, namely class T and int nSize. The first parameter represents the basic type of the dynamic array. The second template parameter is an int-type parameter that specifies the number of array elements. Thus, the template arrays support a special version of nondynamic array in which the number of elements is decided during the instantiation process.

The TEMPLAT2.CPP program declares the class mySortedArray as the descendant of the class myArray. The class myArray supports only indexing and displaying array elements. The descendant class template mySortedArray supports sorting the array elements. The program instantiates the class template mySortedArray to create, initialize, display, sort, and redisplay arrays of integers and characters. To keep the listing short, I did not include a user-defined class (such as myString) as I did in Listing 12-1.

Here is the output from the TEMPLAT2.CPP program:

```
Unsorted array is:
89 34 32 47 15 81 78 36 63 83

Sorted array is:
15 32 34 36 47 63 78 81 83 89

Unsorted array is:
C W r Y k J X Z y s

Sorted array is:
C J W X Y Z k r s y
```

Listing 12-2 shows the source code for the TEMPLAT2.CPP program.

Listing 12-2	**TEMPLAT2.CPP**

```cpp
// A C++ program that illustrates
// descendant class templates

#include <iostream.h>
#include <iomanip.h>

enum Logical { FALSE, TRUE };

template <class T, int nSize>
class myArray
{
  public:
    myArray(T InitVal);
    T& operator[](int nIndex)
      { return m_Array[nIndex]; }
    void Show(const int nNumElems,
          const char* pszMsg = "",
          const Logical bOneLine = TRUE);

  protected:
    T m_Array[nSize];
    int m_nSize;
};

template <class T, int nSize>
```

(continued)

Listing 12-2 (continued)

```cpp
class mySortedArray : public myArray<T, nSize>
{
  public:
    mySortedArray(T InitVal)
      : myArray<T, nSize>(InitVal) {}
    void Sort(int nNumElems);
};

template <class T, int nSize>
myArray<T, nSize>::myArray(T InitVal)
{
  m_nSize = nSize;
  for (int i = 0; i < m_nSize; i++)
    m_Array[i] = InitVal;
}

template <class T, int nSize>
void myArray<T, nSize>::Show(const int nNumElems,
                const char* pszMsg,
                const Logical bOneLine)
{
  cout << pszMsg << endl;
  if (bOneLine) {
    for (int i = 0; i < nNumElems; i++)
      cout << m_Array[i] << ' ';
    cout << endl;
  }
  else {
    for (int i = 0; i < nNumElems; i++)
      cout << m_Array[i] << endl;
    cout << endl;
  }
}

template <class T, int nSize>
void mySortedArray<T, nSize>::Sort(int nNumElems)
{
  int nOffset = nNumElems;
  Logical bSorted;
```

```
    // check argument of parameter nNumElems
    if (nNumElems < 2)
      return;

    do {
      nOffset = (nOffset * 8) / 11;
      nOffset = (nOffset < 1) ? 1 : nOffset;
      bSorted = TRUE; // set sorted flag
      // compare elements
      for (int i = 0, j = nOffset;
           i < (nNumElems - nOffset);
           i++, j++) {
        if (m_Array[i] > m_Array[j]) {
          // swap elements
          T nSwap = m_Array[i];
          m_Array[i] = m_Array[j];
          m_Array[j] = nSwap;
          bSorted = FALSE; // clear sorted flag
        }
      }
    } while (!bSorted || nOffset != 1);
}

main()
{
  const int MAX_ELEMS = 10;
  int nArr[MAX_ELEMS] = { 89, 34, 32, 47, 15,
                81, 78, 36, 63, 83 };
  int cArr[MAX_ELEMS] = { 'C', 'W', 'r', 'Y', 'k',
                'J', 'X', 'Z', 'y', 's' };

  mySortedArray<int, MAX_ELEMS> IntegerArray(0);
  mySortedArray<char, MAX_ELEMS> CharArray(' ');

  // assign integers to elements of array IntegerArray
  for (int i = 0; i < MAX_ELEMS; i++)
    IntegerArray[i] = nArr[i];
  // assign characters to elements of array CharArray
  for (i = 0; i < MAX_ELEMS; i++)
    CharArray[i] = cArr[i];
```

(continued)

Listing 12-2 *(continued)*

```
// test array IntegerArray
IntegerArray.Show(MAX_ELEMS, "Unsorted array is:");
IntegerArray.Sort(MAX_ELEMS);
IntegerArray.Show(MAX_ELEMS, "Sorted array is:");
cout << "\n\n";

// test array CharArray
CharArray.Show(MAX_ELEMS, "Unsorted array is:");
CharArray.Sort(MAX_ELEMS);
CharArray.Show(MAX_ELEMS, "Sorted array is:");


cout << "\n\n";

return 0;
}
```

Listing 12-2 declares the class template myArray with the template parameters
class T and int nSize. The listing also declares the descendant class
template mySortedArray with the same template parameters. Notice that the
declaration of the descendant class template refers to the parent class template
as myArray<T, nSize> and not just myArray. The class template myArray
declares a constructor, the operator [], and the member function Show().
The descendant class template declares a constructor and the member
function Sort().

The function main() creates the objects IntegerArray and CharArray by
instantiating the class template mySortedArray using the int and char
types (for the first template parameters), respectively. The source code for
assigning values to these objects and manipulating them is very similar to the
code in Listing 12-1.

Summary

This chapter shows you the versatility of class templates. You've read that by
using a class template you can create a single (and general) version of a class
that supports various kinds of data types. You've also read about how to
instantiate a class template using predefined or previously defined data types.
The power of class templates takes code reuse one very important step further.

Chapter 13

Exceptions: Run-Time Errors, OOP Style

● ●

In This Chapter

▶ Understanding exceptions

▶ Declaring exception classes

▶ Learning about standard exceptions

▶ Throwing an exception

▶ Using the `try` block

▶ Working with the `catch` clauses

▶ Using nested `try-catch` blocks

▶ Rethrowing an exception

▶ Associating functions and exceptions

● ●

*R*un-time errors are somewhat akin to car accidents. They are unfortunate and very aggravating. This chapter shows you how to deal with run-time errors in C++. The interesting aspect of error handling in C++ is that it involves classes and objects. In other words, C++ supports error handling by using object-oriented programming techniques.

This chapter discusses the throw-and-catch metaphor for error handling in C++ and talks about the syntax for generating and managing run-time errors. The chapter also covers issues related to fine-tuning error handling in your C++ programs.

What's an Exception? Yet Another Buzzword?

The more complex a program is, the more prone it is to run-time errors. How do you handle run-time errors? The answer depends on the programming language that you're using.

In languages such as C++, the programmer needs to resort to *defensive programming* techniques (not too thrilling, if you ask me). Many C++ functions return error codes if they cannot perform their task (such as opening a file for I/O operations). This kind of function enables you to test the waters, so to speak, before you jump in feet first. In other words, your program can check for these error codes before continuing with whatever tasks it's performing. Other languages, such as Microsoft MS-BASIC and Visual Basic, have formal error handling features. Such features enable the program flow to jump to another part of a routine if an error occurs (if you're one of those people who puts down BASIC, better think again).

C++ supports exceptions and exception handling to detect and manage run-time errors. The word *exception* comes from the *exceptional program flow* that occurs in response to a run-time error. In answer to the second part of the heading of this section, yes, *exception* is a new buzzword. I think that some OOP gurus are not busy enough!

To handle exceptions, C++ uses classes and objects and the metaphor of throwing and catching exceptions. Either the run-time system or your code *throws* exceptions. You need to insert statements in your code to *catch* and handle these thrown exceptions.

Exception Classes: Ready to Take the Blame!

C++ uses classes to represent and encapsulate exceptions. Two general kinds of classes model exceptions:

- ✔ **Skeleton classes:** These classes have no members because their names are sufficient to refer to and handle the exception.

- ✔ **Classes with data members:** These classes declare data members that enable them to better describe the exception.

Here are some examples of exception classes:

```
class badNumberException {};
class badLogicException {};
class badFileException
{
  public:
    char m_pszFilename[31];
};
```

The first two examples are skeleton classes that model exceptions that handle input and a range of values. These classes have no members. The last example declares an exception class that has the data member m_pszFilename. The class, supposedly, uses this data member to describe which file failed a file I/O operation.

Introducing Standard Exceptions

C++ defines a set of basic exception classes that represent the most common run-time errors. Table 13-1 lists these exceptions and indicates their lineage.

Table 13-1	The Standard Exceptions	
Exception Class	*Parent Class*	*Purpose*
exception	(none)	The base class for all of the exceptions thrown by the C++ standard library
logic_error	exception	Reports logical program errors that can be detected *before* the program proceeds with executing subsequent statements
runtime_error	exception	Reports run-time errors that are detected *when* the program executes certain statements
ios::failure	exception	Reports stream I/O errors
domain_error	logic_error	Reports the infraction of a condition
invalid_argument	logic_error	Signals that the argument of a function is not valid
length_error	logic_error	Signals that an operation attempts to create an object with a length that exceeds or is equal to NPOS (the biggest value of the type size_t)
out_of_range	logic_error	Signals that an argument is out of range
bad_cast	logic_error	Reports an invalid dynamic cast expression during run-time type identification
bad_typeid	logic_error	Reports a null pointer in a type identifying expression
range_error	runtime_error	Signals an invalid postcondition
overflow_error	runtime_error	Signals arithmetic overflow
bad_alloc	runtime_error	Signals the failure of dynamic allocation

Throwing an Exception: Let's See How Tough Your Code Is

C++ offers the `throw` statement to throw an exception (which is either a predefined data item or an instance of an exception class). Here is the general syntax for the `throw` statement:

```
throw exceptionObject;
```

The `exceptionObject` can be a predefined type or an exception class instance. An exception class instance can be a previously declared instance or a temporary instance that was created by using the constructor of the exception class. Here are examples of throwing exceptions:

```
class badValueException {  public:
    badValueException(int nVal = 0)
      { cout << nVal << " is a bad value\n"; }
};

int nBadVal;

throw badValueException(100);
throw nBadVal;
```

This code snippet shows two `throw` statements. The first one throws an instance of an exception class. The second throws an `int`-type variable. Please keep in mind that I have not yet introduced you to the `try` statement that should contain the `throw` statements. Also, I have not yet introduced you to the `catch` statement that catches the exceptions.

The `try` Block: To Err Is Human!

Throwing an exception occurs in a `try` block that causes the compiler to pay special attention to generating code for handling exceptions. Here is the general syntax for the `try` block:

```
try {
  // statements that may throw one or more exceptions
}
```

The `try` block contains any statement that may raise an exception, including `throw` statements. Here is an example of a `try` block:

```
class badValueException
{
  public:
    badValueException(int nVal = 0)
      { cout << nVal << " is a bad value\n"; }
};

main()
{
  int nBadVal;

  try {
    throw badValueException(100);
  }
  // statements to handle the exception
  return 0;
}
```

This code snippet shows a `try` block that contains a `throw` statement. The statements that follow the `try` block handle the exceptions that are raised in the `try` block. The next section discusses the `catch` clause, which handles exceptions.

The `catch` *Clauses: To Forgive Is Divine!*

C++ offers the `catch` clauses (or handlers, if you prefer) to work with the `try` block. The logic of the `catch` handlers is similar to that of the `case` clauses of a `switch` statement. The general syntax for a `catch` handler is:

```
catch(exceptionType [exceptionObject]) {
  // statements that handle or rethrow the exception
}
```

A `catch` clause declares an exception type and an optional exception parameter. You need this parameter if it passes additional information related to the exception. In this sense, a `catch` clause *looks like* a function that has one or more parameters. You can use multiple `catch` handlers as well as the special `catch(...)` clause to catch and handle exceptions, as shown in the following general syntax:

```
catch(exceptionType1 [exceptionObject1]) {
  // statements that handle or rethrow the exceptionType1
}
catch(exceptionType2 [exceptionObject2]) {
  // statements that handle or rethrow the exceptionType2
}
catch(exceptionType3 [exceptionObject3]) {
  // statements that handle or rethrow the exceptionType3
}
catch(...) {
  // statements that handle or rethrow all other exceptions
}
```

Unlike the `else` or `default` clauses of an `if` or `switch` statement, use the `catch(...)` handler very carefully because it can trap errors that you did not anticipate! You may be in for more than you bargained for.

Here is an example of using a `try` block with `catch` clauses:

```
class myError1 {};
class myError2
{
  public:
  myError2(int nErrorCode)
    { m_nErrorCode = nErrorCode; }
  int m_nErrorCode;
};

main()
{
  int nErrorCode = -1;

  try {
    throw myError1(nErrorCode);
  }
  catch(int nErrorCode) {
    cout << "Handling int exception\n";
    cout << nErrorCode << " is invalid\n";
  }
  catch(myError1) {
    cout << "Handling myError1 exception\n";
  }
  catch(myError2 errObj) {
    cout << "Handling myError2 exception\n";
    cout << errObj.m_nErrorCode << " is invalid\n";
```

```
    }
    catch(...) {
      cout << "Handling other errors\n";
    }

    return 0;
}
```

This example declares the exception classes myError1 and myError2. The first exception class is a skeleton class, whereas the second class has the public data member m_nErrorCode. The class myError2 has a constructor that initializes the data member m_nErrorCode. The function main() declares and initializes the int-type variable nVal. The function has a try block that contains a throw statement which throws a myError1 exception (using the value in the variable nErrorCode). The function main() has the following catch clauses:

- ✔ The catch(int nErrorCode) clause, which catches exceptions that have the int type. This clause displays a message and the value of the parameter nErrorCode.

- ✔ The catch(myError1) clause, which catches myError1 exceptions. This clause has no parameter and simply displays a message.

- ✔ The catch(myError2 errObj) clause, which catches myError2 exceptions. This clause displays a message and then displays the data member errObj.m_nErrorCode. This clause shows you how to use the exception parameter.

- ✔ The catch(...) clause, which catches all other exceptions.

Want to Play catch?

The following sample program, ERROR1.CPP, uses a skeleton exception class, two nonskeleton exception classes, and exceptions that are of a predefined type. The program has several try blocks that test each of these kinds of exceptions.

Here is the output from the ERROR1.CPP program:

```
Testing throwing an int
-32768 is not a valid int
Testing throwing an Exception1 exception
Handling Exception1 exception
Testing throwing an Exception2 exception
Handling Exception2 exception
```

(continued)

(continued)

```
32767 is not a valid int
Testing throwing an Exception3 exception
Handling Exception3 exception
-32768 is not a valid int
```

Listing 13-1 shows the source code for the ERROR1.CPP program.

Listing 13-1	ERROR1.CPP

```
// A C++ program that illustrates
// exception classes, throwing exceptions,
// and catching exceptions

#include <iostream.h>

// declare a skeleton exception class
class Exception1 {};

// declare a nonskeleton exception class
class Exception2
{
  public:
    Exception2(int nErrorCode)
      { m_nErrorCode = nErrorCode; }
    int m_nErrorCode;
};

// declare a nonskeleton exception class
class Exception3
{
  public:
    Exception3()
      { m_nErrorCode = 0; }
    void setErrorCode(int nErrorCode)
      { m_nErrorCode = nErrorCode; }
    int getErrorCode()
      { return m_nErrorCode; }
  protected:
    int m_nErrorCode;
};

main()
{
```

```
int nNum = -32768;
Exception2 errorObj2(32767);
Exception3 errorObj3;

// test throwing a predefined-type object
cout << "Testing throwing an int\n";
try {
  throw nNum;
}
catch (int nErrorCode)
{
  cout << nErrorCode << " is not a valid int\n";
}
catch (char cErrorCode)
{
  cout << cErrorCode << " is not a valid char\n";
}
catch (long lErrorCode)
{
  cout << lErrorCode << " is not a valid long\n";
}

// test throwing an Exception1 exception
cout << "Testing throwing an Exception1 exception\n";
try {
  throw Exception1();
}
catch (Exception1)
{
  cout << "Handling Exception1 exception\n";
}
catch (char cErrorCode)
{
  cout << cErrorCode << " is not a valid char\n";
}
catch (long lErrorCode)
{
  cout << lErrorCode << " is not a valid long\n";
}

  // test throwing Exception2 class
cout << "Testing throwing an Exception2 exception\n";
```

(continued)

Listing 13-1 *(continued)*

```
try {
    throw errorObj2;
}
catch (Exception2 err)
{
    cout << "Handling Exception2 exception\n";
    cout << err.m_nErrorCode << " is not a valid int\n";
}
catch (char cErrorCode)
{
    cout << cErrorCode << " is not a valid char\n";
}
catch (long lErrorCode)
{
    cout << lErrorCode << " is not a valid long\n";
}

    // test throwing an Exception3 exception
cout << "Testing throwing an Exception3 exception\n";
try {
    errorObj3.setErrorCode(nNum);
    throw errorObj3;
}
catch (Exception3 err)
{
    cout << "Handling Exception3 exception\n";
    cout << err.getErrorCode() << " is not a valid int\n";
}
catch (char cErrorCode)
{
    cout << cErrorCode << " is not a valid char\n";
}
catch (long lErrorCode)
{
    cout << lErrorCode << " is not a valid long\n";
}

    return 0;
}
```

Listing 13-1 declares the exception classes Exception1, Exception2, and Exception3, and defines the function main(). I describe these exception classes and the function main() in the following sections.

The class Exception1

The listing declares the class Exception1 as a skeleton exception class. The class has no members and relies on its name to throw and catch an exception.

The class Exception2

The class Exception2 is an exception class that has the public data member m_nErrorCode. The class has a constructor that initializes the data member. Making that member public simplifies assigning and retrieving values to it. The source code for the class Exception2 suggests that you may throw temporary instances of that class.

The class Exception3

The class Exception3 is an exception class that has the protected data member m_nErrorCode. The class has a constructor that initializes the data member and the member functions setErrorCode() and getErrorCode() to access the data member. The source code for the class Exception3 suggests that you throw nontemporary instances of that class.

The function main()

The function main() declares the int-type variable nNum and the objects errObj2 and errObj3 as instances of the classes Exception2 and Exception3, respectively. The function main() performs the following tasks:

- Throwing the variable nNum in a try block. This try block is followed by three catch clauses that handle int-type, char-type, and long-type exceptions. Each clause has a parameter and displays the value of that parameter. The program invokes the first catch clause to handle the int-type exception.

- Throwing the Exception1 exception in a try block. This try block is followed by three catch clauses that handle Exception1-type, char-type, and long-type exceptions. The first catch clause handles the Exception1 exception and has no parameters. This clause simply displays an error message. Each of the latter two clauses has a parameter and displays the value of that parameter. The program invokes the first catch clause to handle the Exception1-type exception.

✔ Throwing the errorObj2 object to trigger an Exception2-type exception in a try block. This try block is followed by three catch clauses that handle Exception2-type, char-type, and long-type exceptions. The first catch clause handles the Exception2 exception and has the parameter err. This clause displays an error message and the value of the data member err.m_nErrorCode. Each of the latter two clauses has a parameter and displays the value of that parameter. The program invokes the first catch clause to handle the Exception2-type exception.

✔ Assigning a value to the object errObj3 (using the value in the variable nNum) and then throwing the errObj3 object to trigger an Exception3-type exception in a try block. This try block is followed by three catch clauses that handle Exception3-type, char-type, and long-type exceptions. The first catch clause handles the Exception3 exception and has the parameter err. This clause displays an error message and the value of the data member err.m_nErrorCode (by sending the C++ message getErrorCode() to the object err). Each of the latter two clauses has a parameter and displays the value of that parameter. The program invokes the first catch clause to handle the Exception3-type exception.

Nested try-catch *Blocks:* *Resorting to Plan B*

In handling really sophisticated exceptions, you may wonder about the ability to nest try blocks and catch clauses inside other catch clauses. C++ allows you to nest try blocks. In other words, you can handle one exception by throwing another exception. The nature of such an action depends on the first exception that you're handling.

The ERROR2.CPP program is a simple example of source code that uses nested try blocks. This program throws a main exception and then throws a secondary error in the catch clause that handles the main exception. This clause contains a nested try block and nested catch clauses. The catch clauses display messages telling about the exception that they are handling.

Here is the output from the ERROR2.CPP program:

```
Throwing the main exception
Handling main exception
Handling exception Exception3
```

Listing 13-2 shows the source code for the ERROR2.CPP program.

Listing 13-2	ERROR2.CPP

```cpp
// A C++ program that illustrates
// nested try blocks

#include <iostream.h>

// declare skeleton exception classes
class mainError {};
class Exception1 {};
class Exception2 {};
class Exception3 {};

main()
{
  int nNum = 123;

  // throw an exception
  cout << "Throwing the main exception\n";
  try {
    throw mainError();
  }
  catch (mainError)
  {
    cout << "Handling main exception\n";
    try {
      if (nNum < 10)
        throw Exception1();
      else if (nNum < 100)
        throw Exception2();
      else if (nNum < 1000)
        throw Exception3();
    }
    catch (Exception1)
    {
      cout << "Handling exception Exception1";
    }
    catch (Exception2)
    {
      cout << "Handling exception Exception2";
    }
}
```

(continued)

Listing 13-2 *(continued)*

```
    catch (Exception3)
    {
cout << "Handling exception Exception3";
    }
    catch (...)
    {
      cout << "Handling other errors\n";
    }
  }
  catch (int nErrorCode)
  {
    cout << nErrorCode << " is not a valid int\n";
  }
  catch (char cErrorCode)
  {
    cout << cErrorCode << " is not a valid char\n";
  }
  catch (long lErrorCode)
  {
    cout << lErrorCode << " is not a valid long\n";
  }

  return 0;
}
```

Listing 13-2 declares the skeleton exception classes mainError, Exception1, Exception2, and Exception3. The listing defines the function main( ), which declares and initializes the int-type variable nNum. The function displays a message and then throws the exception mainError in a try block. This try block is followed by four catch clauses that handle exceptions of the mainError, int, char, and long types. The first catch clause displays an error message and then executes the multiple-alternative if statement inside a nested try block. This if statement throws the Exception1, Exception2, or Exception3 exception, depending on the value in the variable nNum. The nested try block is followed by four catch clauses that handle Exception1 exceptions, Exception2 exceptions, Exception3 exceptions, and all other exceptions. Each catch clause simply displays an error message.

Rethrowing an Exception: The Ball Is in Your Court

C++ allows you to rethrow an exception after partially handling it or after determining that the exception handler cannot deal with it at all. Rethrowing an exception preserves its state and passes it to a higher level of exception handlers. Typically, you rethrow an exception in a function that is called by another function. Consequently, the caller must then handle the rethrown exception. Here is the syntax for rethrowing an exception:

```
throw;
```

That's all! (Yes, I'm sure.)

The ERROR3.CPP program demonstrates how to rethrow exceptions. This simple program declares the functions main() and solver(), each with try blocks and catch clauses. The function main() calls the function solver(). The function solver() handles one kind of exception and rethrows all other kinds to the caller — which in this example is the function main(). The function main() handles all exceptions rethrown by the function solver().

Here is the output from the ERROR3.CPP program:

```
Handling main exception in function solver
Cannot handle secondary exception in function solver
Handling secondary exception in function main
```

Listing 13-3 shows the source code for the ERROR3.CPP program.

Listing 13-3	ERROR3.CPP

```
// A C++ program that illustrates
// rethrowing exceptions

#include <iostream.h>

// declare skeleton exception classes
class mainError {};
class secError {};

void solver(int nErrorCode)
{
try {
```

(continued)

Listing 13-3 *(continued)*

```
    if (nErrorCode >= 0)
      throw mainError();
    else
      throw secError();
  }
  catch(mainError)
  {
    cout << "Handling main exception "
         << "in function solver\n";
  }
  catch(...)
  {
    cout << "Cannot handle secondary exception "
         << "in function solver\n";
    // rethrow exception to caller
    throw;
  }
}

main()
{
  // throw an exception
  try {
    solver(1);
    solver(-1);
  }
  catch (mainError)
  {
    cout << "Handling main exception in function main\n";
  }
  catch (secError)
  {
    cout << "Handling secondary exception in function
    main\n";
  }
  catch(...)
  {
    cout << "This is the last resort to "
         << "solve your problems!\n";
  }

  return 0;
}
```

Listing 13-3 declares the skeleton exception classes `mainError` and `secError`. The listing also defines the functions `solver()` and `main()`, which I describe in the following sections.

The function `solver()`

The function `solver()` has an `int`-type parameter `nErrorCode`. The function uses the value of that parameter to throw a `mainError` exception when the value of the parameter is nonnegative. Otherwise, the function throws the `secError` exception. The `try` block in the function `solver()` is followed by the `catch (mainError)` and `catch(...)` clauses. The first `catch` clause handles the exception by displaying an error message. The second `catch` clause displays a message and then rethrows the exception using the `throw;` statement.

The function `main()`

The function `main()` calls the function `solver()` twice, inside a `try` block. The first call has the argument `1`, and the second call has the argument `-1`. Thus, the first call results in having the function `solver()` throw and handle the exception `mainError`. In contrast, the second call results in having the function `solver()` throw the exception `secError`, partially handle it, and then rethrow that exception to the function `main()`. The function `main()` has three `catch` clauses to handle the `mainError` exception, the `secError` exception, and all other unspecified exceptions. The second call to the function `solver()` causes the program flow to jump to the `catch(secError)` clause and displays the string literal `"Handling secondary exception in function main"`;.

Associating Exceptions and Functions

By default, a function can raise any known exception. That's a lot of exceptions to anticipate! C++ allows you to prototype functions in a way that lists the exceptions that are raised by that function. You use the following syntax for this kind of function prototype:

```
returnType functionName(parameterList)throw(listOfExceptions);
```

The syntax shows that the function prototype includes the keyword `throw` (after the function's parameter list), which declares the comma-delimited list of exceptions raised by the function. Here is an example:

```
void solver(int nCode) throw(mainError, secError);
```

This example declares the function solver(), which can throw the exceptions mainError and secError. Thus, the following try block and catch clauses can safely deal with the exceptions raised by the function solver():

```
try {
  solver(-11);
}
catch(mainError)
{
  cout << "Handling mainError exception\n";
}
catch(secError)
{
  cout << "Handling secError exception\n";
}
```

This code snippet does not need the catch(...) clause because the exceptions raised by the function solver() are known.

To declare that a function does not throw any exception, use the following general syntax:

```
returnType functionName(parameterList) throw();
```

The syntax shows that the function prototype includes the keyword throw with an empty list of exceptions. Here is an example:

```
void superSolver(int nCode) throw();
```

This example declares the function superSolver(), which throws no exceptions (this is the kind of function you wish all software libraries offered).

The ERROR4.CPP program illustrates how to associate exceptions with functions. This program declares the functions solver() and main(). The prototype of the function solver() lists the exception raised by that function.

Here is the output from the ERROR4.CPP program:

```
Handling main exception
```

Listing 13-4 shows the source code for the ERROR4.CPP program.

Listing 13-4	ERROR4.CPP

```cpp
// A C++ program that illustrates
// associating exceptions with functions

#include <iostream.h>

// declare skeleton exception classes
class mainError {};
class secError {};

void solver(int nErrorCode) throw(mainError, secError);

main()
{
  // throw an exception
  try {
      solver(1);
  }
  catch (mainError)
  {
    cout << "Handling main exception\n";
  }
  catch (secError)
  {
    cout << "Handling secondary exception\n";
  }

  return 0;
}

void solver(int nErrorCode) throw(mainError, secError)
{
  if (nErrorCode >= 0)
    throw mainError();
  else
    throw secError();
}
```

Listing 13-4 declares the skeleton exception classes mainError and secError. The listing also declares the prototype of the function solver(). This proto-type indicates that the function raises the exceptions mainError and secError. The definition of the function solver() raises either kind of exception based on the value of its int-type parameter nErrorCode. The function main() calls the function solver() inside a try block. The function has two catch clauses that handle the mainError and secError exceptions that are raised by the function solver().

Summary

This chapter discusses managing exceptions using C++ classes. This error-handling mechanism injects OOP features into C++ programs. You've learned about using the try block and the catch clauses. The next chapter discusses two methods for relating classes with each other (other than inheritance and containment): nested classes and friend classes.

Chapter 14

Friend Classes and Nesting: Still More Class Relations

*T*his chapter looks at two ways to relate classes, namely, friend classes and nested classes. Friend classes establish special access privileges between classes that are not part of the same hierarchy. The nested classes feature allows the declaration of one class (the host class) to contain a nested class that focuses on supporting the host class.

What Is a Friend Class? The Opposite of an Enemy Class?

In Chapter 10, I discuss containment, introduce you to friend classes, and show you how to use friend classes in containment. In general, C++ allows you to declare friend classes that have access to all the members of the befriended classes. The privilege is available for classes that are not in the same hierarchy.

Of course, this kind of relationship is not part of pure OOP thinking. As expected, some OOP gurus complain that friendship between C++ classes is not a genuine part of object-oriented programming. The gurus are technically correct, but friendship between classes does reduce the software red tape, so to speak.

Declaring Friend Classes: Party Time!

You use the following general syntax for declaring a friend class in C++:

```
class className
{
    friend friendClassName;
    // declaration of other members
};
```

To declare a friend class, you use the keyword friend followed by the name of the class.

You typically declare friend classes in a set of classes that you design simultaneously. You cannot declare friend classes as an add-on feature.

Typically, you use friend classes in one of two ways:

- ✔ The friend classes can access the nonpublic members of the befriended classes in function parameters or as local instances declared in member functions.

- ✔ The friend classes are also contained in other classes. The friendship between the contained and host classes allows the host classes to directly access data members of the friend classes without the overhead of using access member functions.

Using Friend Classes: It's Not What You Think!

Using friends is morally wrong, but using friend classes in C++ is *not* morally wrong! By eliminating the overhead of access member functions (that is, the extra machine-level instructions that the compiler puts out), using friend classes makes connecting classes easier. In some cases, using friend classes is the only way to make a connection between classes.

Here is a list of typical ways to use friend classes:

- ✔ The befriended class is contained in the friend class as a data member. Chapter 10 describes this type of containment.

- ✔ The befriended class is a parameter of a member function that belongs to the friend class. This use of friend classes allows the statements that define the member function to access the nonpublic members of the class parameter.

✔ The befriended class has local instances in a member function that belongs to the friend class. This use of friend classes allows the statements that define the member function to access the nonpublic members of the class parameter.

 Because friend classes make connecting classes easier (in particular, because friend classes don't need to use access member functions to set and query the values of data members) and allow you to reduce access overhead in critical applications, you may be tempted to abuse friend classes. Don't! If you do, your class hierarchy design will not be robust, and your applications will crash and burn!

The FRIEND1.CPP program illustrates the use of a friend class as a parameter of a member function that belongs to another class. This program declares the classes myArray and myMatrix. The class myArray manages an array of floating-point numbers. Likewise, the class myMatrix manages a matrix of floating-point numbers. The class myMatrix declares a member function that copies the elements of an array (an instance of the class myArray) to one of the matrix rows. This member function has a parameter of the type myArray.

The program creates the objects anArray and aMatrix as instances of the classes myArray and myMatrix and performs the following tasks:

✔ Assigns values to the elements of the object anArray

✔ Copies the elements of the object anArray to the rows of the object aMatrix

✔ Displays the elements of the object anArray

✔ Displays the rows of the object aMatrix

Here is the output from the FRIEND1.CPP program:

```
The array is:
1 2 3 4 5

The matrix is:
1 2 3 4 5
1 2 3 4 5
1 2 3 4 5
1 2 3 4 5
1 2 3 4 5
```

Listing 14-1 shows the source code for the FRIEND1.CPP program.

Listing 14-1	FRIEND1.CPP

```cpp
// A C++ program that illustrates using
// friend classes

#include <iostream.h>
#include <iomanip.h>

const int MIN_ELEMS = 2;
const int MIN_ROWS = 2;
const int MIN_COLS = 2;

enum Logical { FALSE, TRUE };

class myArray
{
  friend class myMatrix;

  public:
    myArray(int nMaxElems = MIN_ELEMS);
    ~myArray()
      { delete [] m_pfArray; }
    int getNumElems()
      { return m_nMaxElems; }
    Logical Store(double fVal, int nIndex);
    Logical Recall(double& fVal, int nIndex);

    void Show(const int nNumElems,
              const char* pszMsg = "",
              const Logical bOneLine = TRUE);
  protected:
    int m_nMaxElems;
    double* m_pfArray;

};
class myMatrix
{
  public:
    myMatrix(int nMaxRows = MIN_ROWS,
             int nMaxCols = MIN_COLS);
    ~myMatrix()
      { delete [] m_pfMatrix; }
    int getNumRows()
      { return m_nMaxRows; }
    int getNumCols()
```

```
        { return m_nMaxCols; }
      Logical Store(double fVal, int nRow, int nCol);
      Logical Recall(double& fVal, int nRow, int nCol);

      void Show(int nRows, int nCols,
                const char* pszMsg = "");
      myMatrix& CopyToRow(myArray& anArray, int nRow);

    protected:
      int m_nMaxRows;
      int m_nMaxCols;
      double* m_pfMatrix;
};
myArray::myArray(int nMaxElems)
{
  m_nMaxElems = (nMaxElems < MIN_ELEMS) ? MIN_ELEMS :↪
  nMaxElems;
  m_pfArray = new double[nMaxElems];
  for (int i = 0; i< m_nMaxElems; i++)
    m_pfArray[i] = 0.0;
}
Logical myArray::Store(double fVal, int nIndex)
{
  if (nIndex >= 0 && nIndex < m_nMaxElems) {
    m_pfArray[nIndex] = fVal;
    return TRUE;
  }
  else
    return FALSE;
}
Logical myArray::Recall(double& fVal, int nIndex)
{
  if (nIndex >= 0 && nIndex < m_nMaxElems) {
    fVal = m_pfArray[nIndex];
    return TRUE;
  }
  else
    return FALSE;
}
void myArray::Show(const int nNumElems,
                   const char* pszMsg,
                   const Logical bOneLine)
```

(continued)

Listing 14-1 *(continued)*

```
{
  cout << pszMsg << endl;
  if (bOneLine) {
    for (int i = 0; i < nNumElems; i++)
      cout << m_pfArray[i] << ' ';
    cout << endl;
  }
  else {
    for (int i = 0; i < nNumElems; i++)
      cout << m_pfArray[i] << endl;
    cout << endl;
  }
}
myMatrix::myMatrix(int nMaxRows, int nMaxCols)
{
  m_nMaxRows = (nMaxRows < MIN_ROWS) ? MIN_ROWS : nMaxRows;
  m_nMaxCols = (nMaxCols < MIN_COLS) ? MIN_COLS : nMaxCols;
  m_pfMatrix = new double[m_nMaxRows * m_nMaxCols];
  for (int i = 0; i < (m_nMaxRows * m_nMaxCols); i++)
    m_pfMatrix[i] = 0.0;
}
Logical myMatrix::Store(double fVal, int nRow, int nCol)
{
  if (nRow >= 0 && nRow < m_nMaxRows &&
      nCol >= 0 && nCol < m_nMaxCols) {
    m_pfMatrix[nRow + nCol * m_nMaxRows] = fVal;
    return TRUE;
  }
  else
    return FALSE;
}
Logical myMatrix::Recall(double& fVal, int nRow, int nCol)
{
  if (nRow >= 0 && nRow < m_nMaxRows &&
      nCol >= 0 && nCol < m_nMaxCols) {
    fVal = m_pfMatrix[nRow + nCol * m_nMaxRows];
    return TRUE;
  }
  else
    return FALSE;
}
void myMatrix::Show(int nRows, int nCols,
                    const char* pszMsg)
```

```
{
  cout << pszMsg << endl;
  for (int i = 0; i < nRows; i++) {
    for (int j = 0; j < nCols; j++)
      cout << m_pfMatrix[i + j * m_nMaxRows] << ' ';
    cout << endl;
  }
}
myMatrix& myMatrix::CopyToRow(myArray& anArray, int nRow)
{
  if (nRow < 0 || nRow >= m_nMaxRows)
    return *this; // exit

  // note: the number of rows = m_nMaxCols and
  // the number of columns = m_nMaxRows
  if (anArray.m_nMaxElems < m_nMaxCols)
    return *this;

  // copy the array elements to the targeted matrix row
  for (int j = 0; j < m_nMaxCols; j++)
    // the next statement directly accesses the
    // elements of the parameter anArray
    m_pfMatrix[nRow + j * m_nMaxRows] = anArray.m_pfArray[j];

  return *this;
}
main()
{
  const int TEST_SIZE = 5;
  myArray anArray(TEST_SIZE);
  myMatrix aMatrix(TEST_SIZE, TEST_SIZE);

  for (int i = 0; i < anArray.getNumElems(); i++)
    anArray.Store(double(i + 1), i);

  // copy the array object to each matrix row
  for (int nRow = 0; nRow < aMatrix.getNumRows(); nRow++)
    aMatrix.CopyToRow(anArray, nRow);

  // display the elements of the array object
  anArray.Show(anArray.getNumElems(), "The array is:");
  cout << endl;
```

(continued)

Listing 14-1 *(continued)*

```
// display the elements of the matrix object
  aMatrix.Show(aMatrix.getNumRows(),
               aMatrix.getNumCols(),
               "The matrix is:");

  return 0;
}
```

Listing 14-1 declares the class myArray, the class myMatrix, and the function main().

The class myArray

The class myArray models dynamic arrays that store floating-point numbers. The class declares public and protected members and declares the class myMatrix as a friend. Here are the protected members:

- ✔ The int-type data member m_nMaxElems, which stores the number of elements in the dynamic array
- ✔ The double*-type data member m_pfArray, which is the pointer to the dynamic array

The public members of the class myArray are the following:

- ✔ The constructor, which creates the dynamic array and assigns the number of its elements to the data member m_nMaxElems.
- ✔ The destructor, which frees the memory used by the dynamic array (accessed by the data member m_pfArray).
- ✔ The member function getNumElems(), which returns the number of array elements — that is, the value stored in the data member m_nMaxElems.
- ✔ The Logical member function Store(), which stores the value of the double-type parameter fVal in an array element. The int-type parameter nIndex specifies the index of that element. The function returns TRUE if the argument for the parameter nIndex is valid. Otherwise, the member function yields FALSE.
- ✔ The Logical member function Recall(), which recalls the value in an array element. The double-type reference parameter fVal returns the value in the targeted array element. The int-type parameter nIndex specifies the index of that element. The function returns TRUE if the argument for the parameter nIndex is valid. Otherwise, the member function yields FALSE.

✔ The member function Show( ), which displays some or all of the elements in the dynamic array.

The class myMatrix

The class myMatrix models dynamic matrices that store floating-point numbers. The class declares public and protected members. Here are the protected members:

✔ The int-type data member m_nMaxRows, which stores the number of rows in the dynamic matrix.

✔ The int-type data member m_nMaxCols, which stores the number of columns in the dynamic matrix.

✔ The double*-type data member m_pfMatrix, which is the pointer to the dynamic matrix.

The public members of the class myMatrix are the following:

✔ The constructor, which creates the dynamic matrix and assigns the number of its rows and columns to the data members m_nMaxRows and m_nMaxCols, respectively.

✔ The destructor, which frees the memory used by the dynamic matrix (accessed by the data member m_pfMatrix).

✔ The member function getNumRows( ), which returns the number of rows in the matrix — that is, the value stored in the data member m_nMaxRows.

✔ The member function getNumCols( ), which returns the number of columns in the matrix — that is, the value stored in the data member m_nMaxCols.

✔ The Logical member function Store( ), which stores the value of the double-type parameter fVal in a matrix element. The int-type parameters nRow and nCol specify the row and column indices of that element. The function returns TRUE if the arguments for the parameters nRow and nCol are valid. Otherwise, the member function yields FALSE.

✔ The Logical member function Recall( ), which recalls the value in a matrix element. The double-type reference parameter fVal returns the value in the targeted matrix element. The int-type parameters nRow and nCol specify the row and column indices of that element. The function returns TRUE if the arguments for the parameters nRow and nCol are valid. Otherwise, the member function yields FALSE.

✔ The member function Show() displays some or all of the elements in the dynamic matrix.

✔ The member function CopyToRow() copies the elements of an array to a targeted matrix row. The myArray-type reference parameter anArray specifies the array that provides the source values.

The definition of the member function CopyToRow() shows the effect of the friendship between the classes myArray and myMatrix:

✔ The second if statement in the function main() directly accesses the data member m_nMaxElems of the class myArray, using the expression anArray.m_nMaxElems.

✔ The for loop, which copies the array elements, directly accesses these elements by using the data member m_pfArray.

Without the friendship between these classes, the second if statement becomes the following:

```
if (anArray.getNumElems() < m_nMaxCols)
  return *this;
```

and the for loop statement becomes the following:

```
for (int j = 0; j < m_nMaxCols; j++)  {
  double fX;
  anArray.Recall(fX, i);
  m_pfMatrix[nRow + j * m_nMaxRows] = fX;
}
```

Although the changes in the if statement are rather minor, the change in the for loop is significant. The loss of friendship causes the loop to add a declaration and a statement that sends the C++ message Recall() to the myArray-type parameter anArray.

The function main()

The function main() declares the objects anArray and aMatrix as instances of the classes myArray and myMatrix, respectively. The function uses the local constant TEST_SIZE to assign the number of elements, rows, and columns to the two objects. The function main() then performs the following tasks:

✔ Assigns values to the elements of the object anArray. This task uses a for loop that sends the C++ message Store() to that object. The arguments for this message are the expression double(i + 1) and the loop control variable i.

✔ Copies the values in the object anArray to the rows of the object aMatrix. This task uses a for loop that iterates over the rows of the object aMatrix. Each loop iteration sends the C++ message CopyToRow() to the object aMatrix. The arguments for this message are the object anArray and the loop control variable nRow.

✔ Displays the elements in the object anArray by sending the C++ message Show() to that object. The arguments for this message are the string literal "The array is:" and the result of sending the message getNumElems() to the object anArray.

✔ Displays the elements in the object aMatrix by sending the C++ message Show() to that object. The arguments for this message are the string literal "The matrix is:" and the results of sending the message getNumRows() and getNumCols() to the object aMatrix.

What Is a Nested Class?

C++ allows you to declare a class nested inside another class. The nested class mainly serves to support the host class. Nested classes are *not* contained classes (that is, nested classes and containment are two different concepts), because the entire declaration of the nested class appears in the host class. This differs from containment, in which the host class has data members that are instances of or pointers to other classes declared outside the host class.

Why use nested classes? In some cases, some operations of a class are best modeled by a nested class. This nested class has data members and member functions that serve the host class better than any outside class can. In other words, you can code the nested class to include data members and member functions whose main (and only) purpose is to boost the operations of the host class. The host class declares instances of the nested class to obtain its support.

In contrast, using unnested classes instead of nested classes may be undesirable because unnested classes can be used to create other instances outside the host class. You can say that the difference between using nested and unnested classes is parallel to the difference between private and publicly owned companies. The privately held companies need not answer to the public stockholders, because there are none. In contrast, publicly owned companies must answer to the public stockholders. Likewise, nested classes don't give a hoot as to how well they work in generating instances, because they're not meant to work that way. Instead, the main purpose of a nested class is to please the host class.

Declaring Nested Classes

C++ allows you to declare nested classes (as well as nested enumerated types and structures) using the following general syntax:

```
class hostClass
{
   public:
     // declarations of public members
   class nestedPublicClass {
       // declarations of members
   };
   protected:
     // declarations of protected members
   class nestedProtectedClass {
       // declarations of members
   };
   private:
     // declarations of private members
   class nestedPrivateClass {
       // declarations of members
   };
};
```

The nested class may have public, protected, and private sections. However, if you declare the nested class in a protected section, it cannot be accessed by the instances of the host class. Therefore, you can declare the members of this kind of nested class as public and not worry about access by the instances of the host class.

If you declare the nested class as public, you can use it in nonmember functions. In this case, you have to qualify the name of the nested class with the name of the host class (that is, you have to use the form `hostName::nestedPublicClass`). Remember that the nonmember functions can access only the public members of the nested public classes. If you declare the nested class as protected, then the member functions of the descendant classes can access these nested classes using the form `hostName::nestedProtectedClass`. The chief point remains that nested classes mainly serve the host classes.

Using Nested Classes: Also Morally OK in C++

The NESTED1.CPP program illustrates nested classes. This program has a class that models a fixed-size stack of long integers. The stack uses a nested class that models fixed-size arrays to store the stack elements. In other words, the program uses a fixed-size array to do behind-the-scenes support for most of the operations of the fixed-size stack.

The program creates a stack object and performs the following tasks:

▸ Displays the initial stack height (which is zero)

▸ Pushes data onto that stack

▸ Displays the current stack height

▸ Pops data off the stack until the stack is empty

▸ Displays the final stack height (which is zero)

Here is the output from the NESTED1.CPP program:

```
Stack height is 0
Pushing 586 onto the stack
Pushing 487 onto the stack
Pushing 461 onto the stack
Pushing 956 onto the stack
Pushing 931 onto the stack
Stack height is 5
Popping 931 off the stack
Popping 956 off the stack
Popping 461 off the stack
Popping 487 off the stack
Popping 586 off the stack
Stack height is 0
```

Listing 14-2 shows the source code for the NESTED1.CPP program.

Listing 14-2	NESTED1.CPP

```
// A C++ program that illustrates
// nested classes
```

(continued)

Listing 14-2 *(continued)*

```cpp
#include <iostream.h>
#include <iomanip.h>

enum Logical { FALSE, TRUE };

class myFixedStack
{
  public:
    myFixedStack(unsigned nMaxSize = 10)
      {
        m_pArrObj = new Array(nMaxSize);
        m_uHeight = 0;
      }
    ~myFixedStack()
      { delete m_pArrObj; }
     Logical isEmpty()
      { return (m_uHeight == 0) ? TRUE : FALSE; }
    unsigned getHeight()
      { return m_uHeight; }
    void push(long lNum);
    Logical pop(long& lNum);
    void clear()
      { m_pArrObj->erase(); }

  protected:
    // declare nested class Array
    class Array
    {
      public:
        Array(unsigned lArraySize)
          { m_plArray = new long[m_lArraySize = lArraySize];
            m_uWorkSize = 0;
          }
        ~Array()
          { delete [] m_plArray; }
        Logical insert(long lNum)
          {
            if (m_uWorkSize < m_lArraySize) {
              m_plArray[m_uWorkSize++] = lNum;
              return TRUE;
            }
            else
```

```
              return FALSE;
            }
          Logical remove(long& lNum)
            {
              if (m_uWorkSize > 0) {
                lNum = m_plArray[--m_uWorkSize];
                return TRUE;
              }
              else
                return FALSE;
            }
          void erase()
            {  m_uWorkSize = 0;  }

      protected:
        unsigned m_uWorkSize;
        unsigned m_lArraySize;
        long* m_plArray;
    };
    Array* m_pArrObj;
    unsigned m_uHeight;    // height of stack
};
void myFixedStack::push(long lNum)
{
  if (m_pArrObj->insert(lNum))
    m_uHeight++;
}
Logical myFixedStack::pop(long& lNum)
{
  Logical ok = m_pArrObj->remove(lNum);
  if (ok)
    m_uHeight--;
  return ok;
}
main()
{
  const int ARRAY_SIZE = 5;
  myFixedStack Stack(ARRAY_SIZE);
  long lVal;
long lArr[ARRAY_SIZE] = { 586, 487, 461, 956, 931 };

  cout << "Stack height is " << Stack.getHeight() << endl;
  // push integers onto the stack
```

(continued)

Listing 14-2 *(continued)*

```
for (int i = 0; i < ARRAY_SIZE; i++) {
    cout << "Pushing " << lArr[i] << " onto the stack\n";
    Stack.push(lArr[i]);
}
cout << "Stack height is " << Stack.getHeight() << endl;
// pop elements off the stack
while (Stack.pop(lVal))
    cout << "Popping " << lVal << " off the stack\n";

cout << "Stack height is " << Stack.getHeight() << endl;
return 0;
}
```

Listing 14-2 declares the class myFixedStack, which contains the nested class Array. The class myFixedStack models a fixed stack of integers and relies on the nested class to store and manage the data.

The nested class Array

The class Array supports dynamic arrays of integers and declares protected and public members. The protected members are as follows:

✔ The unsigned-type data member m_uWorkSize, which stores the working size (the number of array elements that contain meaningful data). This member also works as an index for storing data in the array and retrieving data from the array.

✔ The unsigned-type data member m_uArraySize, which stores the number of array elements.

✔ The data member m_plArray, which is a pointer to the dynamic array.

The class declares the following public members:

✔ The constructor, which creates the dynamic array and initializes the data members.

✔ The destructor, which removes the dynamic array.

✔ The member function insert(), which inserts the value of the long-type parameter lNum in the next available array element. The function returns TRUE when successful and yields FALSE if the array is already full.

▱ The member function remove(), which obtains an array element from the index m_uWorkSize - 1. The member function returns TRUE if there is an element to retrieve and yields FALSE if the data member m_uWorkSize is 0.

▱ The member function clear(), which sets m_uWorkSize to 0.

The class myFixedStack

The class myFixedStack supports stacks whose sizes are fixed during the creation of the class instances. The class declares protected and public members. Here are the protected members:

▱ The data member m_pArrObj, which is a pointer to the nested class Array.

▱ The unsigned-type data member m_uHeight, which stores the stack height.

The class declares the following public members:

▱ The constructor, which creates a dynamic instance of the class Array and initializes the stack height.

▱ The destructor, which removes the dynamic instance of the nested class.

▱ The member function isEmpty(), which returns a Logical value that indicates whether the stack is empty.

▱ The member function getHeight(), which returns the stack height.

▱ The member function push(), which pushes a value onto the stack.

▱ The member function pop(), which pops a value off the top of the stack.

▱ The member function clear(), which clears the stack.

The member functions push(), pop(), and clear() use the member functions of the nested array to perform the stack operations.

The function main()

The function main() declares the constant ARRAY_SIZE, the object Stack as an instance of the class myFixedStack (which can store up to ARRAY_SIZE elements), the long-type variable lVal, and the long-type array lArr. The function initializes the array lArr and then performs the following tasks:

✔ Displays the initial stack height by sending the C++ message getHeight() to the object Stack.

✔ Pushes the values in the array lArr onto the top of the stack. This task uses a for loop whose statements send the C++ message push() to the object Stack. The argument for the message is lArr[i].

✔ Displays the current stack height by sending the C++ message getHeight() to the object Stack.

✔ Pops the elements off the stack by using a while loop. The condition of this loop sends the C++ message pop() to the object Stack. The argument for this message is the variable lVal, which obtains the value popped off the stack. This task pops off all the stack elements.

✔ Displays the current stack height by sending the C++ message getHeight() to the object Stack.

Summary

This chapter presents programming features (that are unique to C++) which contribute to relating classes. You've learned that friend classes have the special privilege of accessing the nonpublic data members of the befriended classes. This feature allows you to relate classes that are not part of the same hierarchy. You've also learned about nested classes and how they support special operations to help the host class. Typically, nested classes are custom versions of more general-purpose classes that support the host class in a unique and efficient way.

Part IV
The Part of Tens

The 5th Wave   By Rich Tennant

"THIS IS YOUR GROUPWARE?! THIS IS WHAT YOU'RE RUNNING?!
WELL HECK — I THINK THIS COULD BE YOUR PROBLEM!"

In this part. . .

The chapters in Part IV list class components, provide guidelines for using virtual member functions, and describe common stream I/O components.

Chapter 15

The Checklist of Ten Class Components (Plus One)

· ·

In This Chapter

▶ Parent classes

▶ Friend classes

▶ Class sections

▶ Constructors

▶ The destructor

▶ Static members

▶ `const` member functions

▶ Abstract member functions

▶ Virtual member functions

▶ The `operator =`

▶ Friend functions and operators

· ·

A s you write more and more classes, it becomes more practical to develop a general template (not to be confused with a C++ class template) that you can use as a starting point. This kind of template contains the typical components of a class. This chapter lists and describes these typical components. I present a version of the general template in most sections and update it as I introduce another component. Keep in mind that some components appear more consistently than others.

Parent Classes

When you declare a descendant class, list the name of the parent class (if you are using single inheritance) or parent classes (if you are using multiple inheritance) after the name of the class that you are declaring. Don't forget to separate the name of the declared class from the names of its parents with a colon. Here is the general template for a descendant class:

```
class className : public parentClassName
{
  // declare members
};
```

Friend Classes

List the names of the friend classes that have special access privileges to the nonpublic members of the declared class. The following general template includes a friend class:

```
class className : public parentClassName
{
  friend class buddyClass;
  // declare members
};
```

Class Sections

Determine which members go in the public, protected, and private sections. The private section contains highly sensitive data members and member functions. The private section contains members that are accessed only by the member functions of the class.The protected section contains the data members and auxiliary member functions. The protected section contains members that are not accessible by class instances but are accessible to the member functions of the class and the member functions of the descendant classes. The public section contains the constructors, the destructor, access member functions, and other member functions (and operators) that you want the class instances to access.

The following general template includes the sections in a class:

```
class className : public parentClassName
{
  friend class buddyClass;

  public:
    // declare public members
  protected:
```

```
      // declare protected members
  private:
      // declare private members
};
```

Constructors

Classes typically require a default constructor, a copy constructor, and probably one or more custom constructors. Use the default constructor to perform
default initialization of class instances. Use the copy constructor to create new
instances by copying existing instances. Employ the custom constructors to
initialize class instances in a nondefault way. The following general template
includes the constructors in a class:

```
class className : public parentClassName
{
  friend class buddyClass;

  public:
    className(); // default constructor
    className(className& anObject); // copy constructor
    // declare other public members
  protected:
    // declare protected members
  private:
    // declare private members
};
```

The Destructor

Declare a destructor if a constructor initializes the class instances using special
resources such as dynamic memory and stream file I/O. The destructor should
free the resources used by the class instances. The following general template
includes the destructor in a class:

```
class className : public parentClassName
{
  friend class buddyClass;
```

(continued)

(continued)

```
public:
  className(); // default constructor
  className(className& anObject); // copy constructor
  ~className(); // destructor
  // declare other public members
protected:
  // declare protected members
private:
  // declare private members
};
```

Static Members

Declare static data members if you want them to relate conceptually to the class itself rather than the class instances. Make sure that you initialize the static data members outside the class declaration. In addition, declare static member functions to access and manipulate the static data members. The following general template includes a static member function and a static data member in a class:

```
class className : public parentClassName
{
  friend class buddyClass;

  public:
    className(); // default constructor
    className(className& anObject); // copy constructor
    ~className(); // destructor
    // declare the static member function
    static returnType getStaticMember();
    // declare other public members
  protected:
    // declare the static data member
    static memberType m_staticMember;
    // declare other protected members
  private:
    // declare private members
};
```

```
// initialize static data member
memberType className::m_staticMember = initialValue;
```

const *Member Functions*

Insert the keyword const after the parameter list of every member function that should not alter the value of a data member (either declared or inherited).

Abstract Member Functions

Insert = 0 after the parameter list of a member function to declare the host class as abstract. Also, don't forget to insert the keyword virtual before the return type of that member function.

Virtual Member Functions

Declare those member functions that support polymorphic behavior as virtual. Insert the keyword virtual before the return type of these member functions.

The Operator =

Declare the operator = to allow copying of class instances. Make sure that the statements defining that operator perform a deep copy. The following general template includes the operator = in a class:

```
class className : public parentClassName
{
  friend class buddyClass;

  public:
    className(); // default constructor
    className(className& anObject); // copy constructor
    ~className(); // destructor
    className& operator=(className& anObject);
    // declare other public members
```

(continued)

(continued)

```
protected:
    // declare protected members
private:
    // declare private members
};
```

Friend Functions and Operators

Declare friend functions and operators that perform tasks complementing those of the member functions. Regarding the friend operators, don't be creative (in other words, don't get smart with us) and use them for nonintuitive uses. For example, don't declare the operator + to subtract. The following general template includes a friend operator in a class:

```
class className : public parentClassName
{
    friend class buddyClass;

    public:
        className(); // default constructor
        className(className& anObject); // copy constructor
        ~className(); // destructor
        className& operator=(className& anObject);
        friend className& operator +(className& object1,
                                     className& object2);
        // declare other public members
    protected:
        // declare protected members
    private:
        // declare private members
};
```

Chapter 16

The Ten Commandments of Virtual Functions

*C*hapter 7 discusses how C++ virtual member functions support poly-morphism. This chapter lists the ten most important rules and features about virtual member functions. In a way, this chapter is like a brief version of *Everything You Ever Wanted to Know About Virtual Member Functions, But Were Afraid to Ask*.

When to Declare Virtual Member Functions

Declare a member function as virtual when you want that function to support polymorphic behavior. The virtual member function should be called by other member functions that are declared either in the same class or in a parent class.

The Syntax of Virtual Member Functions

To declare a member function as virtual, place the keyword `virtual` before the function's return type in the class declaration. The C++ compiler does not require you to use the keyword `virtual` with the definition of a virtual member function. As a reminder, the general syntax for declaring a virtual member function is:

```
virtual returnType functionName(parameterList);
```

The declaration starts with the keyword `virtual` and proceeds as with nonvirtual member functions.

Using Virtual Functions to Override Nonvirtual Functions

You can declare a virtual member function to override an inherited nonvirtual member function. The parameter list for the virtual member function does not need to be the same as the list for the member function that the virtual member function is overriding. The following code snippet shows how a virtual member function overrides an inherited member function:

```
class myFirstClass
{
  public:
    int foo();
   // declaration of other members
};

class mySecondClass : public mySecondClass
{
  public:
    virtual int foo(int nVal);
   // declaration of other members
};
```

This example shows the class `myFirstClass` and its descendant `mySecondClass`. The class `myFirstClass` declares the nonvirtual member function `foo()`, which has no parameters. The class `mySecondClass` declares the virtual member function `foo()`, which overrides the inherited member function `myFirstClass::foo()`. The member function `mySecondClass::foo()` has the parameter list of `int nVal`.

Overriding Virtual Member Functions

You can override a virtual member function by using another virtual member function. The two member functions must have the same parameter lists. The following code snippet shows how a virtual member function overrides an inherited virtual member function:

```
class myFirstClass
{
  public:
    virtual int foo(int nVal);
    // declaration of other members
};

class mySecondClass : public mySecondClass
{
  public:
    virtual int foo(int nVal);
    // declaration of other members
};
```

This example shows the class myFirstClass and its descendant, mySecondClass. The two classes declare the virtual member function foo(), which has the same parameter int nVal.

Overloading Virtual Member Functions

You can overload a virtual member function by using nonvirtual member functions. Keep in mind that nonvirtual member functions do not support polymorphic behavior. Instead, they serve the operations of the host class. The following code snippet shows how a virtual member function overloads an inherited virtual member function:

```
class myFirstClass
{
  public:
    virtual int foo(int nVal);
    // declaration of other members
};

class mySecondClass : public mySecondClass
{
```

(continued)

(continued)

```
  public:
    virtual int foo(int nVal);
    int foo(char* pszStr);
    int foo(double fX);
  // declaration of other members
};
```

This example shows the class myFirstClass and its descendant mySecondClass. The two classes declare the virtual member function foo(), which has the same parameter int nVal. However, the class mySecondClass also declares the nonvirtual member functions foo(char* pszStr) and foo(double fX), which override the virtual member function.

Inheriting Virtual Member Functions

When a class declares a virtual member function and overloads it with a nonvirtual member function, it can only make the descendant class inherit the virtual member function.

Invoking Inherited Virtual Member Functions

Consider the virtual member function foo declared in class ClassA and its descendant ClassB. The virtual member function ClassB::foo(), which overrides the inherited virtual member function ClassA::foo(), can invoke the latter as *part* of its operations. The following code snippet shows how to invoke an inherited virtual member function:

```
class myFirstClass
{
  public:
    virtual int foo(int nVal);
  // declaration of other members
};

class mySecondClass : public mySecondClass
{
  public:
```

```
    virtual int foo(int nVal);
    // declaration of other members
};

int mySecondClass::foo(int nVal)
{
  int nResult = myFirstClass::foo(nVal);
  return nResult * nResult + 1;
}
```

This example shows the class myFirstClass and its descendant mySecondClass. The two classes declare the virtual member function foo( ), which has the same parameter int nVal. The code snippet shows the implementation of the member function mySecondClass::foo( ), which invokes the inherited member function myFirstClass::foo( ).

Speed and Virtual Member Functions

Virtual member functions are slower to execute than nonvirtual member functions. Therefore, declare member functions as virtual only when necessary.

Virtual Member Functions and Abstract Classes

When you place = 0 after the parameter list of a virtual member function, you declare the host class as abstract. In this case, the class does not define the virtual member function; it only declares the virtual member function. Here is an example of declaring a pure virtual member function:

```
class myAbstractInt
{
  public:
    virtual void setInt(intnInt) = 0;
    virtual int getInt() = 0;
};
```

The class myAbstractInt declares the pure virtual member functions setInt( ) and getInt( ) by placing the = 0 clause after the parameter list of each member function. The class does not define these member functions.

Virtual Member Functions and Class Templates

Virtual member functions work just fine with class templates and provide polymorphic behavior for a hierarchy of class templates. Here is an example:

```
template <class T>
class myOwnInt
{
  public:
    virtual void setInt(T anInt)
       { m_Data = anInt; }
    virtual T getInt();
       { return m_Data; }
  protected:
    T m_Data;
};
```

The class template myOwnInt declares the virtual member functions setInt() and getInt(). The member function setInt() uses the template parameter T in its argument list. The member function getInt() uses the template parameter T in its return type.

Chapter 17

The Ten Most Common Stream I/O Components

. . . .

. . . .

*T*his chapter looks at common objects, operators, and manipulators that are declared in the C++ stream library. What is so special about the stream I/O library from the OOP point of view? The answer is that the stream I/O library supports object-oriented-style input and output. You can expand the library by including I/O operators in your own classes.

The Object cout *and the* operator <<

The operator << works with the object cout to display characters, numbers, and strings.

The Object cin and the operator >>

The operator >> works with the object cin to input characters and numbers.

The Object cin and the Member Function getline()

To obtain a string from the console, send the C++ message getline() to the object cin. The declaration of the overloaded member function getline() is as follows:

```
istream& getline(char* pszStr, int nCount, char cDelim
='\n');
istream& getline(signed char* pszStr, int nCount,
                 char cDelim = '\n');
istream& getline(unsigned char* pszStr, int nCount,
                 char cDelim = '\n');
```

The parameter pszStr is a pointer to an ASCIIZ string. The parameter nCount specifies the maximum number of input characters. The parameter cDelim specifies the string delimiter.

Here is an example of using the member function getline():

```
const int MAX = 30;
char cName[MAX + 1];
cout << "Enter your name : ";
cin.getline(cName, MAX);
cout << "Hello " << cName << "\n";
```

This example prompts you to enter your name. The input involves sending the C++ message getline() to the object cin. The arguments for this message are the array of characters cName and the constant MAX. The array stores your input, which cannot exceed a MAX number of characters.

The Object cerr and the operator <<

The operator << works with the object cerr to display run-time error messages.

The Manipulator dec

The manipulator dec displays the next integer (sent to a stream output object, such as cout) as a decimal number.

The Manipulator hex

The manipulator hex displays the next integer (sent to a stream output object, such as cout) as a hexadecimal number.

The Manipulator oct

The manipulator oct displays the next integer (sent to a stream output object, such as cout) as an octal number.

The following examples demonstrate using the formatting flags hex and oct:

```
// example 1
cout.flags(ios::hex | ios::uppercase);
cout << 15 << "\n"; // displays F
// example 2
cout.flags(ios::oct | ios::showbase);
cout << 8 << "\n"; // displays 010
// example 3
cout.flags(ios::hex | ios::uppercase | ios::showbase);
cout << 15 << "\n"; // displays 0xF
```

The first example sets the hex and uppercase flags to display the integer 15 as a hexadecimal number using uppercase characters, which results in showing the hexadecimal digit F. The second example sets the oct and showbase flags to display the integer 8 as the octal number 010. This output shows the base indicator 0. The third example sets the hex, uppercase, and showbase flags to display the integer 15 as the hexadecimal number 0xF. This output shows the base indicator 0x and the uppercase hexadecimal digit F.

The Manipulator setfill()

The manipulator setfill() sets the stream output fill character. The argument for this manipulator is the output fill character. The default padding character is ' '. Here is an example:

```
// example:  displays 0000125
cout << setw(7) << setfill('0') << 125 << endl;
```

The example uses the manipulators setw and setfill to specify an output that is 7 characters wide, with 0 as the padding character. The output statement displays the integer 125 as 0000125.

The Manipulator setprecision()

The manipulator setprecision() sets the precision for the output of a floating-point number. The parameter for this manipulator specifies the precision of the output. The default value is 6. Here is an example:

```
// example: display 12.12
cout << setprecision(2) << 12.12345 << endl;
```

The example uses the manipulator setprecision to display the number 12.1234 to two decimal places. The argument of the manipulator is 2, the desired number of decimal places.

The Manipulator setw()

The manipulator setw() sets the field width for the next output. The argument for this manipulator is the minimum width of the next field (the default value is 0, which specifies adequate width for the output). Here is an example:

```
// example:  displays 00125
cout << setw(5) << setfill('0') << 125 << endl;
```

The example uses the manipulators setw and setfill to specify an output that is 5 characters wide, with 0 as the padding character. The output statement displays the integer 125 as 00125.

Glossary

• •

abstraction: A concept of generalization that simplifies the representation of a real-world object by focusing on its basic elements.

abstract class: A class that has one or more pure virtual member functions. You cannot create instances of an abstract class.

base class: A class that is the root of a class hierarchy.

C++ message: The invocation of a C++ class member function.

catching an exception: Intercepting a run-time error.

child class: A class that is derived from one or more classes. The child class inherits the member functions and the data members of its parent classes.

class: A category of objects.

class member: A data member or a member function of a class.

constructor: A special class member function that the run-time system invokes automatically when you create a class instance.

containment: The declaration of data members that are instances of other classes or pointers to these other classes.

copy constructor: A constructor that creates new class instances as copies of existing instances.

custom constructor: A constructor that is neither a default (or void) constructor, nor a copy constructor. A custom constructor allows you to initialize class instances to particular states.

data member: A member of a class that stores data.

deep copy: Copying the data members of a class instance and any dynamic data associated with that instance.

default constructor: A constructor that has no parameters. Same as a void constructor.

destructor: A special member function that the run-time system automatically invokes to destroy an object when that object reaches the end of its scope.

exception: A run-time error.

friend class: A class that accesses the nonpublic members of a befriended class, even though the friend class is not a descendant of the befriended class.

inheritance: The capability to create new classes that assume the members of other classes.

instance: An object that belongs to a specific class.

member function: A member of a class that supports a method.

method: A class member function. A method tells an object how to respond to a message.

message: The invocation of a class member function. A message tells an object what to do.

multiple inheritance: An inheritance scheme in which a descendant class has two or more parent classes.

nested class: A class that is declared within another class.

object: An instance (that is, an example) of a class.

object-oriented programming (OOP): A programming method that focuses on modeling and managing objects.

parent class: A class from which other classes are derived.

polymorphism: The abstract-base feature of making classes in a hierarchy offer a consistent response.

private: A class section that declares members that cannot be accessed by the class instances or the member functions of descendant classes.

protected: A class section that declares members that cannot be accessed by the class instances but can be accessed by the member functions of descendant classes.

public: A class section that declares members that can be accessed by the class instances and the member functions of descendant classes.

pure virtual member function: A virtual member function that has no implementation.

raising an exception: Generating a run-time error.

scope: The lifetime of a constant, a variable, or an object.

shallow copy: Copying the data members of a class instance but not any dynamic data associated with that instance.

single inheritance: An inheritance scheme in which a descendant class has only one parent class.

state: The combination of values in the data members of an object.

static data member: A data member that conceptually belongs to the class and not to its instances. There is only one copy of a static data member.

static member function: A special member function that accesses one or more static data members.

throwing an exception: Generating a run-time error.

virtual member function: A member function that supports polymorphic response. In C++, you declare a member function as virtual by using the keyword `virtual` before the function's return type.

void constructor: A constructor with no parameters. The same as a default constructor.

Index

• *K* •

• *L* •

• *M* •

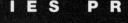

The Internet For Macs® For Dummies® 2nd Edition	by Charles Seiter	ISBN: 1-56884-371-2	$19.99 USA/$26.99 Canada	10/31/95
The Internet For Macs® For Dummies® Starter Kit	by Charles Seiter	ISBN: 1-56884-244-9	$29.99 USA/$39.99 Canada	
The Internet For Macs® For Dummies® Starter Kit Bestseller Edition	by Charles Seiter	ISBN: 1-56884-245-7	$39.99 USA/$54.99 Canada	
The Internet For Windows® For Dummies® Starter Kit	by John R. Levine & Margaret Levine Young	ISBN: 1-56884-237-6	$34.99 USA/$44.99 Canada	
The Internet For Windows® For Dummies® Starter Kit, Bestseller Edition	by John R. Levine & Margaret Levine Young	ISBN: 1-56884-246-5	$39.99 USA/$54.99 Canada	

MACINTOSH

Mac® Programming For Dummies®	by Dan Parks Sydow	ISBN: 1-56884-173-6	$19.95 USA/$26.95 Canada
Macintosh® System 7.5 For Dummies®	by Bob LeVitus	ISBN: 1-56884-197-3	$19.95 USA/$26.95 Canada
MORE Macs® For Dummies®	by David Pogue	ISBN: 1-56884-087-X	$19.95 USA/$26.95 Canada
PageMaker 5 For Macs® For Dummies®	by Galen Gruman & Deke McClelland	ISBN: 1-56884-178-7	$19.95 USA/$26.95 Canada
QuarkXPress 3.3 For Dummies®	by Galen Gruman & Barbara Assadi	ISBN: 1-56884-217-1	$19.99 USA/$26.99 Canada
Upgrading and Fixing Macs® For Dummies®	by Kearney Rietmann & Frank Higgins	ISBN: 1-56884-189-2	$19.95 USA/$26.95 Canada

MULTIMEDIA

Multimedia & CD-ROMs For Dummies® 2nd Edition	by Andy Rathbone	ISBN: 1-56884-907-9	$19.99 USA/$26.99 Canada
Multimedia & CD-ROMs For Dummies® Interactive Multimedia Value Pack, 2nd Edition	by Andy Rathbone	ISBN: 1-56884-909-5	$29.99 USA/$39.99 Canada

OPERATING SYSTEMS:

DOS

MORE DOS For Dummies®	by Dan Gookin	ISBN: 1-56884-046-2	$19.95 USA/$26.95 Canada
OS/2® Warp For Dummies® 2nd Edition	by Andy Rathbone	ISBN: 1-56884-205-8	$19.99 USA/$26.99 Canada

UNIX

MORE UNIX® For Dummies®	by John R. Levine & Margaret Levine Young	ISBN: 1-56884-361-5	$19.99 USA/$26.99 Canada
UNIX® For Dummies®	by John R. Levine & Margaret Levine Young	ISBN: 1-878058-58-4	$19.95 USA/$26.95 Canada

WINDOWS

MORE Windows® For Dummies® 2nd Edition	by Andy Rathbone	ISBN: 1-56884-048-9	$19.95 USA/$26.95 Canada
Windows® 95 For Dummies®	by Andy Rathbone	ISBN: 1-56884-240-6	$19.99 USA/$26.99 Canada

PCS/HARDWARE

Illustrated Computer Dictionary For Dummies® 2nd Edition	by Dan Gookin & Wallace Wang	ISBN: 1-56884-218-X	$12.95 USA/$16.95 Canada
Upgrading and Fixing PCs For Dummies® 2nd Edition	by Andy Rathbone	ISBN: 1-56884-903-6	$19.99 USA/$26.99 Canada

PRESENTATION/AUTOCAD

AutoCAD For Dummies®	by Bud Smith	ISBN: 1-56884-191-4	$19.95 USA/$26.95 Canada
PowerPoint 4 For Windows® For Dummies®	by Doug Lowe	ISBN: 1-56884-161-2	$16.99 USA/$22.99 Canada

PROGRAMMING

Borland C++ For Dummies®	by Michael Hyman	ISBN: 1-56884-162-0	$19.95 USA/$26.95 Canada
C For Dummies® Volume 1	by Dan Gookin	ISBN: 1-878058-78-9	$19.95 USA/$26.95 Canada
C++ For Dummies®	by Stephen R. Davis	ISBN: 1-56884-163-9	$19.95 USA/$26.95 Canada
Delphi Programming For Dummies®	by Neil Rubenking	ISBN: 1-56884-200-7	$19.99 USA/$26.99 Canada
Mac® Programming For Dummies®	by Dan Parks Sydow	ISBN: 1-56884-173-6	$19.95 USA/$26.95 Canada
PowerBuilder 4 Programming For Dummies®	by Ted Coombs & Jason Coombs	ISBN: 1-56884-325-9	$19.99 USA/$26.99 Canada
QBasic Programming For Dummies®	by Douglas Hergert	ISBN: 1-56884-093-4	$19.95 USA/$26.95 Canada
Visual Basic 3 For Dummies®	by Wallace Wang	ISBN: 1-56884-076-4	$19.95 USA/$26.95 Canada
Visual Basic "X" For Dummies®	by Wallace Wang	ISBN: 1-56884-230-9	$19.99 USA/$26.99 Canada
Visual C++ 2 For Dummies®	by Michael Hyman & Bob Arnson	ISBN: 1-56884-328-3	$19.99 USA/$26.99 Canada
Windows® 95 Programming For Dummies®	by S. Randy Davis	ISBN: 1-56884-327-5	$19.99 USA/$26.99 Canada

SPREADSHEET

1-2-3 For Dummies®	by Greg Harvey	ISBN: 1-878058-60-6	$16.95 USA/$22.95 Canada
1-2-3 For Windows® 5 For Dummies® 2nd Edition	by John Walkenbach	ISBN: 1-56884-216-3	$16.95 USA/$22.95 Canada
Excel 5 For Macs® For Dummies®	by Greg Harvey	ISBN: 1-56884-186-8	$19.95 USA/$26.95 Canada
Excel For Dummies® 2nd Edition	by Greg Harvey	ISBN: 1-56884-050-0	$16.95 USA/$22.95 Canada
MORE 1-2-3 For DOS For Dummies®	by John Weingarten	ISBN: 1-56884-224-4	$19.99 USA/$26.99 Canada
MORE Excel 5 For Windows® For Dummies®	by Greg Harvey	ISBN: 1-56884-207-4	$19.95 USA/$26.95 Canada
Quattro Pro 6 For Windows® For Dummies®	by John Walkenbach	ISBN: 1-56884-174-4	$19.95 USA/$26.95 Canada
Quattro Pro For DOS For Dummies®	by John Walkenbach	ISBN: 1-56884-023-3	$16.95 USA/$22.95 Canada

UTILITIES

Norton Utilities 8 For Dummies®	by Beth Slick	ISBN: 1-56884-166-3	$19.95 USA/$26.95 Canada

VCRS/CAMCORDERS

VCRs & Camcorders For Dummies™	by Gordon McComb & Andy Rathbone	ISBN: 1-56884-229-5	$14.99 USA/$20.99 Canada

WORD PROCESSING

Ami Pro For Dummies®	by Jim Meade	ISBN: 1-56884-049-7	$19.95 USA/$26.95 Canada
MORE Word For Windows® 6 For Dummies®	by Doug Lowe	ISBN: 1-56884-165-5	$19.95 USA/$26.95 Canada
MORE WordPerfect® 6 For Windows® For Dummies®	by Margaret Levine Young & David C. Kay	ISBN: 1-56884-206-6	$19.95 USA/$26.95 Canada
MORE WordPerfect® 6 For DOS For Dummies®	by Wallace Wang, edited by Dan Gookin	ISBN: 1-56884-047-0	$19.95 USA/$26.95 Canada
Word 6 For Macs® For Dummies®	by Dan Gookin	ISBN: 1-56884-190-6	$19.95 USA/$26.95 Canada
Word For Windows® 6 For Dummies®	by Dan Gookin	ISBN: 1-56884-075-6	$16.95 USA/$22.95 Canada
Word For Windows® For Dummies®	by Dan Gookin & Ray Werner	ISBN: 1-878058-86-X	$16.95 USA/$22.95 Canada
WordPerfect® 6 For DOS For Dummies®	by Dan Gookin	ISBN: 1-878058-77-0	$16.95 USA/$22.95 Canada
WordPerfect® 6.1 For Windows® For Dummies® 2nd Edition	by Margaret Levine Young & David Kay	ISBN: 1-56884-243-0	$16.95 USA/$22.95 Canada
WordPerfect® For Dummies®	by Dan Gookin	ISBN: 1-878058-52-5	$16.95 USA/$22.95 Canada

DUMMIES PRESS™ QUICK REFERENCES

BOOK SERIES
FROM IDG

IDG
BOOKS
WORLDWIDE

10/

Fun, Fast, & Cheap!™

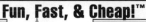

NEW!

NEW!

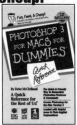

SUPER STAR

SUPER STAR

The Internet For Macs® For Dummies® Quick Reference
by Charles Seiter

ISBN:1-56884-967-2
$9.99 USA/$12.99 Canada

Windows® 95 For Dummies® Quick Reference
by Greg Harvey

ISBN: 1-56884-964-8
$9.99 USA/$12.99 Canada

Photoshop 3 For Macs® For Dummies® Quick Reference
by Deke McClelland

ISBN: 1-56884-968-0
$9.99 USA/$12.99 Canada

WordPerfect® For DOS For Dummies® Quick Reference
by Greg Harvey

ISBN: 1-56884-009-8
$8.95 USA/$12.95 Canada

Title	Author	ISBN	Price
DATABASE			
Access 2 For Dummies® Quick Reference	by Stuart J. Stuple	ISBN: 1-56884-167-1	$8.95 USA/$11.95 Canada
dBASE 5 For DOS For Dummies® Quick Reference	by Barrie Sosinsky	ISBN: 1-56884-954-0	$9.99 USA/$12.99 Canada
dBASE 5 For Windows® For Dummies® Quick Reference	by Stuart J. Stuple	ISBN: 1-56884-953-2	$9.99 USA/$12.99 Canada
Paradox 5 For Windows® For Dummies® Quick Reference	by Scott Palmer	ISBN: 1-56884-960-5	$9.99 USA/$12.99 Canada
DESKTOP PUBLISHING/ILLUSTRATION/GRAPHICS			
CorelDRAW! 5 For Dummies® Quick Reference	by Raymond E. Werner	ISBN: 1-56884-952-4	$9.99 USA/$12.99 Canada
Harvard Graphics For Windows® For Dummies® Quick Reference	by Raymond E. Werner	ISBN: 1-56884-962-1	$9.99 USA/$12.99 Canada
Photoshop 3 For Macs® For Dummies® Quick Reference	by Deke McClelland	ISBN: 1-56884-968-0	$9.99 USA/$12.99 Canada
FINANCE/PERSONAL FINANCE			
Quicken 4 For Windows® For Dummies® Quick Reference	by Stephen L. Nelson	ISBN: 1-56884-950-8	$9.95 USA/$12.95 Canada
GROUPWARE/INTEGRATED			
Microsoft® Office 4 For Windows® For Dummies® Quick Reference	by Doug Lowe	ISBN: 1-56884-958-3	$9.99 USA/$12.99 Canada
Microsoft® Works 3 For Windows® For Dummies® Quick Reference	by Michael Partington	ISBN: 1-56884-959-1	$9.99 USA/$12.99 Canada
INTERNET/COMMUNICATIONS/NETWORKING			
The Internet For Dummies® Quick Reference	by John R. Levine & Margaret Levine Young	ISBN: 1-56884-168-X	$8.95 USA/$11.95 Canada
MACINTOSH			
Macintosh® System 7.5 For Dummies® Quick Reference	by Stuart J. Stuple	ISBN: 1-56884-956-7	$9.99 USA/$12.99 Canada
OPERATING SYSTEMS:			
DOS			
DOS For Dummies® Quick Reference	by Greg Harvey	ISBN: 1-56884-007-1	$8.95 USA/$11.95 Canada
UNIX			
UNIX® For Dummies® Quick Reference	by John R. Levine & Margaret Levine Young	ISBN: 1-56884-094-2	$8.95 USA/$11.95 Canada
WINDOWS			
Windows® 3.1 For Dummies® Quick Reference, 2nd Edition	by Greg Harvey	ISBN: 1-56884-951-6	$8.95 USA/$11.95 Canada
PCs/HARDWARE			
Memory Management For Dummies® Quick Reference	by Doug Lowe	ISBN: 1-56884-362-3	$9.99 USA/$12.99 Canada
PRESENTATION/AUTOCAD			
AutoCAD For Dummies® Quick Reference	by Ellen Finkelstein	ISBN: 1-56884-198-1	$9.95 USA/$12.95 Canada
SPREADSHEET			
1-2-3 For Dummies® Quick Reference	by John Walkenbach	ISBN: 1-56884-027-6	$8.95 USA/$11.95 Canada
1-2-3 For Windows® 5 For Dummies® Quick Reference	by John Walkenbach	ISBN: 1-56884-957-5	$9.95 USA/$12.95 Canada
Excel For Windows® For Dummies® Quick Reference, 2nd Edition	by John Walkenbach	ISBN: 1-56884-096-9	$8.95 USA/$11.95 Canada
Quattro Pro 6 For Windows® For Dummies® Quick Reference	by Stuart J. Stuple	ISBN: 1-56884-172-8	$9.95 USA/$12.95 Canada
WORD PROCESSING			
Word For Windows® 6 For Dummies® Quick Reference	by George Lynch	ISBN: 1-56884-095-0	$8.95 USA/$11.95 Canada
Word For Windows® For Dummies® Quick Reference	by George Lynch	ISBN: 1-56884-029-2	$8.95 USA/$11.95 Canada
WordPerfect® 6.1 For Windows® For Dummies® Quick Reference, 2nd Edition	by Greg Harvey	ISBN: 1-56884-966-4	$9.99 USA/$12.99/Canada

For scholastic requests & educational orders please call Educational Sales at 1. 800. 434. 2086

FOR MORE INFO OR TO ORDER, PLEASE CALL ▶ 800. 762. 2974

For volume discounts & special orders please Tony Real, Special Sales, at 415. 655. 3048

Order Center: **(800) 762-2974** *(8 a.m.–6 p.m., EST, weekdays)*

Quantity	ISBN	Title	Price	Total

Shipping & Handling Charges

	Description	First book	Each additional book	Total
Domestic	Normal	$4.50	$1.50	$
	Two Day Air	$8.50	$2.50	$
	Overnight	$18.00	$3.00	$
International	Surface	$8.00	$8.00	$
	Airmail	$16.00	$16.00	$
	DHL Air	$17.00	$17.00	$

*For large quantities call for shipping & handling charges.
**Prices are subject to change without notice.

Ship to:

Name _____

Company _____

Address _____

City/State/Zip _____

Daytime Phone _____

Payment: ☐ Check to IDG Books Worldwide (US Funds Only)

☐ VISA ☐ MasterCard ☐ American Express

Card # _____ Expires _____

Signature _____

Subtotal _____

CA residents add
applicable sales tax _____

IN, MA, and MD
residents add
5% sales tax _____

IL residents add
6.25% sales tax _____

RI residents add
7% sales tax _____

TX residents add
8.25% sales tax _____

Shipping _____

Total _____

Please send this order form to:

IDG Books Worldwide, Inc.
7260 Shadeland Station, Suite 100
Indianapolis, IN 46256

Allow up to 3 weeks for delivery.
Thank you!

IDG BOOKS WORLDWIDE REGISTRATION CARD

RETURN THIS
REGISTRATION CARD
FOR FREE CATALOG

Title of this book: **Object-Oriented Programming For Dummies®**

My overall rating of this book: ❑ Very good [1] ❑ Good [2] ❑ Satisfactory [3] ❑ Fair [4] ❑ Poor [5]

How I first heard about this book:

❑ Found in bookstore; name: [6] _____

❑ Book review: [7] _____

❑ Advertisement: [8] _____

❑ Catalog: [9] _____

❑ Word of mouth; heard about book from friend, co-worker, etc.: [10]

❑ Other: [11] _____

What I liked most about this book:

_____
_____

What I would change, add, delete, etc., in future editions of this book:

_____
_____

Other comments:

_____

Number of computer books I purchase in a year: ❑ 1 [12] ❑ 2-5 [13] ❑ 6-10 [14] ❑ More than 10 [15]

I would characterize my computer skills as: ❑ Beginner [16] ❑ Intermediate [17] ❑ Advanced [18] ❑ Professional [19]

I use ❑ DOS [20] ❑ Windows [21] ❑ OS/2 [22] ❑ Unix [23] ❑ Macintosh [24] ❑ Other: [25]_____
(please specify)

I would be interested in new books on the following subjects:
(please check all that apply, and use the spaces provided to identify specific software)

❑ Word processing: [26] _____

❑ Spreadsheets: [27] _____

❑ Data bases: [28] _____

❑ Desktop publishing: [29] _____

❑ File Utilities: [30] _____

❑ Money management: [31] _____

❑ Networking: [32] _____

❑ Programming languages: [33] _____

❑ Other: [34] _____

I use a PC at (please check all that apply): ❑ home [35] ❑ work [36] ❑ school [37] ❑ other: [38] _____

The disks I prefer to use are ❑ 5.25 [39] ❑ 3.5 [40] ❑ other: [41]_____

I have a CD ROM: ❑ yes [42] ❑ no [43]

I plan to buy or upgrade computer hardware this year: ❑ yes [44] ❑ no [45]

I plan to buy or upgrade computer software this year: ❑ yes [46] ❑ no [47]

Name: _____ Business title: [48] _____ Type of Business: [49] _____

Address (❑ home [50] ❑ work [51]/Company name: _____)

Street/Suite# _____

City [52]/State [53]/Zipcode [54]: _____ Country [55] _____

❑ **I liked this book!** You may quote me by name in future
IDG Books Worldwide promotional materials.

My daytime phone number is _____

IDG BOOKS

THE WORLD OF
COMPUTER
KNOWLEDGE

 **YES!**
Please keep me informed about IDG's World of Computer Knowledge.
Send me the latest IDG Books catalog.

COMPUTER
BOOK SERIES
FROM IDG